M-D Chenu's Christian Anthropology: Nature and Grace in Society and Church

Janette Gray

M-D Chenu's Christian Anthropology: Nature and Grace in Society and Church

Janette Gray

Adelaide
2019

© Institute of Sisters of Mercy Australia and Papua New Guinea

Photo: M-D Chenu and others circa 1940. Archives of the Dominican Province of France, with thanks to Bruno Dominique Lafille OP

Cover design: Myf Casdwallader

978-1-925872-65-1 soft
978-1-925872-66-8 hard
978-1-925872-67-5 epub
978-1-925872-68-2 pdf

Text: Minion Pro 10 & 11

Published by:

An imprint of the ATF Press Publishing
Group owned by ATF (Australia) Ltd.
PO Box 504
Hindmarsh, SA 5007
ABN 90 116 359 963
www.atfpress.com
Making a lasting impact

Table of Contents

Editor's Note		ix
Foreword		xi
Preface		xvii
Introduction		xix

Chapter 1	History of a Theology	1
	Situating Chenu	1
	Two images of 'présence'	5
	Church-World context of 'deux Chenu'	6
	Post-Vatican II reception of 'deux Chenu'	9
	Post-Vatican II absence of Chenu's theology	13
	A history of Chenu's theology	20
Chapter 2	Chenu's Theological Project	25
	Introduction	25
	Faith as contemplation	28
	Faith in understanding	36
	Theology as faith in reason	43
	La théologie comme science au XIIIe siècle	44
	'La nouvelle théologie'	55
Chapter 3	Anthropological Dimensions of Chenu's Ecclesiology before Vatican II	65
	Chenu's early ecclesiology	65
	Anthropological condition of faith	69
	'Dimension nouvelle de la Chrétienté'	70
	'La Loi de l'Incarnation'	74

	Later pre-Vatican II ecclesiological writing	82
	Mission and reform	82
	Church as historical and social	83
	Beyond 'spiritualisme' or theocracy	85
	Theology and authority in the Church	89
	Sacraments and the priesthood	91
	Conclusion	96
Chapter 4	**Anthropological Shift of Vatican II Ecclesiology**	**99**
	A Council called	99
	Vatican II: a different 'présence'	103
	Signs of the times	109
	Consecratio mundi	113
	Conclusion	116
Chapter 5	**Chenu's Theology of History**	**119**
	Total history for a total theology	120
	'L'histoire de la théologie est intérieure à la théologie même.'	130
	From the development of doctrine to a theology of change	135
	'Je me présente comme historien de l'Évangile dans le Peuple de Dieu'	141
	Conclusion	144
Chapter 6	**Chenu's Socio-political Christian Anthropology**	**145**
	A theology of work?	146
	Definition of work	148
	Chenu's theology and Marxism	151
	Pour une théologie du travail—a thematic Framework	152
	Human condition	153
	Humanity and the universe	158
	Humanity in the whole economy of salvation	161
	Criticism of Chenu's theology of work	165
	Chenu's Christian anthropology and work	174
	Conclusion	176

Chapter 7	**The Human Truth of Matter:**	
	Towards a Christian Anthropology	**179**
	The problem of matter	185
	'The truth of matter'	188
	Anthropological implications of this consubstantiality	191
	'La loi de l'incarnation'	195
	Matter and theology of the world	199
	Implications of Chenu's theology of matter on theological anthropology	203

Conclusion   **207**

Bibliography   **215**

Editor's Note

Janette Gray valued education highly. Initially she received a BA, DipEd, from Macquarie University, NSW. Her first love was history, which she taught in several Secondary Colleges in Adelaide, South Australia, before completing a BTheol degree at Melbourne College of Divinity (now University of Divinity). She described this experience as "opening to me the very rich storehouses of our Catholic tradition." Subsequently she completed an MTheol from the MCD. Her supervisors and examiners recognised the unique quality of the thesis she wrote for the MTheol and requested that she publish it. The result was her first book, *Neither Escaping Nor Exploiting Sex: Women's Celibacy* (1995), in which she explored the sexuality of celibate women and assessed how their response to personal challenges established ideas about human relationships and ecological awareness. (It is interesting to note that Janette was alert to ecological concerns some twenty years before they became popular.)

Over the years Janette lectured at several academic centres in Western Australia: Edith Cowan University, Murdoch University, teaching systematic and pastoral theology, and the University of Notre Dame (Fremantle), where she was Senior Lecturer in Theology from 1999–2003. In Melbourne she was Faculty Member of Jesuit Theological College, Parkville Melbourne, 2004–2014; Principal of Jesuit Theological College, 2012–2014; and Lecturer and postgraduate research Supervisor at the United Faculty of Theology, Pilgrim College, and Yarra Theological Union, all member colleges of what is now the University of Divinity, Melbourne.

For some years Janette was also book review editor for *Pacifica*, a journal recognised in its day as making a leading contribution to ecumenical theological conversation in Australia.

During her time in Cambridge, while she was reading towards her PhD, Janette lectured at the Margaret Beaufort Institute of Theology, and for the Cambridge Federation of Theological Colleges. She also participated in the PACT program at Providence College, Rhode Island.

Her continuing research areas of interest were the theological forerunners to Vatican 11, Vatican 11, the Christian anthropology of Marie-Dominique Chenu, contemporary religious life, and women and religious experience. Much in demand as a public speaker, she delivered talks across Australia on the fruits of her research in these areas.

In 2010 Janette received her PhD in Theology at the University of Cambridge, UK, for a dissertation on "The Christian Anthropology of M.-D. Chenu". At the time of her death, she was working on a book based on her dissertation topic, with the intended title, *Theology for Global People: Chenu*. In the absence of this work, which death sadly prevented her from completing, her doctoral dissertation is now being published.

Kathleen Williams, rsm
Melbourne
March 2019

Foreword
Humanity, History, and Spirit.
Marie-Dominique Chenu's Thought

Thomas F O'Meara, OP

The French historian and theologian Marie-Dominique Chenu, in his long life from 1895 to 1990, offered ideas and inspiration to several generations. Paul Philibert spoke of his 'warm personality and generous heart as he reached out to a range of colleagues and friends from the erudite to the unsophisticated'.[1] Janette Gray composed a study on Chenu's theological project, the forms and approaches underlying the development of his thinking. He was an outstanding historian of the twelfth and thirteenth centuries, even as he was an active voice in the renewal of the Catholic Church in the twentieth century. His studies on Thomas Aquinas remain exceptional, while his writings on the renewal of the local church still influence the move away from the neo-Baroque isolation of the priesthood to the current expansion of ministries. This book on one theologian is also a book of theological history, offering insights into Catholicism in the decades before and after the Ecumenical Council Vatican II. Much of Chenu's work was done before 1962, and Gray saw the event of the Council as being a catalyst for his thought and a separation between periods. In Chenu's career the medieval and the modern, the scholastic and the pastoral, mirror different times.

Seven chapters locate a person of creativity and depth amid the themes of humanity, history, and incarnation. An earlier theological perspective, very much the result of medieval research, has its own themes of divine presence and social relationships. Faith and reason emerge as contemplation and understanding, unfolding first in the

---

1. Philibert, 'M-D Chenu: Situating Theology in History', in Thomas O'Meara and Paul Philibert, *Scanning the Signs of the Times. French Dominicans in the Twentieth Century* (Adelaide: ATF, 2013), 19.

context of science in the thirteenth century and then as the new theology in the twentieth. Gray chose the anthropological dimension of faith and theology as a key to understanding the creative development of this theologian. Incarnation is present not only in Jesus but in people and societies. This human side of reality brings a recognition of the church's structures as historical, the need for reform, and a commitment to new directions for mission. At Vatican II, these themes of presence and person take on new directions aided by Chenu's efforts. If the Dominican was known particularly as a researcher into medieval schools, he is also a theoretician of history. History is not a background to culture but part of the interior reality of culture, and so of theology. These themes were drawn by Chenu into the ministerial and social situation of France after World War II. A concluding chapter sums up these currents in terms of history and incarnation, truth and anthropology.

Yves Congar described meeting the young Chenu, the friar who would be his professor, his colleague, and his friend. 'How to speak of Père Chenu as one ought? The friendship and the fellowship that we had with him for more than twenty years was of a kind so tied up with our lives, with the most simple and the most profound happenings of our lives, that it is not possible to point to a moment when it came about, nor even to indicate its beginnings. I still remember being presented to the lecturers when I arrived at Le Saulchoir. What a magnificent man was Chenu! Then, having got through a light veneer of timidity, one encountered in him the brother, the enlightening, generous brother, open to everything, friendly and ready to help as one struggled to express an idea, ready to help in any research . . . One encountered a master, a friend, and a brother without peer.'[2]

Early theologies became contemporary movements. Even in writings about Thomas Aquinas, the reader has the impression of meeting a theologian as someone contemporary. Chenu liked to refer to a passage from William of Tocco, a student of Aquinas at the University of Naples from 1272 to 1274 and his biographer.

---

2. Congar, *Journal of a Theologian (1946–1956)*, edited with notes by Étienne Fouilloux with the collaboration of Dominique Congar, André Duval and Bernard Montagnes, translated by Mary John Ronayne, OP, and Mary Cecily Boulding and Denis Minns (Adelaide: ATF, 2015), 49.

> One can hardly avoid noting that in these ten lines the word *"novus"* appears eight times. This must be an intentional repetition. Is not the word itself a direct indication of the situation William observed? Tocco wrote: Having been named a bachelor (an assistant professor) and beginning to unveil what his quiet personality had held in his spirit, Friar Thomas appeared to have received from God remarkable knowledge, for he surpassed all the professors. In his courses he stated new problems, discovered new methods, and used new sequences of proofs. To hear him teach was to be in contact with a new doctrine supported by new argumentation. One could not doubt that God by touching him with a new light and with a newness of inspiration led him to teach, from the beginning of his professor-ship, openly and directly, in word and in writing, new views.[3]

In the post-war decades, in the university, in the church, in cities, people are searching for life and truth. A healthy theology and spirituality should never be piously cut off from the individual's society with its aspirations and achievements. Thus the revolution of seeing theology as an Aristotelian science in the thirteenth century is not unrelated to the call after World War II for a 'new theology', a renewed church. In the 1280s at Oxford, John Peckham, Archbishop of Canterbury, in opposition to Aquinas and Albert the Great, condemned a *novella quaedam philosophia,* and now seven centuries later the Vatican was condemning what was new, a *Nouvelle théologie.*

Christian community and thinking flow from the extension of incarnation. Anthropology and mission, reform and education– these are all incarnational. Recent decades have seen studies by Ulrich Engel, Guido Vergauwen, and Christophe Potworowski on Chenu's expansion of incarnation into being the depth of all that is Christian and as a dynamic for all that is contemporary.[4] Gray sums up: 'The dynamic of the in-breaking of the Kingdom of God not only confounds a view of history that depicts humanity as passive before an unfolding progression in time, but it re-instates ordinary human affairs as revelatory of the divine will and its ends, just as the Incar-

---

3. William of Tocco, *Ystoria sancti Thomae de Aquino* (Toronto: Pontifical Institute of Medieval Studies, 1996), 121–22.
4. Ulrich Engel, 'Theologale Mystik im Konflikt. Marie-Dominique Chenu und die Grundintuitionen seiner Theologie', in *Gott der Menschen. Wegmarken dominikanischer Theologie* (Ostfildern: Matthias-Grünnewald, 2010), 154ff.

nation made revelatory Christ's humanity and the ordinary human affairs Jesus inhabited. Chenu drew his understanding of history from Paul's and Irenaeus' doctrine of recapitulation of all things in Christ, that the Incarnation continues to renew all of creation, including humanity, until it reaches its fullest eschatological resolution in history.'[5]

Incarnation was expressed by Aquinas in the friendly interplay of nature and grace. Chenu wrote of this medieval theology: 'Grace leads nature to itself in a cultural density and historicity. Cultural dimensions in the course of history go beyond academic teaching. They emerge in new images and lead the religious dimension to new mental categories and vocabularies, to new disciplines like sciences treating the human person. Albert the Great, Thomas' teacher, wrote that science was far from complete: there are new sciences yet to be discovered. Theology appears as a historical dimension of the life of the church at the same time as the life of the church enters into the breadth of theology.'[6] This happened in past centuries; it was happening again in the course of the twentieth century. The changes in society and in the understanding of the human person provoked fresh readings of the Gospel and gave opportunities for the church to liberate itself from dead theological and ecclesiastical strictures. Chenu's addresses and articles helped people go beyond the end of an ossified regime. He wrote of how the reality of law in society held a creative energy capable of implanting itself in new human areas and to assist the church in being planted in a wider world. This recalled a powerful line from Aquinas: 'That which is most powerful in the law of the New Testament and in which its entire power consists is the grace of the Holy Spirit given by Christ to believers.'[7]

---

5. Gray, 142.
6. Chenu, 'Thomas Aquinas, an Innovator in a New World', in Thomas O'Meara, editor, *Exploring Thomas Aquinas. Essays and Sermons* (Chicago: New Priory Press, 2017) 1f, a translation of *S. Thomas Innovateur dans la créativité d'un monde nouveau Tommaso d'Aquino nella Storia del Pensiero I. Le fonti del Pensiero di S. Tommaso* (Naples: Edizioni Domenicane Italiane, 1974), 39–50.
7. Aquinas, *Summa theologiae*, I-II, q. 106, a 1. Speaking of Aquinas' structures in the *Summa theologiae* he wrote that the 'systematic spirit of Thomas' work is made to respect at all cost the strange logic of the Kingdom of God whose designs are expressed as much in the secrets of divine mystery as in the happy outcomes of human hopes' (Chenu, *Aquinas and His Role in Theology* [Collegeville; Liturgical Press, 2002]), 138.

Revolutionary modern philosophies had asserted that history is not merely a chronological background but a temporal dynamic penetrating everything. Chenu explained: 'History in theology lies at the inner reality of theology itself.'[8] Gray insightfully links the textual issue of the evolution of dogma to the cultural history of theology. Up to 1960, one of the few progressive topics of neo-scholastic theology was the development of doctrine. How was change possible within eternal dogma? Dogmatic evolution remained largely textual research and Aristotelian logic. Beyond concepts and books, however, changes in society raised the issue of change in the church itself, in its mission, structure, and liturgy. Chenu saw himself not as a medieval theologian but as an ecclesial theologian of change and newness at the service of evangelism and church, as a historian of the Gospel amid the People of God. His theology drew from cultural history and became a Christian variation on that theme, so prominent and influential in French culture in the 1950s: *The Human Condition*. 'What matters is the communication of God's word as a kind of dialogue with people through and in a church that understands itself to be missionary. God's word speaks today.'[9]

Gray called Chenu's ideas and movements for a new church a Socio-Political Christian Anthropology.[10] The seminary professor became a theological adviser to the priest-workers.[11] That movement was soon accused of being Communist because it sought a new relationship between church and factory. Chenu addressed the nature and hopes of socialism in pages that would later find narrow critiques. Forms of socialism are forms of humanism, of the struggle to humanise terrestrial society and history. He wrote articles and books on a theology of work, exploring work not from a religious nostalgia for past guilds nor from today's issues of social justice, but from how the breadth of work intersected with the breadth of Christian teaching. A theology of work reaches from the beginnings of *Genesis* to the vast cosmos beginning to be understood in new ways. Work is an aspect

---

8. Chenu, 'Avant-propos', *La théologie au douzième siècle* (Paris: J Vrin, 1957), 14.
9. Chenu, "Un Concile 'Pastoral'," *L'Évangile dans le temps, Cogitatio Fidei* 11 (Paris: Éditions du Cerf, 1964), 663.
10. Gary, chapter 6.
11. See O'Meara, 'Jacques Loewe: Ministry on the Docks', in Thomas O'Meara, Paul Philibert, *Scanning the signs of the times. French Dominicans in the Twentieth Century* (Adelaide: ATF, 2013), 81–96.

of the dynamic where humanity is a collaborator and participant in the continuation of creation. In contrast to a deist view of God's separateness from creation, Chenu asserted that God did not create a finished universe, and men and women are called to participate in the divine creativity, and work is one of humanity's relationships to the Creator in the transformation of matter.[12] Chenu's dialogue with Communism remains of interest; its critics and defenders range from Charles Curran to John Paul II. Some demeaned this degree of optimism. But Gray observes:

> Chenu's theology of work is limited by its contemporary situatedness. His advocacy of socialism as a signal of greater humanization can suggest an uncritical acceptance of socialist politics. Yet I would understand these as the necessary outcomes of a theology focused on dialogue with its temporal situation and its then interlocutors.[13]

Gray concluded that, with historical schools and theological systems as the background, what is central is Chenu's Thomist refusal to see any human situation as beyond the activity of grace. Creation and human activity are open to and responsive to divine invitation to be transformed, even given its inherent sinfulness and resistance. Chenu, however, joined theology and praxis to pursue eschatological possibilities already being realised in new ways in local churches.

---

12. *Pour une théologie du travail* (Paris: Seuil, 1955), 19.
13. Gray, 174.

Preface

Père Marie-Dominique Chenu OP was one of the great between-the-wars French theologians who led the renewal of research on Thomas Aquinas. Chenu also pioneered a new approach to doing theology in the twentieth century. He is the least known of the Catholic reformers in the English-speaking theological world, which has intrigued me throughout the process of this dissertation. My interest in his theology was initiated by reading an English translation of his *Pour une théologie du travail* while working on an Aboriginal Mission in the Kimberley region of Western Australia. Later I drew on his historical theology of the religious vow of poverty through another translation: *Nature Man and Society*. Following the suggestion of Professor Nicholas Lash, my study of the extent of his contribution to Roman Catholic theology was pursued at Cambridge, in a number of libraries in Paris, particularly the Bibliothèque Nationale de France and the Dominican library and archive at Le Saulchoir, and at the Dalton-McCaughey Library in the United Faculty of Theology, Melbourne, Australia.

This study of the Christian anthropology of Marie-Dominique Chenu OP began under the guidance of Professor Lash, to whom I am deeply grateful for his confidence in the project and his patience with my difficulties writing this dissertation. Mrs Janet Lash also offered, me generous hospitality and supportive diversions. After some years interruption due to the commitments of my ministry, Professor Janet Soskice generously accepted to supervise my final draft for submission. I wish to thanks the others who have helped bring this study to completion: for encouragement, scholarly advice and unstinting hospitality, Fr David Sanders OP, Professor Nicholas and Mrs Rosemary

Boyle, Dr Anne Dillon; Dr Catherine Pickstock, who read through an earlier draft in 2001 when Prof Soskice was on study leave; and the support of my colleagues and religious community in Australia, Prof Michael Jackson, Dr Maryanne Confoy RSC, Rev Dr Geoffrey King SJ, Rev Dr Antony Campbell SJ, Rev Dr Brendan Byrne SJ, Sr Rosemary Day RSM, Sr Beverley Stott RSM, Sr Mary Densley RSM, Sr Christine Keain RSM, Sr Patricia Fox RSM, and Sr Nerida Tinkler RSM. During my time in Cambridge I was supported with scholarships from Emmanuel College, the Overseas Research Scholarship and a grant from the British Federation of Women Graduates. In 2001, I received an Australian Government Research Grant that allowed me to spend three weeks in Cambridge to continue my research.

This dissertation is the result of my own work and includes nothing which is the outcome of work done in collaboration, except where specifically indicated in the text.

Introduction

'Les mots ont une histoire, toujours significative'
Chenu, La 'doctrine sociale' de l'Eglise comme idéologie
(Paris: Editions du Cerf, 1979), 87.

This thesis seeks to identify the pivotal concerns of Marie-Dominique Chenu OP's theology, to follow their development, and to determine whether these elements in his theology coalesce into a Christian anthropology. Chenu's long life spanned a century of social and political upheavals in the life of the Church in France and the wider modern world, and even more change in what constituted Catholic theology.[1] Previous studies of his work have registered Chenu's interest in humanity and history, but have insufficiently gauged the anthropological direction of his work, due to their preference for forcing it into a systematic elaboration. The emphasis on pastoral and systematic theology that became dominant after Vatican II overshadowed the more anthropological particularity of 'ad hoc apologetics' like Chenu's.[2] From a systematic viewpoint, the readily identifiable

---

1. Born Marcel-Léon Chenu at Soisy-sur-Seine near Paris on 7 January 1895, died 11 February 1990.
2. Nicholas M Healy describes an 'ad hoc apologetics' 'develops arguments the force of which remains situation-relative', addressed 'not to some abstract unbeliever, but to one who lives within a particular concrete historical and cultural situation' (616). 'Indirect methods in theology: Karl Rahner as an ad hoc apologist', The Thomist, 56 (1992): 613–34. Karen Kilby also characterises Rahner's theology as an 'internal apologetics', a reading which I find applicable also to Chenu. 'The Vorgriff auf esse: A study in the relation of philosophy to theology in the thought of Karl Rahner' (PhD, Yale University, 1994), 202–09.

doctrinal characteristics of a pastoral or Incarnational theology are more discernible than are the elements of an historically, materially, and socially attuned Christian anthropology. It is precisely these elements, so easy to underestimate, that frame Chenu's theology of humanity: history, matter, and their conjunction in the social reality of humanity.

In the Rhône valley there is a village named after its early twelfth century bridge, *Pont-Saint-Esprit*. Chenu found in this bridge a word with a history, a material preaching of the Gospel. He saw embodied in the bridge a moment when evangelical awakening to the active presence of the Holy Spirit was accompanied by social change in medieval society. Prior to the emergence of the new economy of commerce and industry occasioned by the rise of the towns, feudal structures of rural land-holding and serfdom had defined the religious life, politics and wealth of western European civilisation. Chenu saw symbolised in this bridge the emergence of a new social order. He observed that a confraternity of urban traders constructed the bridge, which was not merely a pious association but an economic corporation of the prosperous exponents of the new *polis*. Outsiders to feudalism, the members of the confraternity were motivated by the needs of other outsiders who had been caught between the competing pressures of the new and the old economies. Peasants driven from the margins of feudalism and its stagnant rural economy needed easier access to the thriving markets across the river in the town. For this, the confraternity built a bridge called '*Saint-Esprit*'. Chenu emphasised that the bridge was not called *after* the Holy Spirit, in the sense of under its patronage, but was inspired by a sense of the reality of the Holy Spirit that it represented. This witnessed to a 'sensibilité vive au rôle, à la présence active de l'Esprit.' With an intended pun, Chenu described this as 'la foi concrète en l'Esprit-Saint.'[3]

According to Chenu, this naming of the bridge indicated the confraternity's profound theological sense of the present manifestations of the Holy Spirit. 'C'est précisément dans ces nouveaux secteurs sociaux que se manifeste désormais la prise de conscience de la présence de l'Esprit.'[4] He described it as an example of the 'den-

---

3. Chenu, 'Réveil Évangélique et présence de l'Esprit aux XIIe-XIIIe siècles' in *Mélanges E. Schillebeeckx: L'expérience de l'Esprit* (Paris: Édition Beauchesne, 1976), 167–71 (167).
4. 'Réveil Évangélique', 170.

sity' and authority of an 'orthopraxis', a conjunction of doctrine and action, faith and experience, grace and nature. *Pont-Saint-Esprit* reflected the communion of the Trinity as revealed in the mission of the Holy Spirit in its bringing people together for commercial and social interests, as much as for the sacred meetings of pilgrimage and feast days. 'La liberté de circuler est considérée et pratiquée comme une condition de la liberté de l'Esprit.'[5] Building the bridge allowed movement beyond the immobility of the paternal relations of feudal dependence to the communal fraternity of town commerce. The new freedom of spirit raised by re-distribution of wealth also revealed the economy of Christ and the mission of the Holy Spirit active in human history.[6] Like the love of the Holy Spirit between the persons of the Trinity, the bridge expressed the collectivity of fraternal love between people.

Chenu saw this same theological understanding embodied in the proliferation of banks throughout Europe entitled 'Holy Spirit'. He considered the mission of the Holy Spirit to be operative in the fraternal workings of these associations, involving the more democratic circulation of wealth, the promotion of collective consciousness through communal life in the towns, and the sharing of production and marketing techniques.[7] Chenu stressed that the Christian medieval confraternity grew from the solidarity of these trades-people, the sacred emerged from the profane. Fraternal love is the consecration of this solidarity.[8] Their praxis was not merely charitable generosity, but the extension of their confraternal solidarity to others outside the confraternity. 'Il ne s'agit pas tant, en effet, d'opérations de vertus personnelles, en moralité ou en dévotion, mais bien de solidarité collective, dont l'amour fraternel est la consécration.'[9]

---

5. 'Réveil Évangélique', 168.
6. See also 'Civilisation technique et spiritualité nouvelle' (1948) in *La Parole de Dieu II. L'Évangile dans le temps* (Paris: Cerf, 1964), 137–158, 83.
7. 'Réveil Évangélique', 168.
8. Chenu recognised in this 'les rapports de la nature et de la grâce': 'Car telle est l'économie de la grâce, et premièrement de la lumière de la foi, de se couler dans les formes, dans les structures et les rhythmes, dans le dynamisme de la nature humaine, et non pas de se poser sur une nature comme sur un domaine hétérogène dans ses comportements.' 'Les communautés naturelles, pierres d'attente de cellules d'Église' (1964) in *Peuple de Dieu dans le monde* (Paris: Les Éditions du Cerf, 1966), 129–43.
9. 'Réveil Évangélique', 169.

Chenu's elaboration upon this bridge as an historical–theological artefact encapsulates many features of his theological project. His theology was framed by the recognition of certain 'événements' and crises throughout history that were flagged by the resurgence of the freedom and fraternity of the Gospel and by 'provoquent la mise en question critique des appareils les plus légitimes.'[10] This theological awareness of the dynamic of 'rupture' was reflected by events in his life. His theological output was repeatedly disrupted by ecclesiastical censure, yet he found these setbacks expanded the sources of his theology to include historical and contemporary human experience: 'L'expérience est alors une précieuse ressource d'intelligence et d'expression.'[11] Such engagements with the wider reality of faith inhabiting life alerted him to the gulf between the 'aristocratique' condition of much contemporary theology and that of common humanity. This he sought to bridge through his explorations of the theology of work and the newer forms of Church and evangelisation that emerged in the mid-twentieth century.

Chenu's account of the bridge illustrates the dynamic of faith as relational and historically conditioned. It also represents the theological possibility of materiality, as embodied in the transformation of relations brought about by the construction of the bridge, a material artefact of the Holy Spirit's communion. Indeed, this bridge and the way in which Chenu analysed and applied its doctrinal implications summarise the scope, method, and major concerns of his theology. His theology spanned the theological and socio-political turbulence of the twentieth century, from the Thomist revival at the opening of the century to the new anthropological dilemmas and social injustices raised by mass industrialisation, totalitarianism, and war.

In the thousand and more articles and monographs he published, Chenu foreshadowed a theology of history, a theology of matter, and a theology of the world. This study attempts to show that underpinning all these was his principal project, a theology of humanity. The evidence for Chenu's Christian anthropology is introduced in Chapter 2 through his early study of the dynamic of human understanding and faith, then further developed in Chapters 3 through 6 his theological reflection on the actual human situations of socialisation in the church, history, and industrialised work. Finally in Chapter 7,

---

10. 'Réveil Évangélique', 170.
11. 'Réveil Évangélique', 167.

Chenu's articulation of the nexus of matter and spirit in humanity is examined for the authenticity he claimed for human engagement in the world. Despite collectivist and evolutionary themes in his theological anthropology, Chenu employed these twentieth century concerns in dialectical tension with pre-modern theological understanding, situating current struggles over society and individuality, immanence and transcendence in their broadest historical and philosophical context. While advocating engagement with the full force of issues raised by modernity, I hope to demonstrate that Chenu's theology mostly avoided being colonised by modernity's agenda and thereby stagnated in only modern concerns.

Across a range of contemporary theological topics, Chenu explored a Christian anthropology that articulated the experiential and concrete 'history' of human life in relation to faith. That a Christian anthropology was crucial to his work is attested by the lament of Yves Congar, his student and colleague:

> On eût aimé qu'il s'attaquât . . . à une étude plus systématiquement menée d'anthropologie: l'homme dans le temps, l'homme social. Quelle magnifique étude il eût pu nous donner![12]

Yet Chenu resisted constructing a new *summa* or a systematic account of theological subjects, on the Incarnation or ecclesiology, although he wrote extensively on both of these. For Chenu, theology must be responsive to contemporary questions. Rather than a system, his theology assumed the occasional and apologetic format of fundamental theology, addressing those outside the confessional discourse of the Church, the unbelievers, the un-evangelised, and the secularised. He understood these modern audiences required a theological account of humanity's relation to God that did not shirk the critical criteria of contemporary historical and social theory. Chenu's theology is constructed on the 'theandric' dynamic of a Christian anthropology, which continues to act like another bridge between the theological inheritance that led to Vatican II and the theological and pastoral needs that remain unresolved and polarised since the Council.

---

12. Yves Congar OP, 'Le Père M-D Chenu', in *Bilan de la théologie du XXe siècle*, volume II, edited by Robert van der Gucht and Herbert Vorgrimler (Paris: Casterman, 1970), 772–90, 789.

Chapter 1
History of a Theology

'L'homme ne devient une personne que dans un corps;
son "incarnation" est à la fois le principe d'individualité,
de sociabilité, d'historicité.'
Chenu, 'Création et histoire' (1974), 394.

Situating chenu

This chapter positions Chenu's theology in its historical context and in Chenu's own history in order to establish what his theological project sought to address in contemporary Catholic theology and the controversies this engendered. Chenu's theology and the history of twentieth century Catholic theology turns on the recurring challenge to the Church of the historicity of doctrine.[1] The scholastic reduction of theology to abstract essentialist categories had rendered doctrine timeless. Repeatedly the 'official theology' of the Holy See judged as 'relativist' any attempt to admit historical contingency as recognition of the historical condition of Christianity, however tentative, amounted to heresy. The development of doctrine was equated with Darwinian evolution and Protestant rejection of tradition. For Chenu, the philosophical explication of theology had impaired the Church's capacity for relating the Gospel to contemporary society. Chenu understood theology to be historically conditioned by its 'situation dans le temps (historicité de l'homme), situation dans un

---

1. Chenu, *Introduction à l'étude de Saint Thomas d'Aquin* (Montréal/Paris: Institut d'études médiévales/Vrin, 1950), 60, n 1.

corps'.[2] Whether textually tracing the innovation of Thomas Aquinas or reflecting theologically on the life-concerns of workers, Chenu attended to the historical and social contexts of his subjects:

> le théologien, lui, travaille sur une histoire. Son «donné», ce ne sont les natures des choses ni leurs formes intemporelles; ce sont des événements, répondant à une *économie*, dont la réalisation est liée au temps, comme l'étendue est liée au corps, par-dessus l'ordre des essences.[3]

Chenu's theology of humanity, while historically conditioned, is also attentive to the social reality of humanity and the materiality of these realities.

> Or, dans cette anthropologie «chrétienne», plus ou moins explicite dans les énoncés théologiques, ce sont trois attributs, trois attributs co-essentiels de l'homme qui se dégageaient: l'homme est par nature social, l'homme est lié à l'univers de telle sort que la matière du cosmos lui-même est engagée dans son destin, enfin l'homme existe dans l'histoire.[4]

Throughout his theology Chenu explored these attributes, not as abstract categories, but as they appeared in real-life conditions in his time, as attitudes to the material world, work, politics and the economy, and the human society of the Church. This historical character of Chenu's understanding of theology requires that any study situate him historically, in order to locate his particular contribution to twentieth century theology and estimate his enduring value: 'L'homme est impensable en dehors de l'histoire.'[5]

---

2. Chenu, 'Situation humaine: corporalité et temporalité' (1958) in *La Parole de Dieu II. L'Évangile dans le Temps* (Paris: Éditions du Cerf, 1964), 411–435, 413.
3. Chenu, 'Position de la théologie' (1935) in *La Parole de Dieu I. La Foi dans intelligence* (Paris: Cerf, 1964), 115–138, 128.
4. Chenu, 'Histoire du salut', 29–30.
5. 'L'homme est impensable en dehors de l'histoire, en même temps qu'il confère à l'univers une dimension historique.' Chenu, 'Création et histoire' in AA Maurer, editor, *St Thomas Aquinas 1274–1974 Commemorative Studies*, volume II (Toronto: Pontifical Institute of Medieval Studies, 1974), 391–399, 392.

History is the ground on which all Chenu's thinking is built.⁶ This chapter will survey and attempt to synthesise his understanding of humanity from his historical works and other theological reflections on history. In his early work he used the concept of *'présence'* to describe the engagement of a theologian's reflection with contemporary social and political life: 'Le théologien a les yeux grand ouverts sur la Chrétienté en travail. Ainsi est-il *présent* à son temps: c'est la loi même de son savoir.'⁷ This 'loi' is contrasted with the failure of scholastic theology since the sixteenth century to respond to new social and philosophical challenges:

> Mais lorsque de nouveaux complexes culturels, littéraires, esthétiques, idéologiques, religieux, ont transformée le climat et les techniques d'un milieu, la théologie ne sait pas toujours assurer cette «présence», humaine et chrétienne, qui, sous la lumière de foi, procure à son labeur rationnel la fraîcheur d'une création continuée.⁸

The hermeneutic of *'présence'* is also found throughout Chenu's historical writings. While considering the twelfth century Gospel revival, he comes to see the Church's immersion in the new economic and social order, through the cathedral schools, the artisan confraternities, and the mendicants, as revitalising the *'présence'* of the Gospel in this world.⁹

'Présence' also bears an anthropological significance for Chenu, expressing historical, ecclesiological, material, and sacramental meaning. In his usage it is a charged concept which tests the condition of evangelical efficacy, understood as the capacity to preach the Gospel in a way that renews each age.

---

6. 'C'est a l'intérieur d'une histoire qu'elle [la théologie] rencontre le problème des rélations ontologiques.' 'Histoire du salut', 26.
7. Chenu, *Dimension nouvelle de la Chrétienté* (Paris: Les Éditions du Cerf, 1937), 31.
8. Chenu, *Une école de théologie: le Saulchoir* (Kain-lez-Tournai/Etiolles: Le Saulchoir/Casterman, 1937) [2nd edition (Paris: Les Éditions du Cerf, 1985)], 27 [108]. (Following citations from this text give page references for each edition).
9. 'ce sera l'expression suprême de cette Chrétienté où le retour à l'Évangile a procuré au croyant une présence au monde, au théologien une sensibilité parfaite à la nature, et à l'apôtre une intelligence efficace de l'homme.' 'Moines, clercs, laïcs. Au carrefour de la vie évangélique', *La théologie au douzième siècle* (Paris: Librairie Philosophique J Vrin, 1957), 225–251, 251.

> Mauvais théologiens, ceux qui, enfouis dans leurs in-folio et leurs scolastiques, ne seraient pas ouverts à ces spectacles, non seulement dans la pieuse ferveur de leur coeur, mais formellement dans leur science: donné théologique en plein rendement, dans la *présence* de l'Esprit.[10]

Chenu articulated through '*présence*' a vision of Church–world relations that emphasised the immanence of the Incarnation, conditioned by the incompleteness of humanity and the world but its eschatological orientation towards full union with God. This union is prefigured in the continuing '*présence*' of the Incarnation.[11] That '*présence*' is so pervasive in Chenu's thought heightens the irony of his apparent absence from contemporary Catholic theology. The irony echoes Michel de Certeau's observation that, while history is built on the rupture between the past (which is its subject) and the present (which is the place where it is practised), it finds the present in what it studies from the past, as it finds the past in its present practice.[12] This thesis will attempt to appraise the debt of contemporary Catholic theology to the revolutionary shift that Chenu effected by elaborating the historicity of theology as he did. To credit Chenu's theology properly demands that it be located first in its place, but also in the situation from which it is evaluated now, the place it fills (or remains absent from) in the conflicts of the present—its outsider place in relation to current theology.[13] Certeau said: 'Un manquant fait écrire'[14]

---

10. *Une école de théologie*, 68 [142–3].
11. The theological historian Schoof notes that '*présence*' was the slogan of activist Catholics of the 1930's who sought to move the Church towards the 'dechristianised' masses. Two other concepts employed by the activists are also characteristic of Chenu and suggest his influence, '*engagement*' and '*incarnation*'. Mark (Ted) Schoof OP, *Breakthrough: Beginnings of the New Theology* (Dublin: Gill and MacMillan, 1970), 98–9.
12. Michel de Certeau, 'Faire de l'histoire', *L'Écriture de l'histoire*, 48.
13. I refer here to Certeau's 'localising sites' for the practice of history, where the interaction of content and operations defines the subject and the perspective (point of view) of the history of this subject (historical production). He suggests that this conjunction is equally appropriate for defining historiography ('making history' with emphasis on the 'making' instead of only the product) and theology. 'Faire de l'histoire', 27, and n 1.
14. This is the epigrammatic conclusion of Certeau's assertion that mourning ('desire') for the missing one generates a 'history' and spirituality ('*mystics*'). Michel de Certeau, *La Fable mystique: XVIe-XVIIe siècle* (Paris: Gallimard, 1987), 9.

and, I would add, generates theological reflection. In short, the situation of Chenu's works, the passage of their themes, the conditions under which his corpus developed (or was curtailed), are integral to a critical investigation of Chenu's theology. Using his motif of '*présence*' as an interpretative key, this chapter will situate historically Chenu's response to the theological and broader ecclesial issues of his times.[15]

Two images of 'présence'

Two photographs of Chenu frame his life while juxtaposing the spheres of his work and influence. In the earlier photograph, there is a placard at the feet of a bespectacled clerical figure, which reads 'DU TRAVAIL ET DU PAIN'. This figure, behind a microphone not in a pulpit, is Père Chenu, surrounded by protesting workers outside the Renault factory near Paris in 1952. This widely circulated photograph carried the explanatory caption:

> Le Père Chenu est représentatif d'un clergé soucieux de présence à la base, au coeur des luttes d'un peuple désormais saisi comme prolétariat.[16]

This image of a priest demonstrating solidarity with militant workers was politically charged, as it was unusual to find the Church so represented outside its traditional ecclesiastical settings. This was not a worker-priest absorbed into the hidden life of the working-classes. Chenu's photograph revealed visible Catholic collaboration with strikers and likely communists: a provocative transgression of the anti-communism of the 'Cold War'. It displaced French Catholic public participation from its counter-revolutionary refusal of Republican

---

15. Chenu's use of '*présence*' predates the later project of making 'present the absent', linking such French thinkers as Foucault, Derrida, and de Certeau (as influenced by Heidegger, Wittgenstein and Buber), yet he shares their anti-foundationalist orientation. See Thomas Guarino, 'Postmodernity and Five Fundamental Theological Issues', in *Theological Studies*, 57 (1996): 654–689, 656; also Michel de Certeau, 'L'opération historiographique', *L'Écriture de l'histoire* (Paris: Éditions Gallimard, 1975), 100–2.
16. François Lebrun et al, *Histoire des Catholiques en France: du XVe siècle à nos jours* (Toulouse: Privat, 1980) (caption to photo XXIII); both photos appear in François Leprieur OP, *Quand Rome condamne: Dominicains et prêtres-ouvriers* (Paris: Plon et Les Éditions du Cerf, 1989), 3.

France and its characteristic anti-clericalism, and from the Church's traditional social and class allegiances, and from its fear of atheistic insurgence. This was a new engagement with the world that the Church had withdrawn from since the French Revolution.

In the other photograph the setting appears neither political nor public.[17] The image is that of Chenu as an aged friar in his Dominican habit reading, bent over a desk full of papers, framed by shelves laden with books and stacked folders. This more familiar ecclesiastical subject depicts the solitary, interior place of scholarship. Far from the world-engagement of the other photograph, this is an enclosed place, free of apparent controversy. Ironically, for Chenu this was not so, as his scholarship engendered as much ecclesial censure as did his activism. This image represents another presence, the scholarly place of the researcher in an ecclesiastical institution.[18] There is an inherent ideological approval represented in this photo of the priest-'clerk', as Chenu often termed his historian persona. It resists any disclosure of the controversy that is missing from this photographic narrative frame.

Church-World context of 'deux Chenu'

The contrast between these two images is also a register of the modulations in the Catholic Church's presence and absence to twentieth century French life. The presence of a 'représentatif d'un clergé souci-

---

17. Émile Poulat comments on such juxtaposition of private and public 'space' in relation to religious '*présence*' in the world since modernity: 'Ce monde moderne—défini par l'avènement économique et politique de la *bourgeoisie*—opère à son tour et à son profit une nouvelle bipartition de l'espace, sans aucune connotation religieuse. L'opposition-clé est ici entre public et privé, dont la séparation proclamée admet toutes les variations et les transgressions de frontière qui n'en compromettent pas le principe . . . Le privé est la catégorie exaltée, mais le public est la catégorie dominante. De plus, le privé est une catégorie ambivalente et instable . . . Tout est rarement d'un seul côté . . . Dépouillée de sa quotidienneté médiévale, le religieux a changé de nom: par pudeur et par politique. Il est devenu le sacré, étrange et lointain, protégé autant qu'interdit: en un mot ambigu, défendu . . . Tel est le service que cette société a demandé aux «sciences religieuses»: grâce à elle, le sacré a pu devenir socialement intelligible et conceptuellement maîtrisé'. *Église contre bourgeoisie: introduction au devenir du catholicisme actuel* (Tournai: Casterman, 1977), 263–4.
18. *Cf* Certeau, 'L'opération historiographique', 68.

eux' ironically underscored the Church's absence from the modern world. The image of Chenu's presence among these workers was recorded and widely distributed precisely because it transgressed the received dechristianisation of the French working populations.[19] Pastorally, under the influence of the *intégristes*, the Church condemned any lay social reform responses to this crisis, such as Marc Sangnier and *Le Sillon*, giving only guarded support to the *Association catholique de la jeunesse française (A.C.J.F.)* and later to Canon Josef Cardijn's *Jeunesse Ouvrière Chrétienne (JOC)*. Politically, French Catholicism remained fixed in its nineteenth century predicament: embattled amid the anti-clerical policies of state secularisation, prerevolutionary nostalgia, and internal conflict between Gallican and Ultramontane stances toward Rome and the Republic. Among the competing ideologies of early to mid-twentieth century France, only the nationalist anti-Semitism of Charles Maurras' *Action française* received widespread ecclesiastical approval, persisting even after the movement's condemnation by Pope Pius XI in 1926.[20] Theologically, the peril of the anti-Modernist purges forestalled the wider propagation of the lay French Catholic philosophical and theological revival led by Maurice Blondel, Jacques Maritain, and Etienne Gilson.[21] The neo-scholastic theology of the late nineteenth and early twentieth century so complied with the Vatican's proscription of any sustained discourse with modernity, that it was ineffective to address the issue

---

19. The meaning of 'dechristianisation' is debated, for example: 'Pour être déchristianisées, il faut bien qu'elles [des populations] aient été un jour christianisées! C'est la mesure de cette *christianisation* qui nous révélera la mesure de la *déchristianisation*.' Jean Delumeau, *Le Catholicisme entre Luther et Voltaire* (Paris, 1971) 322, cited by Certeau in 'Questions de méthode', *L'Écriture de l'histoire*, 123-4, n 2; also Chenu: 'qu'une réalité préexistante s'est défaite', 'Déchristianisation ou non-christianisation?' (1960) in *La Parole De Dieu II. Évangile dans le temps* (Paris: Éditions du Cerf, 1964), 247–253, 248.
20. Michael Sutton, *Nationalism, Positivism and Catholicism: The Politics of Charles Maurras and French Catholics 1890–1914* (Cambridge: Cambridge University Press, 1982), 71–75, 228–32; André Laudouze OP, *Dominicains français et Action Française: 1899–1940. Maurras au Couvent* (Paris: Les Éditions Ouvrières, 1989), 181, 217.
21. Émile Poulat, *Intégrisme et catholicisme intégral: un réseau secret international anti-moderniste: La 'Sapinière' (1909–1920)* (Tournai: Casterman, 1961); *Histoire, dogme et critique dans la crise moderniste* (Paris: Casterman, 1962, revised edition 1979); and 'Critique historique et théologique dans la crise moderniste', in *Recherches des sciences religieuses*, 58 (1970): 535–550.

of alienation from the Church.[22] By mid-century a shift occurred in pastoral strategy, which acknowledged that the Church in France was 'en état de mission', as impoverished as any overseas missionary destination.[23] Fostered by formation programmes like the *Semaines sociales*, this shift was the outcome of an alliance of Catholic activists and intellectuals such as Blondel, Gabriel Le Bras, Chenu, Lubac, and Congar. From it emerged the radical strategies of 'Mission de France', notably the worker-priest innovation. Against this background the two images of Chenu embody this alliance displacing the Church's absence from the industrial world. This new '*présence*' of the Church in the contemporary world led to the radical ecclesial re-alignment of Vatican II.

Throughout his life, Chenu was called to defend the coherence of these two images against this background of ecclesial '*présence*' and absence. Even now this divisive characterisation of the youthful activist theologian and the crusty medievalist persists, itself a measure of continuing dichotomisation of faith and the world.

> On pourrait penser qu'il y a deux Chenu. L'un est un vieux médiéviste, non sans réputation, tout occupé de la lecture des textes anciens, nourris d'érudition, attachés au vieux siècles de Chrétienté, dans une tradition qu'il entretient au milieu du siècle nouveau. Puis, voici l'autre Chenu, jeune, fringant, léger, en pleine mêlée du monde contemporain, tout sensible à ses appels, prompt à l'engagement dans les problèmes les plus délicats, dans le monde et dans l'Église, dès lors discuté, suspect auprès de certains. Eh bien non! il n'y a qu'un seul et même Chenu. Ma vie est très unifiée, je ne peux pas vivre en pièces détachées. A travers l'unité paradoxale de deux

---

22. Roger Aubert: 'it has to be said that the neo-Thomist revival . . . did not bear the expected fruits, at all events not in theology, where the outdated categories of neo-Thomisim left it stranded against the mainstream of modern thought. The position was somewhat different in philosophy'. 'The Half-Century leading to Vatican II: The Life of the Church' in *The Church in a Secularised Society: The Christian Centuries*, volume 5 (New York, Paulist Press: 1978), 608.
23. Yves Congar OP attributed this expression, 'l'Église en état de mission', to Chenu in 'Le Père M.-D. Chenu', 774. Its first recorded use by Chenu was in July 1947. See Robert Wattebled, *Stratégies Catholiques en monde ouvrier dans la France d'après-guerre* (Paris: Éditions Ouvrières, 1990), 128, n 48.

personnages, de deux engagements, c'est l'unité de la théologie qui se manifeste.²⁴

Chenu insisted that his apparent 'deux personnages' were not opposed but in a dynamic dialectic, whose tension demonstrated the unity of theology in contrast to the neo-scholastic divisions of theology that estranged its dogmatic, spiritual, and moral branches from each other. Similarly, Chenu understood these 'deux engagements' as not two different phases of his life but as continuous and homogeneous. His 'jeune' orientation to current affairs coexisted with the 'vieux' activities of historical research in his early and later years and mutually informed each other. While there is development in Chenu's theology, it is not simply from an historical Thomist phase to a later theology concerned exclusively with contemporary realities. The 'deux Chenu' combined embody the critical correlation of theology and history. Chenu foreshadowed this methodological direction and the tension it provokes in late twentieth century theology. Yet the problem of how the same person encompassed both domains continues.

Post-Vatican II reception of 'deux Chenu'

Reading Chenu and reading about Chenu today discloses how the separation of 'deux Chenu' persists in the different receptions currently given to his historical and theological works. His studies of Thomas Aquinas and the intellectual history of the twelfth and thirteenth centuries continue to be cited in medieval research, whereas references to his other theological studies are scant.²⁵ The innovation of his early medieval studies and his influence on such important historians as Jacques Le Goff are widely celebrated. This acclaim extends to numerous contemporary references to his seminal work on recover-

---

24. Chenu, 'Le théologien et la vie: un entrétien avec le Père Chenu', *Informations Catholiques Internationales*, 233 (1 February 1965), 30. also *Un théologien en liberté: Jacques Duquesne interroge le Père Chenu* (Paris: Le Centurion, 1975), 61; 'Post-scriptum 1985', *Une école de théologie: le Saulchoir*, 176.
25. Some examples are: Lester K Little, *Religious Poverty and the Profit Economy in Medieval Europe* (London: Paul Elek, 1978), viii, 135, 175, 188; J Dalarun, *L'impossible sainteté, la vie retrouvée de Robert d'Arbrissel* (Paris, 1985), 221, n 144; J-M Bienvenu, *L'etonnant fondateur de Fontevraud, Robert d'Arbrissel* (Paris, 1981), 34, n 325; Carolyn Walker Bynum, *Jesus as Mother* (Berkeley: University of California Press, 1982), 4, 22 n 24, n 60, n 85, n 102.

ing Thomas Aquinas' theology in its historical context. Two dedicated issues of the journal *Revue des sciences philosophiques et théologiques*, for which Chenu regularly reviewed before World War II, featured critical assessments of his medieval studies and the historical background to his early writing together with the controversy that dogged his career.[26] 'Moyen-Âge et modernité' was the topic of a conference commemorating the centenary of his birth, which examined the reciprocity of Chenu's theological works and his medieval studies.[27]

Despite some recognition of his influence in Europe in surveys of twentieth century theology,[28] only three monographs on Chenu's theology have been published to date.[29] There are two critical editions of his work in French and Italian: the 1985 reprint of his *Une école de théologie: le Saulchoir* accompanied with articles on its historical background; and his Vatican II diaries with detailed annotation by Melloni.[30] An early *festschrift* did not include any critical studies of his theology.[31] Of interest for biographical corroboration rather than for its critical value is 'un hommage' published posthumously by his pas-

---

26. 'Hommage au Père M-D Chenu', in *Revue des sciences philosophiques et théologiques*, 75/3 (1991): 361–504; 'Le Père Marie-Dominique Chenu médiéviste', in *Revue des sciences philosophiques et théologiques*, 81/3 (1997): 371–437.
27. Guy Bedouelle, editor, *Marie-Dominique Chenu: Moyen-Âge et Modernité* (Paris: L'Institut Catholique de Paris/Le Centre d'Études du Saulchoir, 1995).
28. Congar, 'Le Père M.-D. Chenu', 772–790; G Jacquemet, 'Chenu', *Catholicisme: hier, aujourd'hui, demain* (Paris: Letouzey et Ané, 1949), 1042; Maurice A Barth, 'M.D Chenu' in *Tendenzen der Theologie im 20. Jahrhundert. Eine Geschichte in Porträts*, edited by HJ Schulz (Stuttgart: Kreuz-Verlag Stuttgart und Walter-Verlag Olten, 1966), 409–415; Marcel Neusch and Bruno Chenu OFM, *Au Pays de la théologie* (Paris: Centurion, 1994), 66–72.
29. Luis-Antonio Gallo, *La concepción de la salvacion y sus presupuestos en M-D Chenu* (Rome: LAS, 1977); Maria Luisa Mazzarello, *Il rapporto Chiesa-mondo nel pensiero del P Marie-Dominique Chenu* (Città del vaticano: Tipografia Poliglotta Vaticana, 1979); Christophe F Potworowski, *Contemplation and Incarnation. The Theology of Marie-Dominique Chenu* (Montreal and Kingsrton: McGill-Queens University Press, 2001).
30. Chenu, *Une école de théologie: le Saulchoir* (Paris: Les Éditions du Cerf, 1985), with articles by Giuseppe Alberigo, Étienne Fouilloux, Jean Ladrière, and Jean-Pierre Jossua OP; *Notes quotidiennes au Concile: Journal de Vatican II 1962-1963*, edited by Alberto Melloni (Paris: Les Éditions du Cerf, 1995).
31. *Mélanges offerts à M-D Chenu, Maître en théologie* (Paris: Librairie Philosophique J Vrin, 1967).

toral contacts and colleagues.[32] Recent historical studies of Vatican II, particularly those by Joseph Komonchak and Giuseppe Alberigo, refer repeatedly to Chenu's influence on the Council's agenda and its documents. The circumstances surrounding Chenu's condemnations by Roman authorities are well examined by ecclesiastical historians including Alberigo and Fouilloux. Elements of Chenu's theology have been critically assessed by three Dominicans. Ted Schoof has given an favourable account of Chenu and his theological innovations and influence in his survey of early and mid-twentieth century theology; Henry Donneaud has produced three fiercely critical articles on the validity of Chenu's historical reputation and theological methodology; Claude Geffré produced two articles on the central themes of the Incarnation and the 'signs of the times' in Chenu's theology.[33]

Since Vatican II, three centres have generated a small number of unpublished theses on Chenu's theology. From the Gregorian University in Rome came two accounts of Chenu's ecclesiology, one about the influence of his theology of work on *Gaudium et Spes*, the other about the Incarnation as fundamental to the Church's engagement with history;[34] from the University of Strasbourg II, a study of his Vatican II theology of the laity in *Gaudium et Spes*, and another thesis which highlighted the significance of Chenu's historical meth-

---

32. Claude Geffré OP, editor *L'hommage différé au Père Chenu* (Paris: Cerf, 1990).
33. Schoof, *Breakthrough: Beginnings of the New Theology* (1970); for example Henry Donneaud OP, 'Histoire d'une histoire: M.-D. Chenu et «La théologie comme science au XIIIe siècle»', in *Mémoire Dominicaine*, 4 (1994): 139–175; 'La constitution dialectique de la théologie et de son histoire selon M.-D. Chenu', in *Revue Thomiste*, XCVI/1 (1996): 41–66; Claude Geffré OP, 'Le réalisme de l'Incarnation dans la théologie du Père M-D Chenu', in *Revue des sciences philosophiques et théologiques*, 69 (1985): 389–399; 'Théologie de l'Incarnation et théologie des signes des temps chez le Père Chenu', in *Marie-Dominique Chenu: Moyen-Âge et Modernité*, 131–153.
34. Josip Grbac, 'Lavoro e vocazione integrale dell'uomo—pre-storia della constituzione pastorale *Gaudium et Spes* nella teologia cattolica dell'area di langua francese.' (unpublished STD thesis, Gregorian University, 1988); Valentin Zanatta, 'Por una Igreja encarnada na història—linihas de fundo do pensamento eclesiológico de M.-D. Chenu' (unpublished STD thesis, Gregorian University, 1989). Chenu has been also treated in other Roman theses but not as their main topic, eg Protais Safi, 'La «consecratio mundi» et la théologie du laïcat à la veille de Vatican II' (unpublished STD thesis, Pontificia Universita' Lateranense, 1981).

odology for his Incarnational theology;[35] and from Louvain-la-Neuve two reviews of his earlier theology.[36] The more substantial treatment by Gallo of Chenu's work as a whole attempted to systematise Chenu's writings into a theology of salvation. While Gallo outlined Chenu's anthropology as integral to this soteriology, his thesis confirms the suspicion that Chenu was not attempting to write such a systematic theology. Under the supervision of Edward Schillebeeckx, who was Chenu's student, Toine van den Hoogen wrote a thesis on Chenu's pastoral theology, encompassing its focus on praxis and the influence of the *Annales* style of social history on both the subject matter and method of his theology, and its reception by the political activists of the pre- and post-War French Church.[37] This location of Chenu's theology in its intellectual and political contexts is one of the better studies of Chenu. Although its emphasis is on the pastoral role of Chenu's theology, it does not discount his work as 'merely' pastoral.

Chenu's theology is less studied in the English-speaking world.[38] Although listed among the greatest names in Catholic twentieth century thought with Lubac, Daniélou, Bouyer, Balthasar, Blondel, and Guardini, Chenu has not yet been republished in the *Ressourcement* series.[39] In contrast with these esteemed contemporaries, Chenu is missing from most contemporary theology except in footnotes.

---

35. M Graczyk, 'La doctrine de la «consecratio mundi» chez Marie-Dominique Chenu' (unpublished STD thesis, Faculté de Theologie Catholique, Université de Strasbourg II, 1978); and Dominik Kubicki, 'La Logique de l'Incarnation selon M.-D. Chenu' (unpublished PhD thesis, Université de Strasbourg 2, 1994). Kubicki's thesis gives Chenu's historical methodology more significance in relation to his Incarnational theology than does Potworowski or others.
36. J-M Dussart, 'L'Évangile dans la réflexion du Père Chenu. Sur la méthode théologique des années 1936 à 1939' (unpublished PhD thesis, Faculté de Théologie, l'Université Catholique Louvain, 1975); Terry Hanley OP, 'An Exposition of the Major Themes of the Theology of M-D Chenu for the period 1920–1965' (unpublished STL thesis, Faculté de Théologie, l'Université de Louvain-la-Neuve, 1981).
37. Published as: Toine van den Hoogen [Antonius Josephus Maria], *Pastorale Teologie: Ontwikkeling en Struktuur in de Teologie van M.-D. Chenu* (Alblasserdam: Offsetdrukkerij Kanters BV, 1983).
38. This could be largely due to the few translations of his work. (See Bibliography: English titles)
39. Co-published by T&T Clark and Eerdmans, the *Ressourcement* series includes the works of the key Catholic theological precursors to Vatican II and some recent critical studies of their writings.

Theses in English are few, usually employing Chenu's theology in a broader study, for example Robert Keller OP's revisiting the topic of the theology of work.[40] A more substantial study is Christophe Potworowski's compelling thesis on the Incarnation in Chenu's theology.[41] While my own emphases differ at times from his, Potworowski delivers a thorough and valuable study of the Incarnation in Chenu's theology, with many insights into the development of Chenu's thought on the centrality of history, society, and matter. It is also significant because it has attracted the attention of some English-language theologians to the continuing relevance of Chenu's theology.[42]

Overall, this literature on Chenu provides only scant evaluation of his theology. References to his ecclesiology and the Incarnation recur, but even then Chenu is acknowledged as an historical moment in twentieth century theology, but not given any substantial treatment. With the exception of Donneaud, most writing on Chenu's theology has been in the form of an appreciation from those educated by him or positively influenced by him. The critical assessment by Potworowski narrowly turns on Chenu's resistance to producing a systematic theology, 'he has never clarified or developed it [his theology] into a system'.[43] This reflects the systematic preoccupation of post-Vatican II theology. From this literature on Chenu's theology, one could erroneously conclude that he has little to offer that is specifically compelling for theology today.

Post-Vatican II absence of Chenu's theology

Chenu's absence from late twentieth century Catholic theology calls for an historical as much as a theological analysis. It would be

---

40. Robert John Keller OP, 'Toward a Contemporary Roman Catholic Theology of Work' (PhD, Graduate Theological Union, San Francisco, 1993).
41. Christophe F Potworowski, 'The Incarnation in the Theology of Marie-Dominique Chenu' (unpublished PhD, School of Theology, University of St Michael's College, Toronto, 1988)—published as *Contemplation and Incarnation. The Theology of Marie-Dominique Chenu* (Montreal and Kingsrton: McGill-Queens University Press, 2001). His Chapter II of the thesis was published as 'History and Incarnation in the theology of M-D Chenu', in *Sciences et Esprit*, 42 (1990): 237–265.
42. Roger Haight SJ, *Dynamics of Theology* (New York: Paulist Press, 1990), 2–3.
43. Potworowski (thesis), 5.

easy to consign his theology to the status of an historical footnote, passed over because of its particularity and historical proximity to the theological whirlwind of Vatican II. Chenu's invisibility could then be partly accounted for by the dominance of German-language theology since Vatican II and the coterminal decline in Thomist and French theology. As Schoof observes, influential Catholic theological revivals repeatedly shifted between Germany and France during the century.[44] As evidence of this, Chenu retains both authority and currency in French-speaking, Spanish, and Italian social justice circles.[45] The inward-looking dimension of much Catholic ecclesiology since Vatican II would also explain the fate of an advocate of theological dialogue with the world. By contrast, Congar's extraordinary output in ecclesiology and ecumenical theology corresponded more to the need of the post-Vatican II Church's to define itself in terms of its history and in relation to other branches of Christianity. Chenu was not officially present during Vatican II. Held in suspicion under Pope Pius XII, he was the only major theologian not to be rehabilitated by invitation to any of the commissions of the Council. This could also account for his failure to receive wider reception after Vatican II. His activity during the Council included initiating the idea and draft of the 'Message to the World' proclaimed by the assembled bishops, assisting the efforts of the Eastern Rite bishops to have non-Latin

---

44. Schoof, 95–96.
45. This is an observation by Rev Dr Frank McHugh, Director of the Von Hügel Institute for Social Justice, Cambridge. He noted the frequent references to Chenu by French, Spanish and Italian theologians at conferences in Europe on the Church's social teaching. (Personal conversation 1997). This is corroborated by articles on Chenu's influence in Italy and Spain: Antonio Franco, 'La teología de M-D Chenu: itinerario histórico-culturel', *Ciencia Tomista*, 112/2 (1985): 231–265; Alberto Escallada Tijero OP, 'La pasión por la verdad. Tríptico con Chenu al fondo', in *Ciencia Tomista*, 112/2 (1985): 267–276; Gregorio Celada, 'Apotación de la historia a la comprensión de la Palabra', *Ciencia Tomista*, 112/2 (1985): 315–339; Ettore de Giorgis, 'Padre Chenu: una teologia incarnata nella storia', in *Vita Sociale*, XLVII.240/2 (1990): 109–119; Evangelista Vilanova, 'Réception de la théologie du Père Chenu en Espagne', in *Revue des sciences philosophiques et theologiques* 75 (1991): 457–468; G Colombo, 'Il «secondo Chenu» in Italia', in *Revue des sciences philosophiques et theologiques* 75 (1991): 491–504; and the bibliography of Chenu's later writing, Maria Luisa Mazzarello, 'Gli scritti del P Marie-Dominique Chenu 1963–1979', in *Salesianum*, 42 (1980): 855–866.

theology incorporated in the Council's debates and documents, and promoting the Church of the poor. As Chenu remained at its edges, he was easily overlooked once the Council's topicality waned.[46] That is not to say that Chenu's theology has been completely ignored. It can be found in such surprising places as a 1999 reference by Pope John Paul II in his message to artists.[47] Nor has his influence been entirely lost, as is acknowledged in a variety of contemporary theological works, but this seems not to translate into wider theological discourse where Chenu is not today acknowledged in any degree equivalent to his historical influence on the theology of Vatican II.[48]

Providing better explanation might be the influence of the restoration under the pontificate of Pope John Paul II, which promoted a selective pantheon of precursors to the Council. Lubac, Balthasar, Bouyer, and Ratzinger were retrieved because they rejected the liberalisation attributed to Vatican II, while Daniélou (despite also being a

---

46. Chenu, *Notes quotidiennes au Concile: Journal de Vatican II 1962–1963* (Paris: Les Éditions du Cerf, 1995); Giuseppe Alberigo, 'Un Concile à la dimension du monde: Marie-Dominique Chenu à Vatican II d'après son Journal', in *Marie-Dominique Chenu: Moyen-Âge et Modernité*, 155–172; Roberto Tucci SJ, 'Introduction historique et doctrinale: Ferments rénovateurs durant la Troisième Session Conciliaire (14 septembre–21 novembre 1964)', in *L'Église dans le monde de ce temps—réflexions et perspectives*, editor by Yves M-J Congar OP, and M Peuchmaurd OP, Unam Sanctam 65b (tome II) (Paris: Cerf, 1967), 73–127, 102, n 97).
47. *Letter of His Holiness Pope John Paul II to Artists* (Easter Sunday 1999), para. 11. Pope Paul VI also cited him in the section on work in *Populorum progressio* (1967), 27 (n 29), and on the role of the theologian in *Les théologiens et le Collège Episcopal: autonomie et service*. [Istituto Paolo VI, Brescia, *Insegnamenti di Paolo VI*, volume VII] (Vatican: Libreria editrice Vaticana, 1977), 654.
48. Theologians like Schillebeeckx, Hans Küng and Gustavo Guttierrez continue to refer to Chenu beyond his historical significance, for example Gutiérrez, *We Drink from our own Wells* (Maryknoll, New York: Orbis, 1988), 129, 147, n 2. Recent references to Chenu's theological influence in English include: Roger Haight SJ, *Dynamics of Theology* (New York: Paulist Press, 1990), 2–3; Bengt Holmberg, *Sociology and the New Testament: an Appraisal* (Minneapolis: Fortress, 1990), 157; Joseph Komonchak, 'Ecclesiology and Social Theory. A methodological Essay', in *The Thomist*, 45 (1981): 262–283, 270, n 12; John Thornhill, 'Is Religion the enemy of faith?', in *Theological Studies,* 45 (1984): 254–274; Paula Jean Miller OSF, 'Technology and the Theology of Earthly Realities in M-D Chenu', in *Chicago Studies* 40/3 (2001): 299–312.

later critic) and Chenu are passed over.[49] Chenu was criticised as being too optimistic, too taken with the promethean progress of the 1960s, to continue to be credible to the following disillusioned decades.[50] Much of the criticism of Chenu's optimism comes from those who objected to his repeated attacks on pessimism about humanity and on the flight from the world characteristic of contemporary and historical forms of Augustinian spiritualism.[51] There is an echo here of the traditional opposition between Augustinian pessimism and Thomist optimism and its ongoing effect on the different receptions of Vatican II. Following Komonchak, David Tracy attributes to this traditional opposition the source of recent tensions about Catholic theological method.[52] He identified those theologians who had 'spent their early years retrieving either patristic thought (especially Origen) or, among the medieval classics, Bonaventure rather than Aquinas', as withdrawing 'from continuing intellectual and institutional self-reform' after Vatican II.[53] These theologians rejected the 'new post-Modernist

---

49. Selected early writings of Congar are also included in 'restorationist' collections despite his life-long support for Vatican II. Joseph Ratzinger's commentaries on *Gaudium et Spes* from immediately after the Council provide much evidence for such a reading of the conflict since Vatican II. See 'The Dignity of the Human Person', in *Commentary on the Documents of Vatican II*, volume V, edited by H Vorgrimler (New York: Herder, 1969), 115–163; 'its problems and its openness' is Ratzinger's term: *Theological Highlights of Vatican II* (New York: Paulist, 1966), 161.
50. Such an account ignores Christian hope and offers an historically fallacious representation of the sixties. Chenu's 'optimism' pre-existed the Vatican II period and also entailed a critical assessment of contemporary reality.
51. Chenu's critique of such Augustinianism was relentless, although he did distinguish it from Augustine's theology, 'Présentation', *Théologie de la matière. Civilisation technique et spiritualité chrétienne*, coll. Foi Vivante 59 (Paris: Éditions du Cerf, 1967), 8. Throughout Chenu's theology there recurred a sub-text rejecting excessive 'Augustinian' spiritualism ('la tradition augustinienne') as a 'manichéisme larvae', cf 'Spiritualité de la Matière' (1962) in *La Parole de Dieu II*, 453–459, 455. 'Augustinian' for Chenu was rhetorical shorthand for the dualism of the Augustinian-Bonaventure-Duns Scotus tradition and the later Jansenist-Cartesian influence on 'modern-scholasticism', see 'Situation humaine' (418).
52. Komonchak's excursus in 'Vatican II and the Encounter between Catholicism and Liberalism' in *Catholicism and Liberalism*, edited by RB Douglas and D Hollenbach (Cambridge: Cambridge University Press, 1994), 76–99, 86–8.
53. David Tracy cites Lubac, Balthasar, Daniélou and Ratzinger as representative of this *ressourcement*. Tracy, 'The Uneasy Alliance Reconceived: Catholic Theological Method, Modernity, and Postmodernity', in *Theological Studies*, 50 (1989): 548–570, 552–555.

alliance' methodology of the critical correlation of theology with contemporary thought. In contrast, those theologians whose *ressourcement* involved the study of Thomas Aquinas, Chenu, Congar, Rahner, and Schillebeeckx, remained open to the outcomes of the Council and the need for ongoing reform.

According to Joseph DiNoia's critique of postconciliar theology in North America: 'the postconciliar collapse of neo-Thomism regrettably and unnecessarily involved the eclipse, at least in Catholic theological circles, of Aquinas himself.'[54] He saw the reception of Vatican II polarised around its two catch-words *ressourcement* and *aggiornamento*. Those who prioritised 'the reaffirmation of Christian identity' implicit in the *ressourcement* interpreted the Council in terms of the conciliar documents *Dei verbum* and *Lumen Gentium*, whereas a focus on 'modernization, dialogue and social commitment' distinguished those (especially 'numerous and influential' in the American Catholic Church) who emphasised *Gaudium et Spes*.[55] DiNoia argued the need for 'a Thomas after Thomism' to redress Catholic theology's slide into an accommodation with modernity's agenda—a theology faithfully grounded in the Christian tradition, engaging the challenges of contemporary society while creating 'a vital Church life'. Yet Chenu, whose theology was characterised precisely by these attributes and concerns, was not named. While DiNoia's focus was on North American theology, which shared in the English-speaking Church's ignorance of Chenu's theology, Chenu's absence here suggests a more

---

54. JA DiNoia OP, 'American Catholic Theology at Century's End: Postconciliar, Postmodern, Post-Thomistic', in *The Thomist*, 54 (1990): 499–518, 510. The imprecise and polemical uses of the term 'neo-scholasticism' insufficiently distinguished the variety of the historical stages of the 'modern' examples of Thomism encompassed. In chapter 2 Chenu's term 'modern scholasticism' is preferred. In the present chapter, 'Thomist' encompasses the Thomist theologies of Chenu, Congar, Rahner, Lonergan and early Schillebeeckx as to the pre-Vatican II 'neo-scholastic' and 'neo-Thomist' theologies of Garrigou-Lagrange, Journet, Billot, and *Humani Generis*.
55. DiNoia draws on the American Lutheran theologian George Lindbeck for these *ressourcement* and *aggiornamento* categories. Other restorationist commentators nuance the poles as for example in the statement that 'the issue that divided them was not whether *aggiornamento* was needed, but rather precisely what was to serve as the guidelines and norms for the *aggiornamento* process.' Marcellino d'Ambrosiano, '*Ressourcement* theology, *aggiornamento*, and the hermeneutics of tradition', in *Communio*, 18 (1991): 530–555, 554, n 90.

deliberate relegation of his theology by 'restoration' proponents rather than an oversight due to the passage of time. DiNoia's concern for 'an uncompromising unapologetic' together with the pessimism of the current 'restoration'/*ressourcement* ascendancy would seem to have little commerce with Chenu's theological reflection with the world in mind. Yet DiNoia's quest for 'a post-*neo*-Thomistic Aquinas?' corresponding to Pope John Paul II and the then Cardinal Ratzinger's '*reaccentramento*' projects ('balancing tradition-mindedness with modernization'[56]) recalled Chenu's initial and abiding preoccupation with understanding theology as 'la foi *in statu scientiae*' and as in 'le statut historique'. Chenu's theology of engagement does not so much comply with modernity's agenda but critically articulates the faith as historical witness *and* in terms that address the questions of the day. Chenu anticipated the desire of DiNoia's postmodern and neo-*ressourcement* theology to reject both modernist historicism as well as 'the narrower post-Tridentine tradition enshrined by neo-scholastic and neo-Thomistic theology'. DiNoia's approval of postmodern anthropological categories of 'bodiliness, agency, and community' for 'new theological initiatives' as against the modernist categories of 'subjectivity, consciousness, and the autonomous self', would appear also to be anticipated in the material, vocational, and social orientation that characterises Chenu's Christian anthropology.

Alberigo and Kerr welcomed as timely the reissue of Chenu's *Une école de théologie: le Saulchoir* in 1985 precisely because his theological method overcame this opposition between *ressourcement* and reform.[57] Because Chenu's optimistic view of humanity's destiny in the world failed to fit the confessional interests and Augustinian pessimism of current official theology, his blend of traditional teaching and critical correlation with contemporary understanding has not

---

56. DiNoia, 'American Catholic Theology at Century's End', 501.
57. 'Dans le contexte actuel de lassitude, de désorientation, et même nostalgie, le propos méthodologique de P. Chenu révèle pleinement sa capacité à guider un profond renouvellement de la connaissance scientifique du christianisme...fidèle à l'inspiration thomiste, mais également engagé dans les problèmes que pose aux chrétiens la culture contemporaine.' Giuseppe Alberigo, 'Christianisme en tant qu'histoire et «théologie confessante»', in *Une école de théologie: le Saulchoir* (Paris: Cerf, 1985), 11–34, 12. 'amid the enthusiasm and neo-conservatism of the era of Pope John Paul II it may be time to retrieve a classic by an imaginative use of documentation in tandem with speculative reasoning.' Fergus Kerr OP, 'Chenu's Little Book', in *New Blackfriars,* 66 March (1985): 108–112, 112.

been rehabilitated in the latest ressourcement of pre-Vatican II theology. For Chenu's theology to re-emerge would require a more critical engagement with our times rather than the resignation of such timeless pessimism. Instead the ineffective century-long polemic by official teaching against Promethean *techne* and its secularisation remains mute before globalised economic and social violence. Chenu's theology evokes the urgent need to recognise the incarnational presence of the Gospel in the world, not as ideal but real: 'd'avoir à penser ma foi sous l'urgence d'une mutation humaine, cela crée dans ma réflexion théologique une puissance de rénovation étonnante.'[58] The inductive turn of Chenu's theology led way from a confessional ideology to engagement with questions posed by the world to the Gospel:

> ce n'est plus la foi qui interpelle la politique ou l'économique, c'est la politique et l'économique qui interpellent la foi. Le point d'ancrage est le terrestre. Autrement dit, je ne me réfère pas à ma foi pour essayer de voir clair en politique, c'est mon engagement politique qui me provoque à me référer à l'Évangile. Vous voyez le changement de perspective. Il tire toute la conséquence du fait que l'Église n'est pas située hors du monde, en un lieu d'où elle enverrait ses hommes et ses idées vers le monde . . . Elle n'a son existence que dans le monde.[59]

Then theology might more effectively articulate the eschatological completion and transformation of the world in Christ, which saves from the sinfulness and despair of absence.

No doubt there is a contemporary agenda that militates against recognition of Chenu's continuing value, but it must be acknowledged that the simplest explanation of his current neglect resides in his style of '*ad hoc* apologetics'. Unlike most of his Thomist contemporaries, Chenu rejected the superiority accorded to timeless and universal categories in favour of particularity and historical contingency incorporated into theological discourse.[60] For Chenu, theology must be relevant to the time it was written. Just as his optimism may

---

58. *Un théologien en liberté*, 70.
59. *Un théologien en liberté*, 78.
60. In contrast to: 'La sagesse de saint Thomas est au-dessus de toute particularisation', Jacques Maritain, *Le docteur Angélique* (Paris: Desclée De Brouwer, 1930), 24.

seem dated, so does much of his content because it is so historically conditioned by the circumstances in which it was written. The controversies and concerns of his writing can appear banal, since they are now so accepted. Sometimes even his interlocutors are now forgotten, and the sting of his polemic is salved by the outcomes of his influence since Vatican II.[61] Perhaps the inseparability of his method from his content renders it largely irretrievable, hence its demise, except for its interest to historians.

Yet some of Chenu's content does transcend its particularity to be as relevant today as it ever was, for example his retrieval of an anthropology far removed from the negative Manichean tendencies found in Catholic Christianity. Geffré has observed that Chenu's particularity requires that 'une théologie n'est vivante que dans le dépassement d'elle-même en réponse à de nouvelles conjonctures historiques'. He finds Chenu's continuing value is 'à interpréter différemment la conscience historique de l'Église en cette fin du second millénaire'.[62] This would indicate the appropriate orientation for a study of Chenu's Christian anthropology: not only to seek what abiding value can be mined from Chenu's theology, but to understand how the concerns of his time shaped his theological approach to what is human, in order to discern how they might shape theology about what it means to be human today.

A history of Chenu's theology

The historical consciousness active in Chenu's theology in turn demands some location of his work within its historical context. Without such a perspective 'deux Chenu' are perpetuated through a textual periodisation that distinguishes his earlier major historical work from the so-called incomplete and undeveloped theological

---

61. Kerr makes this observation about the current obscurity of Chenu's negative allusions in *Une école de théologie: le Saulchoir* in 'Chenu's Little Book', 110-111. Another more negative example of the disadvantage of this particularity is Henry Donneaud's accusation that Chenu's contemporary concerns distorted his historical and theological reading of developments in 12th-13th, 16th-17th and 19th century theology. (see particularly 'La constitution dialectique de la théologie et de son histoire selon M.-D. Chenu', in *Revue Thomiste* XCVI/1 (1996): 41-66.
62. Claude Geffré OP, 'Théologie de l'Incarnation et théologie des signes des temps chez le Père Chenu', in *Marie-Dominique Chenu: Moyen-Âge et Modernité*, 132.

reflections on contemporary issues of his later life.⁶³ Such a history would locate the constraints on his theological writing, the ruptures they caused in his treatment of key subject-matter, and the means by which he nevertheless continued to work on his major themes. Chenu's own practice of supplying chronological appendices for his *St Thomas d'Aquin et la théologie* and the second of his two 1964 volumes of collected essays furnished 'les contextes religieux ou profanes des articles ici rassemblés'.⁶⁴ To review Chenu's life in relation to his theology would require more than a biographical summary or a list of the influences on his thought.⁶⁵ Some explanation is required of his reasons for taking a different course to that of 'la position qu'avait le christianisme avant 1939 dans la société française (partagé entre un mouvement d'*intériorisation*—avec *Primauté du spirituel* de Maritain (1927) ou *Esprit* de Mounier (1932)—et un *positivisme* religieux des traditionalistes).'⁶⁶ Many questions remain unanswered: How did he become such a theological innovator despite his Roman training and in such a particularly censored period? What led to his unconventional activism for industrial workers given the reactionary politics of the French Church and Dominicans? What theological perspective informed his early rejection of the politics of the Right and their definition of humanity in terms of 'family, work and nation'? What understanding of community and the structures of society allowed him to anticipate the reform of Church–world relations thirty years before Vatican II? What were his formative experiences that initiated

---

63. This is the superficial judgement by Hanley who notably does not refer to the restrictions placed upon Chenu's publishing at crucial moments during his career.
64. Chenu, *St Thomas d'Aquin et la théologie* (Paris: Éditions du Seuil, 1959), 186–7 and 'Repères Chronologiques', in *La Parole de Dieu II. Évangile dans le temps* (Paris: Éditions du Cerf, 1964), 680–687, 680.
65. Given Chenu's eclecticism, I share Certeau's caution about explaining a thinker exclusively in terms of his sources or influences thereby missing the discontinuities or inventive juxtaposition of different ideas and experiences: 'cette remontée sans fin à travers une poussière de fragments, l'évanouissement des totalités, des délimitations, des ruptures qui constituent l'histoire.' 'Faire de l'histoire', 37. Chenu similarly emphasised the significance of discontinuity.
66. Certeau, 'Faire de l'histoire', 33; Émile Poulat specifically cites Chenu as the representative of that other polarity in the French Church: 'Par exemple, comment penser ensemble le *progressisme* du P Chenu et le *traditionalisme* de l'abbé Richard', in *Église contre bourgeoisie*, 59, n 19.

appreciation of the centrality of history and humanity in his theology? These await a substantial biographical treatment not possible for this thesis.

Schoof introduced Chenu as 'one of the few people who seems to survive even the most extreme praise that his friends lavish on him—anyone reading about him is bound to want to meet him'.[67] This observation was repeated by Congar, Schillebeeckx, and Brosse, raising more specifically personal questions about Chenu. Why was his pastoral approach attractive to people of different social classes, genders, degrees of education, disbelief or belief? Who is included (or excluded) in Chenu's understanding of humanity? How did Chenu come to his theological understanding of what it means to be human? What sustained his commitment to the Church despite being repeatedly condemned? As a person and a theologian, Chenu is both of his times and also ahead of them; how is this resolved in him? Such queries are not intended to psychologise his theology and practice, nor to reduce his inspiration to biographically determined factors. There is the danger of isolating the subject in a biography despite locating that person in their context, either through the specificity provided from hindsight or an analysis that over-values individuality above the collaborative and social immersion. Besides, there is a conjunction of forces and challenges that constitute being in any context. Such distinctions as constructed in biography would run counter to the social interactivity of Chenu's theology. Instead, since he privileged socialisation, which bore a theological as well as political meaning for Chenu, indicating the resurgence of Gospel energy in ordinary human lives as well as in the movements of social reform and solidarity in history, it is more probable to discover him through his theological projects. At his funeral in Notre Dame Cathedral in 1990, the eminent atheist French historian Jacques le Goff, who had been his student, proclaimed in his eulogy:

> Vous étiez dans votre pensée comme dans votre existence la vie, la vivacité avec les orages généreux d'un homme qui n'ignore pas les ténèbres, mais qui suit la lumière, toujours présente, même clignotante. Une homme toujours ouvert aux autres, attentif à eux. Humain, trop humain diront certains, mais pas ceux qui vous ont connu . . . Vous nous avez appris

---

67. Schoof, *Breakthrough*, 102.

le courage, la fermeté, l'intrépidité, voire la résistance, mais dans l'humilité.[68]

Chenu's theological life oscillated between acute periods of '*présence*' and influence in the Church's life and chronic periods of absence and disregard. His story echoes that of Certeau's 'missing one' whose absence speaks greater truth than the whole assembly or community combined. Chenu refused the role of outcast by displacing the centre of the Church to a '*présence*' in the modern world: a displacement that encouraged his development of a theology about the humanity present in his times. As 'un manquant fait écrire'[69] Chenu recovered 'la Parole de Dieu' as 'la Foi dans l'intelligence' as well as 'Évangile dans le temps'. The next chapter examines how, in his early theology, Chenu pursued the identification of the human component of 'la Foi dans l'intelligence'.

---

68. Jacques Le Goff, 'Au Père Chenu', in *Lumière et Vie*, 39/196 (1990): 138-139.
69. Certeau, *La Fable mystique*, 9.

Chapter 2
Chenu's Theological Project

> 'Si vraiment l'homme connaît Dieu,
> il le connaîtra humainement.'
> Chenu, 'Position de la théologie' (1935) in
> *La Parole de Dieu I. La Foi dans intelligence*
> (Paris: Cerf, 1964), 115–38, 119.

Introduction

Chenu's theology developed within theological limits set by two events: the endorsement of neo-scholastic Thomism by Pope Leo XIII as the universal theology for Latin Catholicism from 1879, and the proscription of any tendencies to theological 'modernism', from the pontificate of Pius X.[1] The intensely analytical scholasticism that resulted enshrined propositional content and a deductive method for theology. In this chapter, Chenu's early theology is surveyed for its theological anthropological direction, especially the challenge his insistence on historicity posed to the neo-scholasticism of this period. Chenu labelled this 'modern scholasticism' to flag his belief

---

1. In 1879 Leo XIII's encyclical *Aeterni Patris* called Catholic scholarship to reinstate the theological tradition of Aquinas, especially, but also Augustine and other Patristic sources. In Pius X's encyclical *Pascendi* (1907) neo-scholasticism was recruited to police theology. See Roger Aubert, 'The Modernist Crisis and the Integrist Reaction' in *The Church in a Secularised Society* (New York/London: Paulist Press/Darton, Longman and Todd, 1978), 198–203.

that its true paternity was Enlightenment rationalism, not unbroken descent from medieval Thomism.²

> Dans la technique quotidienne, c'est le formalisme logique qui triomphe au détriment de la curiosité, et à la «dispute» médiévale se sont substitués les «exercises scolastiques» qui n'en sont que la parodie dialectique.³

This late scholasticism reduced theology to a philosophical apologetics that took on the rationalist style of the modernity it sought to combat. Theology thus condemned itself to a solipsistic retreat to the margins of the modern world.⁴ Chenu initiated an innovative theological *rapprochement* with contemporary thought to circumscribe this marginalisation. He found authorisation for this in the example of Thomas Aquinas in the thirteenth century. Chenu's diachronic study of Thomas' full opus in its context showed the extent of 'modern scholastic' deviation from Thomas' theology. It revealed the scope

---

2. Chenu called this 'modern scholasticism' or, even more pejoratively, 'baroque scholasticism': 'Sous le patronage de Leibniz, cette qualification de *philosophia perennis* nous invite à reconnaître, puis à situer—historiquement et doctrinalement—certain idéal d'intelligibilité qui marqua la scolastique moderne, et lui donne encore aujourd'hui le plus souvent sa tonalité. Cette scolastique tendit à définir l'intelligible sous forme strictement rationnelle: l'intelligible, c'est le concept qui s'analyse et qui s'attribue; le lien du réel, sa structure intime est imaginée comme un lien de concepts'. *Une école de théologie: le Saulchoir*, 83 [155]; cf also 'il apparaît bientôt que des tranches entières de philosophie médiévale ont disparu, ou du moins ont perdu leur densité spirituelle et systématique, dans la «scolastique» moderne, qui revendique pourtant l'hériage de cette philosophie médiévale.' 'Ratio superior et inferior. Un cas de philosophie chrétienne', in *Revue des sciences philosophiques et théologiques*, XXIX (1940): 84–89, 84.
3. *Une école*, 156. Chenu also termed this neo-scholasticism as the 'thomisme de séminaire' and 'thomisme régénéré par le kantisme'.
4. Chenu, 'Aux origines de la «science moderne»', in *Revue des sciences philosophiques et théologiques*, XXIX (1940): 206–217, 21; and 'Ratio superior et inferior. Un cas de philosophie chrétienne', in *Revue des sciences philosophiques et théologiques*, XXIX (1940): 84–89, 88; See the full elaboration of this view in Michael J Buckley SJ, *At the Origins of Modern Atheism* (New Haven: Yale Unversity Press, 1987). 341–2, 344–7, particularly 357: 'In failing to assert its own competence, in commissioning philosophy with its defense, religion shaped its own eventual negation.' and 358: 'Theology alienated its own nature by generating a philosophy that functioned as apologetics.'

of Thomas' engagement with his contemporary context and classical thought and contrasted Thomas' theology with the narrow systematisation digested into the manual theology of this time.[5]

After the 'modernist crisis' the historical status of theology and Revelation remained unresolved. Chenu's early publications betray his impatience with the atemporality and extrinsicism that passed for a 'super-orthodoxie'.[6] The perspective derived from his teaching of the history of doctrine gave him more critical historical purchase on doctrinal development. His uncommon theological openness to the challenges posed by contemporary philosophies disposed him to regard the 'Modernist crisis' as continuous with, not an aberration from, the celebrated theological achievements of the late nineteenth century.[7] These had awakened the Church to the urgent need for reform of theology through an engagement of faith with each historical situation.[8] Chenu wanted to restore the critical engagement of Catholic theology with contemporary life and thought by reclaiming the unity of the positive and speculative, mystical and doctrinal, and speculative and practical divisions of theology.[9] He advocated a theology that could integrate the experience of faith, situate doctrine within its human history, and draw out the human inclination to reason as constitutive of the dynamic of faith. After the negative allusions to such theology by Pope Pius XII to the Jesuit Congregation and later to the Domini-

---

5. The manual theology of Denzinger received further authorisation from the promotion of the digest of the 'Twenty-Four Theses' in 1914.
6. 'Le thomisme devenait pour eux une super-orthodoxie.' *Un théologien en liberté*, 32.
7. 'Les controverses et les incidents ultérieurs ne doivent ni dissimuler ni compromettre les fruits de cette très féconde activité, à laquelle présidait Léon XIII'. *Une école*, 35 [115]. Chenu provocatively included a 'Modernist' pantheon in *Une école*'s second chapter on 'Esprit et méthodes': Blondel, citation of a letter from George Tyrrel to Baron von Hügel, and a reference to Loisy.
8. 'Si, à tous ces étages, la controverse moderniste donna alors un caractère d'urgence à la «réforme de la théologie», comme on disait, les problèmes posés s'enracinaient en réalité beaucoup plus loin et engageaient toute l'histoire de la théologie moderne: *le statut des disciplines théologiques sur lequel nous vivons est celui des XVI*^{e}*-XVII*^{e} *siècles, non celui des Sommes médiévales*.' *Une école*, 51–2 [129].
9. Chenu outlined the origins and outcomes of the separation of positive and speculative theology, the extremes of 'historicisme et theologisme', in his later summary of his theology: *La théologie est-elle une science?* (Paris: Athème Fayard, 1957), 110–112.

can leadership in Rome, such theology became known as 'nouvelle théologie', although those designated its proponents, Lubac, Chenu, Congar, and Daniélou, neither perceived themselves as nor acted as a movement.

Chenu's earliest theology focused on the rupture between speculative and 'mystical theology'. In Aquinas' teaching on contemplation, he uncovered faith presented as contemplation. For Chenu following Aquinas, faith is the affective experience of God's illuminating self-disclosure to each person that constitutes the desire for union with God and is grounded in human assent to the truths of Revelation. This is not a mindless affirmation of 'truths' or the confession of the 'deposit of faith'. Aquinas established the engagement of human intelligence in faith: that faith is unified in its formal and real qualities, and congruent with the process of all human reasoning. From this teaching, Chenu further derived the coherence of faith and theology in its historical contingency, as attested by the logic or grammar of the Incarnation. In this reading of Aquinas' teaching on faith, Chenu found elements for a theological anthropology more responsive to current epistemological concerns.

Faith as contemplation

'Modernist' claims about theological development were not entirely constrained by the discipline of 'modern scholasticism'. From the early twentieth century there also emerged nascent spiritual, liturgical, missiological, and ecumenical reform movements that would slowly move the Church towards Vatican II. These movements subverted the spiritual and critical deficiencies of the official neo-scholastic theology. They represent the dynamic currents hidden in Catholic theology in the late nineteenth and early twentieth centuries. The 'Modernist crisis' and Blondel's turn to experience an historical consciousness had inflicted an irreversible change of direction in theology. No longer was the Kantian turn to experience resistible by the philosophical exclusivity of neo-scholasticism. It had insinuated itself into Church life and then into theology through the experiential modes and particularity of these reform movements. The epistemological need to engage with the reality of the spiritual life of Christians then raised unavoidable problems from within for the neo-scholastic metaphysics. Chenu's theology was formed within two different schools of this theological revival. He learnt what he termed 'l'équilibre spirituel' at Le Saulchoir led by Ambroise Gardeil, a founding proponent of the return to textual criticism. At the Angelicum, he studied at the heart of the Roman spiritual revival with Réginald Garrigou-Lagrange. Theology at Le Saulchoir was already shaped by the Tübingen School's ecclesiology and a concern for a revived theology of grace. Chenu's 1920 doctoral thesis on contemplation in Aquinas reveals the substantial influence of Tübingen's Möhler and his mystical ecclesiology.[10] Another source was the Jesuit Pierre Rousselot who recovered the intellectual component of contemplation in Aquinas.[11] Chenu contributed his critical *ressourcement* of the complete Aquinas corpus to this revival, which informed his early methodological studies.[12]

Chenu's thesis on contemplation launched not only this *ressourcement* of Aquinas' theological method and development, but several recurring subjects in his theology: the meaning of faith, doctrinal development, reconciliation of the ruptured ascetic and mystical, positive and speculative theology, and the unity of theological understanding and theological contemplation of God. In these are evidenced the characteristic anthropological direction of his later theology. His scepticism about neo-scholastic metaphysics came through his preference for historically locating Thomas' teaching. Chenu's optimistic

---

10. Extracts from Chenu's thesis are cited in CG Conticello's study, '*De Contemplatione* (Angelicum 1920) La thèse inédite de doctorat du P M-D Chenu', in *Revue des sciences philosophiques et théologiques*, 75/3 (1991): 363–422.
11. Chenu was influenced by Gardeil's debate with Rousselot's position on the intrinsically divine value of the human intellect. Chenu approved of Rousselot's teaching that the grace of faith included a divine illumination, which made it possible to see the natural grounds for making the act of faith. Chenu quoted Rousselot in his thesis, cited in Conticello, '*De Contemplatione*', 401: 'Le point capital est que, pour S. Thomas, la faculté qui nous fait capables de cette action transcendante (vision, contemplation de Dieu) est identiquement celle qui, selon une autre mode d'agir, forme nos concepts et combine nos déductions . . .' Pierre Rousselot SJ, *L'intellectualisme de saint Thomas* (Paris: Alcan, 1908), 38–40.
12. 'Ce n'est donc pas par manie d'antiquaire que j'ai recherché et cité quelques textes de théologiens ou philosophes assez obscurs du 13e siècle; mais parce qu'il est indispensable pour atteindre la pensée de S. Thomas de la remettre dans le milieu où elle est née, où elle s'est développée, selon telle ou telle réaction, sous telle influence', in *De Contemplatione*, 5–6, in Conticello, 386.

vision of humanity and the world, countering Augustinian dualism and contempt for the world, also appeared in the thesis and his quest for a theological equilibrium between reality and mystery, nature and grace, contemplation and action, were introduced.

Chenu took as his starting point the current theological debate about the nature and distinction of mystical states and the scope of their occurrence: whether mystical experience and contemplation were restricted to a spiritual elite.[13] For Thomas, mystical contemplation is integral to the Christian life as the normal fruit and end of baptismal grace. In contemplation, the gifts of the Holy Spirit perfect humanity by drawing it to union with God. Evident in Thomas' teaching about this question is his use of Pseudo-Dionysius to reject the aristocratic restriction of mystical experience, invoking his understanding that contemplation consists of a knowledge-experience of God, through the *mystagogy* of divine action, which engages the connaturality of the human's creatureliness with the Creator's initiative in Creation.[14] Chenu's examination of Aquinas' sources, in relation to this debate, disclosed the impact of Greek Patristic theology and neoplatonic thought on Aquinas, particularly his debt to Dionysius as much as to Augustine. This identification of Aquinas' dependence on Augustine's psychological theology and Dionysius' spiritual theology rejected the prevalent reduction of the *Summa theologiae* to a theological Aristotle and provided the key to reclaiming the medieval theological synthesis: a revised theology of faith. The references to Dionysius in this thesis are also significant as the earliest evidence of Chenu's zeal to propagate the importance of the theology of the East for Latin theology, not merely to balance a lopsided Christian theol-

---

13. The key antagonists were A. Poulain SJ, who advocated a pure mysticism, of an extraordinary and miraculous nature restricted to a few blessed souls, and A. Saudreau who held the more ancient concept of spirituality/mysticism as accessible to all, ie 'infused contemplation'. Conticello, 371.
14. Pseudo-Dionysius, *Divine Names*, II, 9 (*PG* 3, 648B), cited in Conticello, 414–5. The Dominican school, promoters of the unity of the spiritual life, defended the argument for a broad mysticism based in a theology of the gifts of the Holy Spirit, as elaborated by Gardeil and Garrigou-Lagrange. Conticello, 373 n 38.

ogy, but to augment deficient interpretations in the Latin tradition.[15] Chenu also employed this teaching on contemplation to overturn the 'aristocratique' distinction of mystical contemplation from the commonplace *ascesis*. Such understanding later informed Chenu's conviction about the Christian vocation of the laity and his involvement in lay formation and other practical anticipations of the 'universal call to holiness' in Vatican II's *Lumen Gentium*.

Even more significant for Chenu's theology was the location of contemplation as integral to the Christian life of faith. The relationship between contemplation and faith then drew Chenu's examination. As he would later describe this: 'La foi est vraiment alors l'amorce de la vision béatifique, la prélibation de la contemplation future.'[16] Chenu was influenced by Gardeil's recovery of Thomas' concept of the supernatural inner illumination of faith (*synderesis*). Through this light, the Holy Spirit who reveals the truths of Revelation also integrates faith as intrinsic to human experience.[17] This understanding of the supernatural character of faith overturned the need for an extrinsic definition of faith: in order to preserve the divine continuity between Revelation, faith, and theology, faith was located outside any possible human contamination. Affirming faith's supernatural integrity, then Chenu outlined the human reality in which faith is grounded. He asserted that the believer's assimilation to God, who as the object

---

15. A later example is found in 'Position de la théologie' (1935), 127: 'Le théologien latin réduira le symbole à une *signe* dont l'intelligibilité va être définissable et l'expression juridiquement classée; mais l'oriental conservera au sacrement son nom de *mystère*, et Denys voit dans le culte un milieu d'opération déifiante.' Chenu did not oppose Latin and Greek theologies, a simplification common in twentieth century theology. Michel René Barnes discredits this false dichotomy in 'Augustine in Contemporary Trinitarian Theology', in *Theological Studies*, 56 (1995): 237–250, 237–242. Chenu's promotion of Eastern theology and his mediation for the Eastern bishops at the Second Vatican Council was his most direct and effective contribution. See *Notes quotidiennes au Concile: Journal de Vatican II 1962–1963* (Paris: Les Éditions du Cerf, 1995), 107–110, 123, 130–132.
16. Chenu, *La théologie est-elle une science?*, 31.
17. Gardeil clarified the formal object of faith and with Garrigou-Lagrange restored the emphasis on faith's supernatural character. Gardeil's recovery of Aquinas' teaching on the illumination of faith, *lumen fidei*, the inward light of the Holy Spirit bridging Revelation and the believer in ways that human understanding can perceive, was particularly influential. Roger Aubert, *Le problème de l'acte de foi*, 587; Schoof, *Breakthrough*, 189–190.

sought and known, is the sole goal and source of all human understanding. This included the activity of both the intuitive and affective properties of contemplation as much as the volitional character of assent.[18] Here Chenu demonstrated his early scepticism about the reductive effect on the doctrine of faith of the deductive metaphysics of modern scholasticism, which marginalised doctrine from the life experience of faith, and segmented the unity of theology into discrete spiritual, doctrinal or pastoral categories. For Chenu, continuity with the patristic and medieval understanding of theology required instead a dynamic nexus between the spiritual, doctrinal, and pastoral aspects of theology. Chenu's later research on the epistemological and psychological structure of the act of faith was anticipated in this analysis of the formal elements in the genesis of the believing act, the assent to attested truths (*auditus fidei*), and the interior call of God. The dynamic of the understanding of the faith (*fides quaerens intellectum*) is not a simple conceptual knowing, but a progressive assimilation to the first Truth through the ways of human understanding.[19] For Chenu, there is no *auditus fidei* without an *intellectus fidei*, and the object of faith is neither of these but God.

Central to Chenu's study of Thomas' understanding of contemplation was a concern for theological realism. Rejecting the Augustinian and neo-scholastic dichotomy between human religious perception and other human conceptualisation, Chenu embraced St Albert the Great's and St Thomas' teaching on the unity of human cognition: the same intellectual faculty that generates all other acts of cognition, for acquiring any other knowledge, is that engaged in contemplation and any graced vision of God.[20] Such an understanding was underpinned by a Dominican optimism about humanity and the world, that homogeneous view of the relationship of nature and grace so characteristic of Thomas' anthropology. Chenu emphasised that, for Aquinas, the gap between humanity and God is not bridged by means of the negation of human freedom, nor by a Buddhist-like renuncia-

---

18. Conticello, 386–88. Conticello notes that Chenu referred frequently to Garrigou Lagrange in his thesis, while Gardeil is seldom cited although his influence pervades the whole work, *cf* 377, and n 44.
19. Conticello, 408.
20. Chenu: 'C'est là le point de divergence, non seulement de deux théories *peri psychés*, mais de deux mentalités, de deux spiritualités, de deux mystiques.' *De Contemplatione*, 40, cited in Conticello, 400–401.

tion of will, but in the human act of recollection. Such recollection is the essential yet freely chosen unifying of all the creature's being and activity with God.[21] This demonstrated for Chenu the homogeneity or continuity between human knowledge of God and the data of God's Revelation, in contrast to the negative view of the human condition prevalent in seventeenth and eighteenth century spiritualities, still influential on twentieth century Catholic life. Consistent with his Dominican background, the horizon of Chenu's thesis is theocentric: God is supremely intelligible. It was thus not specifically Christocentric, which was more characteristic of Augustinian, Franciscan, and Jesuit spiritualities.[22] This was in contrast to his emphasis on the 'loi de l'Incarnation' in his theology after 1937. There is an early orientation towards anthropological theology in the centrality afforded by Chenu to the human understanding of faith in Aquinas' theology of contemplation.

Chenu found in contemporary studies on the psychology of the spiritual life, support for the psychological realism of the unity of theology, of contemplation and faith. He referred particularly to Bergson's vitalist phenomenology and Maréchal's transcendental epistemology of the dynamism of human spirit.[23] These psychological arguments did not meet with Garrigou-Lagrange's approval. Despite recovering the spirituality of St John of the Cross and reinstating the academic study of spiritual theology, Garrigou-Lagrange maintained its separation from dogmatic theology and regarded such interdisci-

---

21. 'La simplicité intellectuelle du contemplatif ne s'opère pas par en bas dans un état negatif, à la façon d'un bouddhiste, mais par en haut: elle est non simplification par appauvrissement—celle des hallucinés—mais par enrichissement. *Totus labor meditationis, cogitationis, reflexionis, etc, quo homo ascendit et pervenit ad simplicem intuitum contemplationis, fundatur psychologice in hac doctrina S. Thomae*', De Contemplatione, 19–20, in Conticello, 396.
22. *De Contemplatione*, 8–9, in Conticello, 384, n 51; 387 n 55.
23. Conticello, 379–80. The influence of Maréchal's transcendental synthesis on Chenu (initially in 'La mystique chrétienne', in *Revue de philosophie*, 2 (1912): 445–446) is not sustained, despite André Hayen SJ's detection of an unacknowledged echo in *La théologie comme science au XIIIe siècle*. 'La théologie comme science aux XIIe, XIIIe et XXe siècles', in *Nouvelle Revue Théologique*, 79 (1957): 1009–1028, 1011–1012, notes 37, 38). The reference cited demonstrates more Chenu's dependence on Maréchal for his valuing the Dionysian theology of contemplation.

plinary scope as insufficiently focused on Thomas.[24] In contrast, these extra-scholastic sources demonstrated for Chenu the psychological realism of the unity of faith and contemplation.[25] Chenu's insistence on the coherence of faith and contemplation repaired the dismemberment of the mystical from doctrinal theology:

> Il faut manifester la valeur contemplative, «mystique», de l'intelligence (*intellectus ut intellectus*), et maintenir sa prépondérance jusque dans les mystérieuses profondeurs de l'union mystique, où, là comme partout ailleurs, elle est puissance d'ordre lumière. Point donc d'opposition fausse et vaine ... Le mysticisme, a-t-on dit, est pour Saint Thomas intellectualisme intégral.[26]

In his thesis, Chenu emphasised the unity of spiritual and speculative theology in Thomas and refuted a common tendency to oppose Thomas' intellectualism with the mysticism of Anselm, Bonaventure, and Scotus.[27] Chenu thus contributed to the spiritual renewal recognising the need to restore the coincidence of *speculatio* and *contemplatio*, that contemplation in faith is constitutive of all theology.[28]

His historical situating of Thomas with 'minor' Franciscan spiritual writings in the thesis, to ascertain the genealogy of Thomas' teaching on contemplation, drew portentous warning from his teacher, Gar-

---

24. 'Garrigou-Lagrange lui-même, qui a patronné généreusement ma thèse, était un peu effarouché par l'introduction de l'analyse psychologique dans un phénomène qui, de soi, est «surnaturel». Heureusement, mon analyse théologique lui plaisait beaucoup.' Chenu, *Un théologien en liberté*, 38.
25. 'En tout cas, il est représentatif qui imprégnait, depuis un siècle, les lettres, les arts, la morale, le droit ... Non plus foi en la Parole, dont l'appétit se nourrit d'intelligence contemplative et rationnelle, *fides quaerens intellectum*, mais combinat hétérogène d'autorité et de raison: après une enquête dite positive, la théologie s'organise en «science des conclusions»—c'est l'expression ingénument employée—, qu'on tire, selon les lois de la logique, d'un dossier extérieur.' Chenu, 'La littérature comme "lieu" de la théologie', in *Revue des sciences philosophiques et théologiques*, LIII (1969): 70–80, 73.
26. *De contemplatione*, 3 (Chenu's brief insertion in French to the introduction). cf also 60, Chenu criticises: 'pseudo-mystici, qui despiciunt cognitionem tanquam impedimentum et obstaculum amoris'.
27. *De contemplatione*, 3, in Conticello, 383.
28. Conticello, 391.

rigou-Lagrange.[29] Chenu later identified this resistance to historical perspective on theology as the point of division between him and Garrigou-Lagrange. Chenu's trawling of the Western spiritual tradition yielded a more nuanced differentiation of Thomas' theology, and of other Dominican theologians, from the dualist spirituality of the neo-Augustinians. This in turn revealed to him the extent of the deviation of the Augustinians from Augustine's thought.[30] Making its debut in these distinctions is Chenu's trademark abhorrence of any psychological dualism or spiritual rejection of the world. More than merely mapping the diversity in scholastic positions, he was detecting a hitherto ignored inclusiveness as integral to Aquinas' theology. This provided an authoritative corrective to the narrow selection and prejudice of 'modern scholasticism's' method and sources. Chenu found modelled in Thomas' synthesis and elucidation of conflicting sources an aversion to exclusive concentration on one theological author or system.

Chenu's doctoral study of contemplation in Aquinas, with its methodological innovation and psychological curiosity, evidences his early concern with the failure of 'modern scholasticism' to preserve the unity of human cognition. Its inability to acknowledge the historical context of Thomas' theology and anthropological concerns boosted the persistence of the dichotomisation of asceticism and mysticism, spirituality and theology, faith and reason, experience of historical event and doctrine. The historian Boureau noted that the historical incarnation of theological thought, which Chenu established in his doctoral thesis, remained his constant conviction from this time in Rome to his activism with workers in 1950s Paris. This tight connection between the intellectual and spiritual in human being is the core of all his theology.[31] Separation of this connection, so marked in the extrinsicism of 'modern scholasticism', is at the dread-

---

29. Conticello, 379–80. Chenu's later explanation of this was that Garrigou-Lagrange was 'a complete stranger to history' and its significance: *Un théologien en liberté*, 38.
30. The Franciscans cited were John Rupellensis, J Peckham and St Bonaventure. His Dominican authorities were Master Eckhardt, Henry Suso, Johannes Tauler. Other later 'spirituels' included Ruysbroeck, Angelo Foligno, Jeanne de Chantal, Francis de Sales, Teresa of Avila and John of the Cross. Pseudo-Dionysis is the most frequently cited source.
31. Alain Boureau, 'Le Père Chenu médiéviste: historicité, contexte et tradition', *Revue des sciences philosophiques et théologiques*, 81 (1997): 407–414, 410–11.

ful cost of denying the divine activity in Creation and Incarnation. Chenu's theological project began as a rejection of these oppositions. In demonstrating faith as contemplation in Aquinas, Chenu began his lifelong commitment to the unity of theology, human inquiry, and contemplation of God.

Faith in understanding

Chenu recognised that the discounting of human experience by 'modern scholasticism' restricted the role of reason in the doctrinal assent of faith.[32] This quarantined neo-scholastic theology in an unchecked extrinsicism. Only a renewed understanding of the intellectual dimension of faith could relieve this theological stand-off to reveal the anthropological condition of faith and reason. For Chenu, this underscored the contemporary need to continue the medieval synthesis of reason and restore human understanding as integral to faith: *la Foi dans intelligence*.[33]

In three seminal studies on *Summa Theologiae* IIa IIae, q. 1, a. 2, Chenu recovered a neglected part of Thomas' teaching regarding the intellectual quality of faith. The object of faith is God, a reality, not those propositions compounded into a deposit or body of dogma.[34] The human subject receives this Revelation in a complex of propositions about the object of faith, because of the ontological difference between God and the creature, and the limitations of human understanding.[35] Chenu emphasised the importance of this formal

---

32. 'Contribution à l'histoire du traité de la foi. Commentaire historique de IIa IIae, q. I, a. 2' (1923) in *La Parole de Dieu I. La Foi dans intelligence* (Paris: Cerf, 1964), 31–50, 48. Louis Dupré commented on 'the clearcut separation between spiritual doctrine and School theology': 'This isolation, in the end fatal to both, freed spiritual life from the burden of an incompatible theology and rendered it more congenial to the modern age. Theology's severance from the religious experience, once an integral part of *contemplatio*, had marginalised it with respect to culture as well as to piety.' *Passage to Modernity* (New Haven: Yale University Press, 1993), 222.
33. Hence Chenu chose this emblematic expression as the title for his first collection of writings: *La Parole de Dieu I: La Foi dans intelligence*.
34. 'Ergo objectum fidei non est enuntiabile, sed res.' *Summa Theologiae* IIa IIae, q. 1, a. 2, ad. 2.
35. 'Contribution à l'histoire du traité de la foi', 48.

distinction, that the object known to us from Revelation is necessarily complex, while the object itself, God, remains simple.

> La connaissance de foi est une connaissance humaine et terrestre, complexe, et donc essentiellement progressive; la vision seule est simple et immobile, «*per modum simplicis intelligentiae*».[36]

Thomas assigned to human understanding, not to human volition, the reception of the self-disclosure of God, thereby categorically affirming the human character of the act of faith.[37]

Chenu found that the key to interpreting Thomas' teaching on faith was the reply to article 2: what is knowable about the object of faith comes by the same means of knowing as all other human knowledge, *cognita sunt in cognoscente secundum modum cognoscentis*.[38] Integral to faith and to human knowledge of God is the same act of judgement, the weighing-up and clarification of what is revealed, and then assent to a complex of propositions. Such coming to judgement is definitive of human understanding not merely accidental to it. This is the action of the governing virtue of prudence.

> La prudence ne s'ajoute pas de l'extérieur à la raison et à la volonté, comme un devoir s'impose à la liberté pour la contraindre: c'est la raison même, rendue parfaite, dans son jugement et dans ses choix. Elle intériorise, elle personnalise la loi, au point que là seulement, dans ma conscience, je puis parler décidément d'obligation.[39]

Dogmatic truth presents itself structurally and dynamically as an affirmation of human understanding, with all the complexity involved in all other human knowledge and judgement.

---

36. *ST* IaIIae, q.1, a.2, ad. 3. Chenu, 'La raison psychologique du développement du dogme d'après Saint Thomas' (1924) in *La Parole de Dieu I*, 52–58, 57.
37. 'Contribution à l'histoire du traité de la foi', 49.
38. *ST* IIa IIae, q. I, a. 2, *responsio*. 'Contribution à l'histoire du traité de la foi', 48–49; 'La raison psychologique', 53. Chenu repeatedly uses this text also to justify the use of sociological method in theological reflection.
39. *St Thomas d'Aquin et la théologie*, 145.

> la lumière de foi ne modifiera pas notre mécanisme conceptual, nos procédés d'élaboration, de penetration . . . sans nuire à l'unité et à l'immutabilité de la foi ni non plus à sa «réalité».[40]

Chenu found in this reply Thomas' heuristic principle. Any descriptions of faith that compromise the unity of human spirit by their heterogenous separation of faith from other human knowing are exposed as deficient through this principle.

Resituating faith in its human condition required an account of the development of doctrine. For Chenu, the problem of the immutability of faith and the development of doctrine is not solved by opposing a timeless concept of faith with a judgement determined in time, because 'la foi est de la terre', faith is ever conditioned by human ways of knowing and history:

> saint Thomas admet désormais que la détermination temporelle est partie essentielle de l'acte de foi, comme d'ailleurs de toute proposition: nous devons croire que «le Christ est né», au passé. Il va donc falloir reconnaître entièrement les «variations» de la foi.[41]

He emphasised also the psychological reality of the subjective cognition involved in dogmatic formulation.[42]

> Complexité et «pluralité» sont notes essentielles de la connaissance de foi parce qu'elle sont notes essentielles de la connaissance humaine. Ainsi le dogme a une histoire parce qu'il est sujet au progrès (homogène et infaillible de par l'assistance de l'Ésprit-Saint) de l'énoncé humain.[43]

Thomas' realism led him to a categorical affirmation of the temporal character of the human act of faith. From this, Chenu drew both the

---

40. 'La raison psychologique', 53–4.
41. 'Contribution à l'histoire', 47.
42. Contra Guillaume d'Auxerre's *Summa aurea*, lib. III, tr. 3, cap. I, q. 5: 'la théorie de l'*explicatio implicatorum*, formule encore un peu simpliste chez lui': 'La raison psychologique du développement du dogme d'après Saint Thomas' (1924) in *La Parole de Dieu I. La Foi dans intelligence* (Paris: Cerf, 1964), 51–58, 52. Chenu noted that this theory applied to the progress of Revelation not the development of dogma, 53, n 4.
43. 'La raison psychologique du développement', 54.

authority and method to approach the problem of the development of doctrine. Chenu recovered Aquinas' method of dialectic, and ability to judge between different readings across the tradition, all of which had escaped other modern Thomist commentators.

> La genèse de cette méthodologie, ses préparations, ses réactions, les résistances qu'elle rencontra, rendaient témoignage à ce grand oeuvre de saint Thomas, dont les textes, ainsi lus dans leur milieu natif, prenaient une vigueur historique, à l'appui d'une interprétation interne solidement tenue depuis sept siècles.[44]

Thomas saw analogy between the development of other human knowledge and the way that dogma evolves and is elaborated. Chenu's *ressourcement* of Thomas thereby undermined the strategy of separation foundational to 'modern scholasticism'.

Chenu's interest in restoring the role of reason in theology drew him to probe Thomas' text for its more nuanced anthropological observations about faith and theology. Thomas had provided such an example in his synthesis of the long-received Augustinian psychology with the new 'science' of Aristotle's epistemology.[45] In what Chenu described as a profound theological echo of St Augustine's famous cry, Thomas asserted that the restlessness of human inquiry is of the nature of faith and is fuelled by its origin and end in the natural human desire to see and know God.[46] Hence desire for union with God, for life eternal, constitutes all action and knowing, and is an analogue of reason within human inquiry. The human restlessness to understand is integral to faith. Thomas' solution was that fidelity to God is not grounded in the passivity of certitude, nor even of willing obedience, but in 'l'inquiétude' that drives all human understanding.

---

44. Chenu, Préface to 1942 edition, *La théologie comme science au XIIIe siècle* (Paris: Vrin, 1957), 11.
45. Chenu, 'La psychologie de la foi dans la théologie du XIIIe siècle. Genèse de la doctrine de saint Thomas Somme théologique, IIa IIae, q. 2, a. 1.' (1932) in *La Parole de Dieu I. La Foi dans intelligence* (Paris: Cerf, 1964), 77–104, 88–92.
46. Augustine: '*Fecisti nos ad te, et inquietum est cor nostrum donc requiescat in te.*' *Confessions*, Book I, chap. 1. Chenu glossed that Aquinas' teaching ('*Imperfectio cognitionis est de ratione fidei, ponitur enim in eius definitione.*' ST Ia IIae, q. 67, a.3) was 'moins pathétique mais non moins profonde' than Augustine's. 'La Psychologie de la foi', 99.

> La densité de ce texte du *De Veritate* dépasse en puissance d'émotion et en valeur religieuse les plus pascaliennes pensées; il ne trouvera réplique que dans les descriptions anxieuses du mystique avançant dans les «ténèbres» de la foi. Mais aux yeux du théologien, ce par quoi il vaut, c'est par la qualification donnée à cette inquiétude, plus encore que par l'angoisse discrète qu'il recèle: pour saint Thomas, cette inquiétude est *dans la nature* même de la foi; c'est par là que la foi se classe et se définit dans la hiérarchie des assentiments, autant que par sa certitude: «*Imperfectio cognitionis est de ratione fidei, ponitur enim in ejus definitione.*» [Ia IIae, q.67, a.3][47]

He found there the ontological warrant for the coherence of human reason and faith:

> Dieu dans son humaine pédagogie, pourra n'éveiller que peu à peu notre intelligence à une lumière trop éblouissante; mais dès le début, sous le régime d'autorité que doit accepter tout disciple, c'est l'intelligence qui abordera le mystère.[48]

Chenu observed in Thomas not merely harmonisation of the seemingly incompatible Aristotelian theory of scientific understanding and the affective adherence of faith, but evidence of the critical presence of Thomas' own spiritual experience.[49] From Thomas' contemplative-scholar life came the evidence for the co-existence of affective and intuitive elements in the act of faith. This coherence of an 'intuition' and a 'mentalité' informed his synthesis.

> L'appétit de béatitude qui détermine son assentiment, loin d'enclore sa raison dans une sécurité trop courte, provoque incessamment sa recherche.[50]

That the profound yearning for knowledge and understanding does not cancel out faith was an insight grounded in the mentality that faith and Revelation are not introduced or developed outside of the laws of our human existence and psychology. Faith is not a divine overriding of human structures of understanding. Here in the Angelic Doctor's own teaching was the turn to human experience,

---

47. 'La Psychologie de la foi', 97.
48. 'La Psychologie de la foi', 95.
49. 'c'est l'âme religieuse de saint Thomas qui la fournit', 96.
50. 'c'est l'âme religieuse de saint Thomas qui la fournit', 96.

well before the feared Kant. As well, it demonstrated that Thomas had evaluated the arguments of his antecedents, in a way that resembled the historical analysis condemned as 'Modernist'. Thomas had incorporated reason into faith. Although each of these propositions was condemned as erroneous by the modern authorities of neo-scholasticism, Chenu had found they already figured in the master authority, Thomas Aquinas.

It is significant that Chenu presented Thomas' innovation in such existential and historical terms. Chenu's *ressourcement* of Aquinas was as concerned with uncovering the Thomas' human experience as with determining the genealogy of his theological and philosophical sources.[51]

In one of a number of his key articles published around *1937*, Chenu examined how faith is both about communion with God and the formal assent to dogma. This apparent conflict lies at the heart of the split between positive and speculative theology.[52] The article was

---

51. Later Chenu described the method of his *ressourcement* of Aquinas as: 'selon toutes les ressources que procure l'application de la méthode à l'étude du texte, de la pensée et de la personnalité intellectuelle d'un écrivain.' (Archives de la province dominicaine de France, Paris, Le Saulchoir—Collège 9 (18)), cited in André Duval OP, 'Aux origines de l'«Institut historique d'études thomistes» du Saulchoir (1920s). Notes et Documents', 435. This interest in Aquinas culminated in Chenu's own favourite book *St Thomas d'Aquin et la théologie* (1959).

52. There is some suggestion of Blondel's influence in Chenu's interest in the active and experiential view of faith, the rejection of extrinsicism, and also of the implications of Blondel's distinction between immanentism and the immanent principle of human knowing. While Chenu did not directly acknowledge Blondel, he seemed to pursue a parallel quest to Blondel's, identifying within Aquinas' corpus what Blondel constructed at a deliberate distance from the wizened contemporary 'scholasticism' that he despised. Yet later, Congar warned against attributing too much influence on Chenu to Blondel, given Chenu's limited study of modern philosophy. Congar: 'Il ne semble pas que le P. Chenu ait beaucoup fréquenté l'oeuvre de Maurice Blondel, ni connu son «monophorisme»', and 'Bien que n'ayant pas une formation philosophique complète, surtout en philosophie moderne, il avait le goût du problème philosophique.' 'Le Père M-D Chenu', in Robert van der Gucht and Herbert Vorgrimler, editors, *Bilan de la théologie du XXe siècle*, volume II (Paris: Casterman, 1970), 772–787, 777, 773. Later Congar admitted he was more influenced by Möhler than Blondel's work on Tradition, even though he cited him: 'J'ai l'habitude—c'est presque une "manie"—de citer des auteurs qui ont dit avant moi ce que je veux dire. Ce ne sont pas toujours des "sources".' Congar, 'Preface' in Charles MacDonald, *Church and World in the Plan of God: Aspects of History and Eschatology in the Thought of Père Yves Congar OP* (Frankfurt: Verlag Peter Lang, 1982).

published in *Vie Spirituelle*, so its tone presents a contrast to his usual more polemical style. Faith is a strictly personal way of seeing that assimilates our understanding to God, and is equally a work of the will and love:

> dans cette lumière, mon regard rejoint, découvre avec étonnement celui que Dieu porte lui-même sur la vie du monde, sur ma vie à moi; moi dans la destinée mystérieuse du monde, avec ma propre destinée, mystérieuse aussi, en face du Dieu Trinité.[53]

In formal terms, faith is an intellectual virtue, socially transmitted and located in the community of faith. There revealed truth is taught across generations, through the Church defining, condemning errors, and affirming the tradition and more contemporary experiences of faith. So faith checks mystical tendencies to solipsism or other-worldliness, and the more general tendency of those captivated to disengage from human reality, to dissociate the inner illumination from its object and source, intuition from the conceptual, the individual from society, and experience from tradition.[54] Chenu identified the issue as the need to restore human understanding as constitutive of faith. To conceive faith exclusively as assent to something extrinsic, as exclusive of human processes of understanding, is a 'fausse exaltation du surnaturel'. The supernatural character of faith is not outside of human experience but inserted intimately in our being, according to its human condition. Chenu observed that the unity of faith revolves on the recognition that the divine encounter of faith occurs humanly:

> Dieu prend l'homme tel qu'il est; la foi, aussi, même si l'âme a peu de ressources de connaissance ou d'amour. Réalisme de la foi, oui, mais réalisme humain!

---

53. Chenu, 'L'unité de la foi. Réalisme et formalisme' (1937) in *La Parole de Dieu I. La Foi dans intelligence* (Paris: Cerf, 1964), 15. Chenu cited three 'traits' of the 'realisme de la foi': 'une *perception*'—'Regard attentif, compréhensif' (characterised in the human analogy of the focused gaze of the nursing mother and child); 'une oeuvre de *volonté* et d'*amour*'—'désirée'; and 'une acte *strictement personnel*'—'personne à personne', 14–15.
54. 'la tentation de dissocier lumière et objet, intuition et notion, individu et société, experience et tradition. La tentation du croyant est de rejeter l'humain, tout l'humain'. 'L'unité de la foi', 17.

and

> Dans le dynamisme même de la foi est inscrit l'appel de la vision. Mais n'oublions jamais que la garantie même du réalisme de la foi est que notre foi soit toujours HUMAINE.[55]

Drawing on Thomas' conviction that faith shares the reality of all human operations, Chenu proposed a revised theological understanding of humanity. The foundation for this coherence of the human and divine, faith and reason, in the unity of faith is the Word made flesh, because the Incarnation assures us that all that is human has been assumed in Christ.

> De même que les actions du Christ sont «théandriques» (oeuvres humaines, pleinement humaines, et cependant divines), de même, toutes proportions gardées, notre raison, et nos concepts, et nos formules dans la foi.[56]

The unity of faith, like the divine-human nature of Christ, holds together without diminishment both the supernatural light of faith and the action of human understanding through recognising the patterning of faith on the divine mystery it reveals. Chenu resolved the problem of dualism in faith and theology by reinstating the anthropological condition of faith, and by analogy the role of reason in constructing theology. This is the earliest explicit Christological analogy in Chenu's earlier writings, and encapsulates the grammar of the Incarnation so characteristic of his later work.

Theology as faith in reason

Chenu's writings between the wars sought to establish the way reason functions in theology. In 'La théologie comme science au XIIIe siècle', he traced the growing critical use of reason in medieval theology, as demonstrated in Thomism's correlation of Christian traditions with

---

55. [Chenu's emphasis] 'L'unité de la foi', 18.
56. 'L'unité de la foi', 19.

Aristotelian philosophy.[57] 'Position de la théologie' developed this theological correlation and proposed new bearings for theology from its location in history and how human understanding constitutes theology.[58] In *Une école de théologie: le Saulchoir*, Chenu distinguished this critical integration of reason from the introverted rationalism of 'modern scholasticism'. This manifesto of his theological reform of the curriculum at *Le Saulchoir* presented theology as a human 'science'. He thus affirmed that in the interplay of the subjective and objective condition of faith there is coherence between Revelation and human reason. If a theology is to be responsive to the mystery of the Incarnation, it must appreciate the importance of history.[59] In these theological works, Chenu promoted the need for theology to continue a critical correlation with contemporary philosophy, while preaching the truths of Revelation in terms of the historical condition of the human experience of faith.[60]

La théologie comme science au XIIIe siècle

Chenu's early studies on Thomas' doctrine of faith retraced Aquinas' arguments for the integration of philosophy in the construction of theology. In an early demonstration of 'ressourcement', Chenu followed the development of a scientific method in theology, 'la foi in statu scientiae', from thirteenth century scholastic texts. He sought authorisation from Thomas for a more critical theological incorporation of reason, which excluded neither the subjective experience of faith, nor the supernatural nature of faith's inner illumination. He presented Thomas' methodological elaboration of Anselm's 'faith

---

57. 'La théologie comme science au XIIIe siècle. Genèse de la doctrine de Saint Thomas. *Sum. Theol., IaPars, q. 1, art. 2 et 8*', in *Archives d'histoire doctrinale et littéraire du Moyen Age (AHDLMA)*, 2 (1927): 31–71. This article was revised in an unpublished manuscript in 1943 then republished in an expanded version in 1957 as *La théologie comme science au XIIIe siècle* (Paris: Librairie Philosophique J.Vrin, 1957).
58. 'Position de la théologie' (1935) in *La Parole de Dieu I. La Foi dans intelligence* (Paris: Cerf, 1964), 115–138.
59. *Une école*, 58–64 [134–139].
60. Chenu later cast this as an ancient and never fully resolved dialectic for Christian theology: 'la curieuse dialectique d'une foi qui, en quête d'éternel, valorise le temps, et d'une raison qui, liée au temps et au lieu, cède à l'éternisme de l'abstraction.' 'Situation humaine: corporalité et temporalité' (1958), 415.

seeking understanding' in the *Summa* as 'l'épisode le plus sensationnel de l'entrée d'Aristote en Chrétienté', an innovative rupture with all that preceded it rather than the summit of an evolution in medieval theological understanding.[61] Such innovation, what Chenu described as a new sap for theology, offered a precedent for justifying similar changes in contemporary neo-Thomist theology.

'La théologie comme science au XIIIe siècle' (1927) described the genealogy of Aquinas' break with the typological and allegorical expositions of *sacra pagina* that was called *sacra doctrina* in the previous centuries.[62] This study of the background to articles 2 and 8 of the Prologue of Thomas' *Summa theologiae* showed how the various attempts by Aquinas' contemporaries to integrate *expositio* of the scriptural and patristic texts with extra-textual theological speculation had faltered on their fear of diluting Revelation with human reasoning.[63] Propaedeutic use of philosophy in defence of the faith had been condoned well before Aquinas. Twelfth century theologians already debated the rational coherence of theological propositions, but their schemas were not systematised.[64] Some thirteenth century theologians, like Fishacre (d 1248), Kilwardby (d 1261) and Alexander of Hales (d 1241), had used Aristotelian categories in disputation but they limited such inferior rational argument to combat with heretics or unbelievers or to the instruction of the faithful.[65] Chenu concluded that while Kilwardby studied Aristotle, giving an account

---

61. 'Préface', 'La théologie comme science au XIIIe siècle' (1943), reprinted with 1957 preface, 13.
62. Chenu, 'Les Magistri. La "science" théologique' in *La théologie au douzième siècle*, 323–350, especially 329–337; and Chenu, 'La décadence de l'allégorisation. Un témoin: Garnier de Rochefort († v. 1200)', in *L'homme devant Dieu: Mélanges offerts au Père Henri de Lubac*, volume II (Paris: Aubier, Éditions Montaigne, 1964), 129–135.
63. *ST* Ia, q.1, a.2: 'Utrum sacra doctrina sit scientia'; a.8: 'Utrum haec doctrina sit argumentativa'.
64. 'La théologie comme science' (1927), 43, 46. Chenu noted approvingly the creative diversity that accompanied the confusion of these theological approaches compared to more recent theology: 'le XIIe siècle présente ici une opulente fécondité que nous dissimule fâcheusement l'uniforme de la scolastique posttridentine.' 'Les Magistri. La "science" théologique', 336. See also *La théologie est-elle une science?* for Chenu's approval of 'Les divers systèmes théologiques' in the history of theology, 99–105.
65. 'La théologie comme science' (1927), 46; *La théologie comme science au XIIIe siècle* (1957), 34.

of the content, procedures and demands of scientific method (*modus artificialis*) in the prologue to his *summa*, he declined to apply this technique to understanding *sacra doctrina*, because he was blocked by an Augustinian mentality that opposed *scientia* (*ratio inferior*) to *sapientia* (*ratio superior*).[66] The function exercised by human reason in theology, for Chenu, was held to be a register of the anthropological awareness and commitment to the human component of faith and correspondingly a measure of his independence from Augustinian suspicions about 'scientia' and the world.

Before Kilwardby, William of Auxerre (d 1231) provided the key to a theological appropriation of scientific methodology by recognising the likeness of the articles of faith to the scientific principles in Aristotle's *Posterior Analytics*.[67] Applying this comparison to *sacra doctrina*, William proposed an objective function for the articles of faith.[68] Chenu judged that, although successive theologians had noted this insight, none expanded on it, and he attributed 'cette pudeur intellectuelle' to an over-concern to protect the supernatural character of faith and Revelation from any mere human analysis.[69] He added pointedly that this is the problem of the Augustinians of all eras.[70] Chenu asserted that Thomas' method and conception of theology as 'science' was not only a leap beyond the understanding of these previous attempts, but marked a new 'discovery' of humanity, an

---

66. 'La théologie comme science' (1927), 44–46. 'Kilwardby l'accepte, mais en la surchargeant de distinctions qui trahissent la résistance irréductible d'une mentalité augustinienne' (1927), 36; and 'Il y a là évidemment autre chose qu'une non-distinction sur le mot reçu de *doctrina sacra* et sur son contenu, dont l'hétérogénéité n'apparaîtrait pas. Il y a une implicite répugnance à admettre dans le domaine de cette donné révélé l'intervention, ou mieux le principe même de l'intervention propre de la raison.' 'La théologie comme science' (1927), 46. (*cf* also, 57). A fuller treatment is presented in 'Ratio superior et inferior. Un cas de philosophie chrétienne', in *Revue des sciences philosophiques et théologiques*, XXIX (1940): 84–89.
67. 'La théologie comme science' (1927), 49–52.
68. 'La théologie comme science' (1927), 51–52.
69. 'Indice révélateur de cette pudeur intellectuelle dans ces esprits tout pénétrés de saint Augustin, ils ont recours, pour qualifier et définir leur amoureuse recherche, au concept augustinienne de *sapientia*, qui, à leurs yeux, se changeait d'affectivité et de dévotion, en même temps qu'il éliminait la dialectique intempérante et le goût terrestre qui sont l'apanage de la *scientia*.' (1927), 57. Chenu indicted this as a 'réserve spontanée, comme une timidité, en face de la vérité révélée et de la réalité.' 'La théologie comme science' (1927), 56.
70. 'La théologie comme science' (1927), 34.

advance in creaturely self-understanding. Chenu interpreted Aquinas' contribution as a dynamic and revolutionary interaction of the 'donné' of Revelation and faith and the human 'construit' of reason and understanding, which provided the moment of dialectical resolution when the opposites of contemplation in faith and Aristotelian 'scientific method' were united.[71] Theology as science, as intellectual faith, enhanced humanity's inherent connaturality with God in a preview of our beatific destiny.[72] Later, Chenu would cite the Tübingen theologian Johann Evangelist Kuhn's epigram to capture the ramifications of such innovation: 'Pas de théologie, sans nouvelle naissance.'[73]

William of Auxerre's analogy of the articles of faith with the principles of science was the first application of the theory of subalternation of one science to another to *sacra doctrina*. According to this theory, a science (or body and method of knowledge) can be verified by the relationship of its content and mode of knowledge to another higher science, in terms of this science's verifiable principles. The lesser science becomes intrinsic to the higher one by being drawn up into its principles. The theory of subalternation of sciences explains how theology can be a 'science' even as it depends on principles or truths that are not self-evident or open to empirical confirmation. Initially even Thomas in his early commentary on the *Sentences* had failed to explain how the articles of faith are not self-evident except to the believer, because he had limited subalternation to faith not theology.[74] Chenu stressed his discovery only emerged in the later commentary on Boethius' *De trinitate* and his more conclusive *Summa* treatment. Thomas recognised that theology's inability to establish evidence for its claims is no different to the derivative qualities of other branches of human knowledge. He found Bonaventure's use of 'subalternation' still restricted to the subordination of theology to Scripture. Yet it held the key to applying William of Auxerre's analogy. Aquinas argued that as optics to geometry is subordinate, or music to

---

71. 'Beau témoignage d'une synthèse très parfaitement une entre la mystique du croyant et la science du théologien, que cette théorie de la subalternation des sciences, qui, légitiment d'une part l'établissement de la dialectique en terrain de révélation, rattache d'autre part toute cette dialectique à la science même de Dieu, *scientia Dei et beatorum*.' 'La théologie comme science' (1927), 70.
72. 'La théologie comme science' (1927), 63.
73. 'Position de la théologie' (1935), 115–138 (115).
74. Chenu cited: *I Sentences*, Prologue, a. 2, obj. 2; a. 5, ad. 4 in (1927), 34, 59.

arithmetic, so theology is a subordinate 'science', which through faith receives its principles from the revealed higher 'science' of God's self-knowledge. So, theology deduces both its method and content from the higher science of God.[75] Because evidence for the articles of faith is afforded by the higher 'science', the 'science' of God, then reason is no longer limited to providing proofs for the articles of faith. Instead, the role of reason in the 'science' of theology is to deduce, from these articles of faith, further understanding of the truth of Revelation. The article of faith is no longer the matter or subject of theological exposition and research, as in twelfth century understanding of *sacra doctrina*, but the principle already known, from which theology works for further understanding.

> L'article de foi trouve son «lieu» dans l'immense genèse de vérité qui va de Dieu, Vérité première, à la modeste conclusion théologique: la théorie de la science qui semblait devoir à jamais consacrer l'hétérogénéité de la lumière divine de la foi avec la laborieuse et humaine spéculation du théologien, en souligne au contraire, sous les distinctions nécessaires, la féconde continuité.[76]

Chenu found that subalternation resolved for Thomas any apparent contradiction between the speculative task of understanding faith, particularly the development of faith, and the contemplative simplicity of faith. Reason is declared not heterogeneous to revealed truth, but is 'une remontée de la foi vers la science de Dieu et la première étape sur la voie de la vision béatifique, *scientia dei et beatorum*'.[77]

In the later editions of *La théologie comme science au XIIIe siècle*, further implications of this subalternation are outlined. Faith is presented as constitutive of theology. In subalternation it is faith that provides the necessary continuity between the 'science of God' and the critical human operation of theology, thereby preserving transcendence while validating human reason as not extrinsic to

---

75. *ST* Ia, q. 1, a. 2.
76. 'La théologie comme science' (1927), 63; *La théologie comme science au XIIIe siècle* (1957), 74.
77. 'La théologie comme science' (1927), 63.

theology.⁷⁸ Theology is a science by the same means that it is mystical; subalternation also explained the integral role of the mystical dimension of theology.⁷⁹ Confidence in the *intellectus fidei* offered Chenu further demonstration of Thomas' ubiquitous application of the principle of the unity between human understanding of Revelation and the way all things are known humanly: 'cognita sunt in cognoscente secundum modum cognoscentis' (*ST* IIa IIae, q. 1, a. 2).⁸⁰ Chenu had already linked the legitimacy of argument in theology with the scholastic axiom, '*Gratia non tollit naturam, sed perficit*'. Chenu observed that Aquinas' favourite axiom found its highest and most fruitful realisation in this subalternation.⁸¹ Yet Chenu observed, the theory cannot completely account for the discrepancy between the relationship of the believer to God, and to that of a physicist to a mathematician. So by the 1943 and 1957 editions, Chenu had added that theology's relationship to the 'science of God' is the 'quasi-subalternation' of an imperfect 'science'.⁸² Subalternation reinforced the conviction that the object of faith is God, and not doctrinal conclusions. This allowed Chenu to insist more on the subjective-objective dynamic of theology, that the end of theology is to know God through Revelation and faith, emphasising more clearly than he had before the place of scripture in theology.⁸³ By locating theology as a science, albeit subalternated, he implied that theology is necessarily concerned with the whole of reality, not merely with specific religious

---

78. 'Non seulement par conséquent livraison d'un donné, d'une série de propositions acceptées d'autorité, par une légitime «obéissance» intellectuelle à Dieu se révélant, mais continuité organique, psychologique et religieuse, selon laquelle la lumière de foi, émanation de la lumière divine dans l'esprit de l'homme, compose le milieu indispensable à la connaissance des propositions révélées.' *La théologie comme science au XIIIe siècle* (1957), 73.
79. *La théologie comme science* (1957), 73-4.
80. *La théologie comme science* (1957), 71, 70 n 1.
81. 'La théologie comme science' (1927), 64-5.
82. *La théologie comme science* (1957), 80-85
83. Chenu emphasised medieval scholasticism's basis in scripture in the opening of his chapter on 'The dialectic of science' with: 'La théologie est la science d'un livre, le livre des livres, la Bible. Elle l'est de droit, car, science de Dieu, elle trouve dans ce livre la parole de Dieu, la révélation de Dieu.' *La théologie comme science* (1957), 15. *Cf* also 13-14, 16-17.

subjects at the periphery of human affairs, which had become its constricted charter under modernity.[84]

The 1927 article drew some discussion, and its subsequent editions continue to be cited in debates on the nature of theology and the meaning of Thomas' treatise on *sacra doctrina*.[85] It is significant that even in subsequent editions, Chenu did not modify his judgment that Thomas' theory of subalternation radically outstepped all previous understanding of 'theology as science'. This contrasted markedly with more evolutionary readings of the development of doctrine, which vindicate passive or only gradual doctrinal and methodological change. For Chenu, Aquinas pre-figured and legitimised the orthodoxy of innovative reform in the critical practice of theology. An early critic of this interpretation was the Franciscan Jean-François Bonnefoy, who was concerned that Chenu had mistakenly attributed Bonaventure's contribution to Aquinas, giving Thomas sole credit for the scientific status of theology. While Chenu registered Bonnefoy's criticism in the 1943 edition's preface, he did not address Bonnefoy's arguments.[86] In the 1927 original version, Chenu's case for Aquinas' innovation depended on a detailed account of Fishacre and Kilwardby. Its sparse treatment of Bonaventure's use of subalternation led to a focus on Thomas' later works that over-emphasised Aquinas' contribution, while playing down his earlier minimal reading of subalternation in the *Commentary on the Sentences*. Following

---

84. *La théologie comme science* (1957), 100. *Cf* also 'On ne manquera pas de donner à cette «continuité», objective et subjective, sa portée épistémologique, si on observe la densité de la *continuatio* dans l'univers—non aristotélicien en cela, certes—de saint Thomas, comme principe d'être et d'intelligibilité des choses, que ce soit en physique, en psychologie des facultés dans l'homme, en analyse de l'action et de la causalité, même instrumentale', 73, n 1. 'Position', 120: '«Le Verbe s'est fait chair»: ma foi en raisonnant contemple volontiers en cette «chair» tout ce que comporte une humanité, depuis une sensibilité soumise à la tentation jusqu'à une intelligence ouverte à la vision de Dieu; et ma raison, *sub lumine fidei*, se charge de résoudre les délicates questions que pose, jusque dans les mots, une pareille révélation.'
85. Chenu's noted at the beginning of Preface to XIII and note 2 articles on it by: M Grabmann, 'De theologia ut scientia argumentativa secundum S Albertum magnum et S Thomam Aquinum', in *Angelicum*, XIV (1937): 39–60; Jean-François Bonnefoy OFM, 'La théologie comme science et l'application de la Foi selon S Thomas d'Aquin', in *Ephemerides theologicae louvainienses*, XIV (1937): 421–446, and 600–631; XV (1938): 491–516.
86. 'Préface' (1943), reprinted with (1957) preface, 11, n 2.

the detailed attention to Kilwardby and Fishacre, the reader is stopped short by the light treatment of the Franciscan's contribution by Chenu.[87] In the 1943 and 1957 editions, Chenu did expand on this shorter article, including Bonaventure's input, but Chenu did not revise his argument or respond to its critics. There was his acknowledgment of an over-emphasis on confining the scientific character of theology to the deduction of conclusions from the articles of faith and he cited Congar's arguments for a univocal meaning for *sacra doctrina*, but left his own equivocal interpretation unrevised.[88]

This revival by Chenu of the importance of the theory of subalternation is credited with initiating the twentieth century engagement of theology with 'earthly realities'. This led to the theological disputes with '*Konklusiontheologie*', which came to define the innovation of the 'nouvelle théologie'.[89] Yet his interpretation of the meaning of *sacra doctrina* in the first Part of the *Summa* has generated much controversy.[90] In two comprehensive deconstructions of Chenu's exegetical and historical arguments, Henry Donneaud OP accuses him of lacking a true historical-critical discipline, not being objective about

---

87. 'Saint Bonaventure avait bien, il est vrai, d'une subordination de la théologie à l'Écriture; mais il s'agissait d'une simple dépendance de fait, en dehors de tout souci de systématisation, puisque chez lui le problème de la «science» n'était pas vraiment posé.' 'La théologie comme science' (1927), 63 and '[Bonaventure] s'agit de subordination au sens commun du mot, non cet agencement technique en vertu duquel une science reçoit d'une autre les «principes» de son raisonnement', 55.
88. *La théologie comme science au XIIIe siècle* (1957), 78–80.
89. Two more recent examples published in English are: Piet Schoonenberg SJ, 'The Theologian's Calling, Freedom, and Constraint' in *Authority in the Church*, edited by Piet Fransen SJ (Leuven: K. U. Leuven Press, 1983), 92–118, 93: 'Chenu's article remains modern because of what he writes concerning faith, the tie between heaven and earth, and its influence upon theology.'; and Roger Haight SJ, *Dynamics of Theology* (New York: Paulist Press, 1990), 2. Chenu's criticised the reduction of theology to 'a science of conclusions' in 'La littérature comme "lieu" de la théologie', in *Revue des sciences philosophiques et théologiques*, LIII (1969): 70–80, 73.
90. Marie-Joseph Congar OP, in *Bulletin thomiste*, 5/8 (1938): 490–505; Victor White OP, *Holy Teaching: The Idea of Theology according to St Thomas Aquinas* (London: Blackfriars Publications, 1958); James A Weisheipl OP, 'Review: Is Theology a Science?', in *New Scholasticism*, XXXV (1961): 241–243; James A Weisheipl OP, 'The Meaning of *Sacra Doctrina* in Summa Theologiae I, q.1', in *The Thomist*, 38 (1974); Michel Corbin SJ, *Le Chemin de la théologie chez Thomas d'Aquin* (Paris: Beauchesne, 1974); John I Jenkins CSC, *Knowledge and Faith in Thomas Aquinas* (Cambridge: Cambridge University Press, 1997).

his sources, and failing in the humility required to revise his faulty conclusions.[91] These are serious charges against a work which was so foundational for Chenu's theology and his historical credentials. Donneaud judges that Chenu applied 'une clef de lecture reçue *a priori*' to discard the univocal meaning for *sacra doctrina* for article 2, in favour of the anachronistic twentieth century meaning of 'theological science'. He also finds that Aquinas' extrapolation from Bonaventure's 'subalternation', in the commentary on the *Sentences*, did not sufficiently distinguish between scripture as *sacra doctrina* and the critical understanding of Revelation that defined 'theology as science' in the later works. Chenu acknowledged that this was not a full exegetical study.[92] Donneaud convincingly argues that his genetic historical method was inadequate as Chenu needed to examine more the relevant texts in Aquinas, instead of his antecedents.[93] Chenu's account, in the 1927 original, of the reference to subalternation in the *Commentary on the Sentences* does suggest that the rupture in the understanding of theology as science claimed for Aquinas' later works may be less clear than he asserted.[94] Yet Chenu's explanation for the halting progress of the other thirteenth century masters' understanding of the scientific nature of theology does not necessarily depend on the discontinuity he proposed between Aquinas' early and later works. Despite the proximity of Bonaventure's use of subalternation, his later rejection of Aquinas' theology clearly distinguished his understanding from the correlation with philosophical method that subalternation generated for Aquinas.

Donneaud does register that Chenu was really answering article 2 even though this discussion is presented instead as an answer to article 1: 'what is *sacra doctrina*?' Donneaud identifies Chenu's 'clef de lecture' as stemming from an unexamined reception through his teachers Gardeil and Garrigou-Lagrange of John of St Thomas' equiv-

---

91. Henry Donneaud OP, 'Histoire d'une histoire: M-D Chenu et «La théologie comme science au XIIIe siècle»', in *Mémoire Dominicaine*, 4 (1994): 139–175, and 'M-D Chenu et l'exégèse de *Sacra Doctrina*', in *Revue des sciences philosophiques et théologiques*, 81 (1997): 415–437.
92. 'N'ayant pas ici à présenter une exégèse textuelle suivie, mais à discerner les points critiques de l'évolution doctrinale': Chenu, 'La théologie comme science' (1927), 61.
93. Donneaud (1997), 422.
94. 'La théologie comme science' (1927), 58–60.

ocal interpretation of *sacra doctrina* in the Prima Pars.⁹⁵ But he also charges Chenu with having a transparent Hegelian agenda, manifested in the stress on conflict and his dialectical portrayal of Aquinas' incorporation of scientific method in theology.⁹⁶ Both charges are feasible. Chenu's theological interest and the object of his concern was to relativise the scientific claims of 'modern scholasticism' against Aquinas' more nuanced ascription of *sacra doctrina* broadly to holy teaching *and* the theology that is derived from it. Chenu argued for the 'theology' reading of *sacra doctrina* more in terms of his understanding of the unity of the relationship of doctrine to faith. He held that *sacra doctrina* meant 'theology' (in the modern sense of the word) because of his need to distinguish neo-scholasticism's uncritical alignment of theological reason with rationalism. This was in contrast to the Thomists of the eighteenth century, influenced by Wolffian rationalism, who reduced *sacra doctrina* to theorems which were deduced independently of faith and contemplation on the Word of God.⁹⁷ Donneaud observes that for Chenu: 'La connaissance humaine ne culmine pas dans la *ratio* et ses procédés dialectiques, mais dans l'*intellectus*, c'est-à-dire dans la saisie intellective de son objet.'⁹⁸ The issue for Chenu was that human understanding requires critical reasoning in theology, not the mechanical neo-scholastic rationalism. This was grounded in his confidence in the intellectual condition of faith and theology. Donneaud finds that Chenu's antagonism to neo-Augustinian separation of faith and reason overwhelmed his scholarship.⁹⁹ Whether this sensitivity compromised Chenu's historical objectivity is surely as debatable as the possibility of objectivity itself. Chenu often referred in his later writing to the competing

---

95. A Gardeil OP, *Le donné révélé et la théologie* (Juvisny: Les Éditions du Cerf, 1932), 250; R Garrigou-Lagrange OP, *De Deo Uno: Commentarium in Primam Partem S. Thomae* (Paris: Éditions du Cerf, 1938), 126–145, as cited in Weisheipl, 'The Meaning of *Sacra Doctrina* in *Summa Theologiae* I, q.1', 60–61.
96. Donneaud (1997), 419, 421, 423.
97. Chenu, *La théologie est-elle une science?*, 88–89.
98. Donneaud (1994), 162.
99. 'Sans doute M-D Chenu garde une réserve spontanée envers les tendances dualistes qui traversent la pensée augustinienne et la rendent selon lui, incapable de saisir, dans une même synthèse, vérités divines et éternelles d'une part (sagesse), réalités temporelles et contingentes d'autre part (science). Une certaine méfiance à l'égard de l'augustinisme accompagnera d'ailleurs toute son oeuvre.' Donneaud (1994), 152.

dialectic of these positions in the history of theology, indicating his preference while insisting that both are necessary because of the tension between immanence and transcendence in Christianity.[100] As he would later assert:

> Sous ce choc épistémologique, c'est un vieux problème qui nous est posé. Saint Thomas, dans une conjoncture culturelle analogue, se faisait déjà cette objection à l'*unité* du savoir théologique: Comment tenir sous le même registre le Créateur et la créature? [101]

That Chenu failed to amend his interpretation even after Congar's correction defies any adequate justification, although some explanation may be found in the proximity of the second edition to his condemnation in 1942. The 1943 version added a note of acknowledgment to both Gardeil and Garrigou-Lagrange, despite his recent humiliation by the latter.[102] Was this failure to revise his position an attempt to establish the orthodoxy of his theology by its overt conformity on *sacra doctrina* with these luminaries of neo-scholasticism? Or was it a stubborn refusal to recant what he regarded as a foundational study for the reform of theology? There is a faint echo of such tenacity in a later related context, the preface to a 1968 French translation of the *Summa theologiae*. Chenu recalled how Aquinas was initially rejected then systematically forgotten, despite his official revival and honours, because of the risk inherent in incorporating reason in theology, and he ends with the battle-cry: 'Il est temps de reprendre l'opération.'[103] Chenu's later works do tend to maintain the equivocal interpretation while paradoxically insisting on the 'unity' of *sacra doctrina*.[104] His objective was to establish the importance that Aquinas had given to understanding theology as scientific and its correlation to reason,

---

100. Chenu, *La théologie est-elle une science?*, 103–4 and 'Vérité et liberté dans la foi du croyant' (1959) in *La Parole de Dieu I. La Foi dans intelligence* (Paris: Cerf, 1964), 337–359.
101. Chenu, 'Définition de l'unité de l'enseignement', in *Seminarium*, XXIII/2 (1971): 267–279, 268.
102. 'Préface', 'La théologie comme science au XIIIe siècle' (1943), reprinted with (1957) preface, 12, n 1.
103. Chenu, 'Préface', in *Somme theeologique. La théologie: la Prologue et question 1*, translated by HD Gardeil OP (Paris: Éditions du Cerf/Desclée, 1968): 5–9, 8.
104. These include reference to Congar's article in: 'Définition de l'unité de l'enseignement', 276.

more than answering the other articles about *sacra doctrina*. Whether Chenu was not convinced that Congar's work demolished his whole argument remains unknown. Could Chenu have regarded his own work as historical, that is not the definitive work on *sacra doctrina*, but a seminal 'événement', to be superseded by the scholarship of his student and colleague, and not subject-matter for continuous revision unlike a textbook would be?[105] It can only be concluded that Chenu's aim to legitimate contemporary theological innovation as consistent with his portrayal of Aquinas' revolution was his overarching concern in the theological climate that preceded Vatican II.[106]

'La nouvelle théologie'

When in 1935 he published 'Position de la théologie', advocating reform of neo-Thomist theological method, Chenu intensified his historical critique of 'modern scholasticism'.[107] He had expressed his dissatisfaction with the authority bestowed in contemporary theological discourse on Denzinger's *Enchiridion*, which gave this handbook equivalent status to Thomas' theology.[108] 'Position de la théologie' took this criticism further by proposing how theology could be reformed from its theological and philosophical foundations with 'new' bearings for constructing a theology, later to be known as '*la nouvelle théologie*'. While in a less polemical and caustic format than *Une école de théologie: le Saulchoir*, which launched his renewal of theological method, this article marks a significant departure from its *ressourcement* antecedents. Congar recalled its origins in an encounter with Chenu before *Le Saulchoir* moved nearer to Paris, where they

---

105. Donneaud applauds Congar's detailed and erudite method as much in judgement against Chenu's. Donneaud (1997), 428.
106. There are further discussions and disputes with other parts of Chenu's groundbreaking work on Thomas Aquinas, especially that on the plan of the *Summa* and Chenu's *exitus-reditus* schema. As these do not touch directly on the anthropological topic I have not discussed them here. See Rudi Te Velde, *Aquinas on God: The 'Divine Science' of the Summa Theologiae* (Farnham: Ashgate, 2006), 10–15.
107. Chenu, 'Position de la théologie' (1935). Surprisingly it was commended by Garrigou-Lagrange although he condemned *Une école de théologie: le Saulchoir*. Garrigou later regretted as too favourable his letter to Chenu about 'Position'. Étienne Fouilloux, 'Autour d'une mise à l'Index', 34, n 3.
108. From Chenu's review of some introductions to theology in *Revue des sciences philosophiques et théologiques* 24 (1935): 705–7.

conspired in 'un accord profond, à la fois intellectuel, vital and apostolique' to undertake the 'liquidation de la théologie'. They planned their respective tasks. 'Ce fut un moment d'intense et totale concordance des esprits.'[109] The plan was not to overturn one set of theological theses for another, Congar insisted, but to propagate a retrieval of the innovation and evangelical intensity of the Thomist tradition. The conspiracy had immediate if not the desired effect. On publishing its manifesto *Une école de théologie: le Saulchoir*, Chenu was condemned for discrediting Thomism and dishonouring Aquinas.[110]

'Position de la théologie' still rings like a declaration of this projected offensive. Its epigram from Johann Kuhn and the dedication to Matthias Scheeben provocatively enlisted the Tübingen reformers as proto-collaborators in this campaign.[111] Chenu's invocation of them situated this article as transitional. It stood between their neo-scholastic reinstatement of the intellectual dynamic in Aquinas' doctrine of faith and the historical direction of Chenu's theological curriculum outlined in *Une école de théologie: le Saulchoir*. The more positivist 'return to the sources' method, associated with Congar and Lubac, was described by their opponents as 'la nouvelle théologie', with the pejorative sense that innovation carried for an immutable system.[112] The 'Conclusion theology', that summarised the rationalist analysis of Thomas into propositions bearing the status of articles of faith, had made its object merely the 'principles' of a method rather than the divine reality that these propositions were intended to communicate. 'Modern scholasticism' objectified its intellectualism into a rationalist creed. Chenu's project attempted an interplay between object and subject in theology that was more true to Thomas' methodology, while it acknowledged the necessary subjectivity demanded by modern psychology. This study of Thomas, uncovered by these innovators, exposed this rationalist theology of 'modern scholasticism' as the actual innovation:

---

109. Yves Congar OP, 'Le frère que j'ai connu' in C Geffré, *L'Hommage differé au Père Chenu* (Paris: Cerf, 1990), 239–245, 242.
110. Père Parente (1942): 'ce discrédit retombe sur saint Thomas.' cited by Chenu in his preface to 'La théologie comme science au XIIIe siècle' (1943).
111. 'Avec eux, c'est la liquidation de la «théologie baroque» qui commence.' 'Position de la théologie', 'Notes documentaires', 137. He also referred to his debt to Gardeil and Garrigou-Lagrange, 138.
112. Contemporary with this period of Chenu's output were Lubac's *Catholicisme* (1938) and *Surnaturel* (1946), and Congar's *Chrétiens désunis* (1937) and *Esquisses du Mystère de l'Église* (1941).

> Le comble du paradoxe sera de voir des théologiens tenir que la théologie peut se construire hors l'expérience de foi. Théologie mort-née, spéculations à vide, et, à la lettre, sans objet.[113]

In 'Position de la théologie', Chenu announced the terms of this reform in theological method. He rehearsed the topics of his earlier discussions on the scientific status of theology, that theology has a quasi-scientific mode explained by the theory of subalternation, insisting on the supernatural dimension of Revelation and the incarnation of the divine in the theological work of human reason. Collected together under another citation of Thomas' principle of epistemological continuity, these topics reiterated the human condition of faith and the perception of Revelation: 'Si vraiment l'homme connaît Dieu, il le connaîtra humainement.'[114]

Then Chenu focused on the reform of theological method in the section, 'La construction de la théologie', by distinguishing the givens of Revelation, which privileges the object of theology, divine reality as revealed, over dogmatic conclusions; and how the speculative construct extrapolates from these revealed givens. The 'donné' is revealed, unlike the givens acquired as extrinsic data in human sciences, but more like the natural law that corresponds to the codified laws of society.[115] The God revealed by Revelation is more interior to humans than we are to ourselves.[116] The construct composed from this data of Revelation is always dependent on it to provide the frame through which the content of Revelation can be understood. Dogmatic formulae are constructed within the limitations of particular times, places, and societies, which never equate with or exhaust the full meaning of Revelation. This distinction privileged revealed data, over the speculative formulation, in relation to the object of faith. It also steered between excessively subjective or extrinsicist theologies of Revelation. In this understanding of the Thomist anthropological dynamic, the divine imprint created in human nature corresponds with contemplation of the divine source of Revelation, otherwise Revelation

---

113. 'Position', 118.
114. 'Position', 119.
115. Chenu used François Gény's juridical analogy from *Science et technique en droit privé positif* (Paris: L. Tenin, 1914), 95 ff: 'la loi inscrite dans la nature même de l'homme individuel ou social, avant qu'un pouvoir positif en ait fixé les inclinations et déterminé les applications concrètes'. 'Position', 124.
116. 'Position', 123.

about God would be humanly inaccessible. The unity of theology is thus preserved through its supernatural source and end. For Chenu, human subjectivity is integral to theology and faith because it is there that God meets us.[117] Theology is constructed on *both* the '*donné*' and the '*construit*'.[118] Chenu asserted that theology requires the historical 'retour aux expériences premières' to test the value of any deduced abstract propositions. This implied that only a *ressourcement* of the experiential and historical sources of theology could overcome the stagnation produced by a concentration on metaphysics and the deduction of abstract formulations.[119] Positive and speculative theology should no longer be maintained separately, as Chenu later commented: 'le dépassement du dualisme théologie positive et théologie speculative, qui, dès le début, lorsque j'y avais recours comme tout le monde, me blessait dans mon *intellectus fidei*.'[120]

Chenu broke from his neo-scholastic background to situate the construction of theology within the historical consciousness of modernity. In order to explain how the construct always remains secondary to Revelation, Chenu introduced the role of historical development in theology, as the counter and corrective of 'l'impuissance de la spéculation'. He concluded that Christian theology is ontologically historical. Historical method, he maintained, was apposite to a faith founded on Revelation in history. While Chenu's understanding of historical development here reflects Hegelian and Bergsonian ideas of progress, he insisted:

> Mais le théologien, lui, travaille sur une histoire. Son «donné», ce ne sont les natures des choses ni leurs formes intemporelles; ce sont des événements, répondant à une *économie*, dont la réalisation est liée au temps, comme l'étendue est liée au corps, par-dessus l'ordre des essences. Le monde réel est celui-là, et non pas l'abstraction du philosophe.[121]

---

117. 'Position', 123–126.
118. Chenu presented this unity as incarnationally verified: 'rejeter la seconde, avec ses espoirs et ses efforts d'intelligibilité, hors la zone de la première, ce serait manquer de réalisme, car si Dieu consent à se livrer à la raison humaine, c'est, après l'avoir habilitée, en acceptant la loi native de cette raison.' 'Position', 116.
119. 'Position', 124.
120. Chenu, 'Préface' in Claude Geffré OP, Un *Nouvel Age de la Théologie* (Paris: Cerf, 1972), 9.
121. 'Position', 128.

The economy of salvation is revealed in the historical contingencies of creation, incarnation, and redemption, and the mission of Christ continued through his mystical body, the Church.[122] Chenu declared that the purpose of theology is contemplation of this sacred history from each theologian's particular place in history, not the deduction from atemporal principles, for the mystery is only recognised in history.[123] This represented a direct attack on the prevailing theological preoccupation with examining eternal causes.[124] To support his claim, Chenu introduced an analogy between the correlation of historical and theological method and the Incarnation of Christ.

> Voici à nouveau la «position» de la théologie. Sachant assumer dans cette vision chrétienne du monde l'ordre des natures, tout comme le Christ a assumé une nature humaine, elle reconnaît dans la raison une lumière issue de la pensée divine, que le don nouveau de la foi intègre en son labeur.[125]

Enlisting first Aquinas then surprisingly Augustine as prototypes of historically grounded theology, Chenu concluded that the historical 'givens' of Revelation, which herald the economy of salvation, are components for the construction of theology.[126]

Having dismissed the position that protected the supernatural end of faith and theology from contamination by the human condi-

---

122. 'Position', 130.
123. Later, Chenu captured this in one of his characteristic aphorisms: 'Le Mystère est dans l'histoire. L'Église est dans le monde.' Chenu, 'Histoire du salut et historicité de l'homme dans le renouveau de la théologie' in L Shook and GM Bertrand, editors, *La théologie du renouveau* (Paris: Cerf, 1968), 21–32, 26.
124. 'La théologie est *réaliste*, parce qu'elle est l'intelligence de l'ordre du salut dans son histoire et sa réalisation concrète.' 'Position', 131.
125. 'Position', 129.
126. Chenu attributed an anthropological significance to Aquinas' historical option: 'il s'en tient, pour déterminer le motif de l'incarnation, à l'histoire contingente du Christ rédempteur du péché, et résiste à la tentation de situer un Homme-Dieu au sommet de l'ordre du monde idéalement achevé.' Augustine is uncharacteristically cast positively by Chenu: 'Ce fut la grandeur de la théologie de saint Augustin, et ce demeure son irrépressible séduction, de rester exclusivement centrée sur l'histoire de l'homme et de son péché, sur les imprévisibles histoires de l'amour gratuit de Dieu. Non point une métaphysique sacrée, mais une *Cité de Dieu* et des *Confessions*.' 'Position', 129–30.

tion, Chenu completed his map of the construction of theology by providing a demonstration of history as a locus for theological reflection. The human condition of the theological enterprise was based in Aquinas' teaching on the theological virtues. Rejecting Peter Lombard's insistence on a direct unmediated infusion of grace by the Holy Spirit, Aquinas declared virtue to be rational, located not in a spiritual zone of humanity, but actually in the seat of the passions. Chenu found the coherence of faith and reason in theology reinforced its anthropological integrity as it resisted the truncation of the 'science' of theology.

> La théologie est ainsi le plus beau fruit d'une confiance audacieuse dans la cohérence de la foi et de la raison, cohérence par l'intérieur, et non pas seulement accord externe par juxtaposition de deux vérités. Cette confiance est audacieuse parce qu'elle est fondée dans la structure même de la foi, de la vertu «théologale» habilitant l'homme à entrer dans la connaissance de Dieu. C'est donc la foi qui est audacieuse, et non pas d'abord la raison.[127]

This amounted to a prolegomenon for his theological anthropology: 'la foi est lumière divine *dans* une intelligence humaine. Elle est possédée par l'homme, et l'homme pense par elle.'[128]

While registering the danger of the reduction to either anthropocentrism or theocentrism, Chenu refused the false dichotomy of humanism opposed to theology as too simplistic. His use of the term 'théologal' in 'l'humanisme théologa' emphasised the divine and human relationship, locating this humanism within the theological order, as a *theo*-logal anthropology, which speaks to humans of God. This signalled an anthropological starting-point, which is qualified and enhanced by its relationship to its divine object: 'la vie théologale, c'est-à-dire de la vie divine en nous participée, selon la triple et unique puissance de la foi, de l'espérance, de la charité.'[129] In a sweep through the historical drama of two renaissances, Chenu juxtaposed 'le haut équilibre spirituel' of Aquinas' response to the Aristotelian humanism of his time, to the inability of theology to correlate critically with

---

127. 'Position', 131.
128. 'Position', 134.
129. *St Thomas d'Aquin et la théologie*, 54.

subsequent revolutions in human thought. Unlike the invention and critical openness of Aquinas' 'theological humanism', humanism was dismissed perfunctorily as error. In contrast, the history of the failure of 'humanist theology' demonstrated to Chenu the limitations of a too apologetic and defensive 'formalism', divorced from the 'realism' of faith. Yet he conceded that this attempt at dialogue with humanism did save Catholic doctrine from the anti-humanist challenges of Lutheranism. Chenu insisted that this 'humanist theology' was at least more theological in its refutation of the reformers than that provided against Erasmus by the Cologne Dominicans; he even praised its rich if severe spirituality, as represented by St Francis de Sales. He observed the dissimilar orientation and ends of each theological approach: 'la théologie humaniste procéda exactement à l'inverse d'un humanisme théologale.'[130] In contrast, the 'theological humanism' of Aquinas disclosed the coherence of reason and faith within the mystery of that same faith, with that critical curiosity that marks all true humanism.[131] Chenu regretted the absence of another Aquinas in this history of doctrinal conflict and development.

'Position de la théologie' drew less attention from the Roman authorities than *Une École de théologie: le Saulchoir*, and yet it drastically broke with the conventions of neo-scholastic method. In it, Chenu's particular version of 'la nouvelle théologie' was introduced as a profound renewal of theological method. While Lubac's *Catholicisme* and *Surnaturel* opened the central doctrines to the breadth of the Patristic and other non-Thomist sources, Chenu's contribution reformed even this methodology, turning '*le retour aux sources*' from a merely positivist retrieval into a '*ressourcement*', drawing on the traditional sources for constructing contemporary theology. Grounded in a retrieval of Thomas' teaching on faith, Chenu also stressed faith's critical orientation of both contemplation and theology. Faith and reason are united in their object, principle, and end, and entwined in the necessary tension between faith and understanding, as expressed by Anselm's formula.

> C'est encore et toujours le *Fides quaerens intellectum* d'Anselme et de Thomas d'Aquin, mais saisi par une perception nouvelle de son objet: le mystère de Dieu entré en communication avec

---

130. 'Position', 135.
131. 'Position', 135.

> l'homme. La nouveauté est en ceci que, sans rejeter, bien sûr, sa référence à Dieu, la foi trouve son objet dans une «histoire sainte»[132]

He paralleled the coherence between faith and reason in theology with that of grace and nature: 'Cette exaltation de la raison dans le travail théologique, c'est la consécration suprême de la nature dans la grâce.'[133] Chenu expanded on this parallel of nature-grace and faith and reason when arguing for the autonomy of the human sciences:

> Théologiens, c'est, pensons-nous, par les exigences mêmes de notre théologie qu'est requis un ordre propre de vérités rationnelles, tout comme la grace requiert une nature. La théologie est, au très fort sens médiéval du mot, une «sagesse»; mais une sagesse dont la transcendance même interdit une préséance *active* en vertu de laquelle elle interviendrait positivement dans l'établissement et la construction des disciplines rationnelles. Elle n'est pas au sommet des sciences, mais hors l'ordre du savoir, plantée qu'elle est par la foi dans la science de Dieu. Le théologian ne porte pas en soi une philosophie, une physique, une métaphysique, pas plus qu'une politique, une sociologie, ou une économie. Il n'y a pas continuité, scientifiquement parlant.[134]

The problem of the coherence of nature with grace, how to avoid the deprecation of nature engendered by excessively spiritual Augustinianism without compromising the divine gift of grace, became the key theme of *'la nouvelle théologie'.* Echoing his earlier claim that Aquinas' genius lay in the conjunction of 'intuition' and 'mentalité', Chenu emphasised the importance of intuition as an expression of faith, because intuition reconciles the separated mystical and speculative forms of theology.[135]

---

132. Chenu, 'La théologie en procès', in *Savoir, faire, espérer: les limites de la raison* (Brussells: Facultés Universitaires St Louis, 1976), 691–696 (692).
133. 'Position', 134–5.
134. *Une école*, 153 [81].
135. Chenu, 'La psychologie de la foi dans la théologie du XIIIe siècle.' (1932), 98: 'L'intuition, c'est l'ame religieuse de saint Thomas qui la fournit, dans l'expérience d'une affecteuse adhésion—infrangible et impatience à la fois—au Dieu béatifiant qui se révèle.'

Chenu's project of outlining the dynamic of faith in reason and theology was a development of the intellectualist theology of his teachers Gardeil and Garrigou-Lagrange. Yet it continued the critical overhaul of the method and presuppositions of 'modern scholasticism' initiated by the 'modernist crisis'. To some extent, Chenu's *ressourcement* of Thomas can be read as continuous with Garrigou-Lagrange's work in returning to the sources of spiritual theology. There is some suggestion of this continuity in Chenu's shock at Garrigou-Lagrange's condemnation of *Une École* in 1937; he appears to have understood his task as adding an historical criticality to his master's Thomism, but he discovered there was no middle ground position between them.[136] His correlation of human reason and historical trends was deemed dangerous to the Church's doctrinal deposit, because it unveiled doctrine's historical development and the historical imperative to communicate the Gospel anew to each age. Chenu regretted how Aquinas' critical correlation of these was absent from theology in subsequent ages, and attributed this to an inadequate understanding of how central to Aquinas' theology was his teaching on faith and human understanding, and the anthropology this was grounded in.

> Toute la théologie de la foi, chez saint Thomas, est élaborée à partir des «conditions» du sujet humain, en même temps que sur l'absolu de sa divine vérité.[137]

This methodological article concluded with Chenu's account of 'l'humanisme théologal' and the concomitant anthropological implications of the Incarnation. He would explore this further in his manifesto *Une école de théologie: le Saulchoir*:

> *Cognita sunt in cognoscente ad modum cognoscentis*: exclure Dieu de cette loi naturelle de toute connaissance, sous prétexte qu'il est transcendant ou qu'il se révèle, ce serait

---

136. There is some support for this view in Garrigou-Lagrange's earlier attacks on incursions of nominalism and idealism into neo-scholastic thought, and his recovery of Thomas' teaching on 'common sense'. Yet his metaphysical commitment is clearly a different register from Chenu's. See particularly the contrast of his approach in *De Deo Uno: Commentarium in Primam Partem S. Thomae* (Paris: Cerf, 1938), 126–145, to Chenu's earlier articles on the *Prima Pars* and *sacra doctrina*.

137. 'Vérité et liberté dans la foi du croyant' (1959), 358.

> céder d'avance au désordre spirituel d'une fausse mysticité. Si vraiment l'homme connaît Dieu, il le connaîtra humainement. Pas plus que la grâce en la nature, la foi n'est une lumière posée à la surface d'une raison: elle vit en elle. Et la foi n'est pas contaminée pas cette incarnation, pas plus que le Verbe n'est amoindri pour s'être fait chair. Double mystère théandrique, mieux, unique mystère, qui est le mystère même du Christ, en qui le divin et l'humain sont un: unique Personne, en laquelle la foi me plante, Fils éternel de Dieu entré dans l'histoire. Le Christ de la foi, dans le Christ de l'histoire.[138]

For Chenu, it is a false mysticism that denies the role of human reason in the phenomenon of faith and thereby risks the unity of human understanding. That a dualist concept of humanity would be the result was for him a compromise of the Incarnation, for it deems humanity as incapable of bearing the mystery of Christ. His slogan, 'Si vraiment l'homme connaît Dieu, il le connaîtra humainement', captured the significance for Christian anthropology of avoiding such a bifurcated understanding. Human understanding is not limited to appreciating creation only, but is open to God's revelation through its very same faculties for knowing. God is known humanly, and any separation of the capacity for faith understanding from other knowledge destabilises the whole concept of what it means to be human. Chenu continued his theological investigation from this human perspective in his early ecclesiological writings, before and after his condemnation in 1937, and the next chapter examines the anthropological nature of his understanding of church.

---

138. *Une école de théologie*, 60–61 [136–137].

Chapter 3
Anthropological Dimensions of Chenu's Ecclesiology before Vatican II

> "L'Eglise est, meme socialement, le people de Dieu."
> 'Présentation' in *Théologie de la matière*
> (Paris: Éditions du Cerf, 1967), 11.

Chenu's early ecclesiology

For Chenu, the crisis caused by his *Une école de théologie: le Saulchoir* represented as much a crisis in the Church's self-understanding, already demonstrated by the reaction to the Modernist Crisis earlier in the century. His ecclesiological concerns emerged from both the debates over the development of doctrine and his involvement with the *Jeunesse Ouvrière Chrétienne (JOC)* movement, which challenged the traditional ecclesial structures, particularly the parish. The issue was how the Church could be a 'présence' in the new world of industrialised France. He recast this perceived threat as a new type of Christianity, not merely a pastoral tactic. In this chapter, Chenu's anticipation of the anthropological turn of Vatican II will be identified through his influential ecclesiology in response to the JOCist movements and to the mission of the worker-priests. His support for other lay consciousness in the Church, particularly with *Esprit* and the followers of Mounier, will also be considered.

Chenu's inter-war ecclesiological writings addressed the issues raised by the French Church's late concern about the long-term effects of nineteenth century 'laicisme' or secularisation on the 'dechristianisation' of urban populations. The impetus for his theological contribution was a series of articles that appeared in the early 1930s in *La vie intellectuelle*, which had assessed the extent and penetration of atheism beyond that secularity limited historically to the educated bourgeoisie. An increase in unbelief throughout the population as the concomitant of the aggressive atheism of organised socialist labour had been earlier noted by pastors such as the young bishop of Bayeux, Suhard, who became Cardinal of Paris. Less expected was the unbelief displayed as passive indifference that pervaded the wider industrial demographic. The ecclesial awakening to this development was spurred by the early success of the original Belgian 'JOC' models of work-place reflection and action. Such approaches engendered further critical and practical challenges to the Church's mission, and Chenu's early ecclesiology substantiated these.

Chenu perceived that this widespread disaffection with existing Church practices demanded the response of a new type of Christianity, formed in experiential reflection and defined in terms of immersion in the current 'milieu' through more extra-ecclesial activity or what he called 'présence'. Focus on parish community and the provision of the sacraments characterised the reforms of the concurrent liturgical movement. Chenu recognised that the Church's future lay in 'une déterritorialisation des communautés d'Église',[1] displacement that refused isolation of the Church from the world inhabited by the majority of the population. Here was a new ecclesial experience of community, defined in terms of 'milieu' and 'présence', which fostered a militancy in ecclesial as well as industrial matters.[2] Instead of socially and politically locating French Catholicism exclusively in the sacred domain, the 'militants' sought to displace its mission to become engaged with the modern world, which forecast the climate that eventually confronted the universal Church at Vatican II. Hence Chenu's early ecclesiology remarkably anticipated most of the agenda and much of the teaching of Vatican II.

---

1. Chenu, 'Paroisses et œuvres. Les exigences de l'Action catholique', in *Revue Dominicaine (Ottawa)* (mars 1934): 343–358. See also Chenu, *Un théologien en liberté: Jacques Duquesne interroge le Père Chenu* (Paris: Le Centurion, 1975), 138.
2. This is Toine van den Hoogen's thesis, *Pastorale Teologie: Ontwikkeling en strukture in de teologie van M-D Chenu* (Alblasserdam: Offsetdrukkerij Kanters BV, 1983), Sommaire (in French): 'la théologie de Chenu comme une fonction autonome de la mutation mentale du catholicisme français, depuis les années 30. Cette mutation produit un nouveau type de chrétien français, le militant. [. . .] La naissance du chrétien-militant donne à penser, aux fidèles, aux prêtres, aux évèques, aux théologiens.'

Crucial to this ecclesiology is Chenu's understanding of 'Chrétienté' and 'l'économie chrétienne'. 'Chrétienté' is used to distinguish the historical relativity of types or expressions of Christianity. It is best defined in Chenu's article 'Chrétienté ou mission?' (1950), where he differentiated between the Church's essential mission to its times and the 'institutional' mentality that limits the Church to parish or other established practices. Chenu admitted that 'le terme «Chrétienté» n'est pas sans ambiguïté'.[3] He used it variously to mean either the institutional Church, the theocentric tendency to sacralise the profane, or the 'new' assembly of networks of the Church engaged in an evangelisation, which were open to proclaiming the Incarnation in the changing social dimensions of current human history. For Chenu, 'Chrétienté' is measured by the degree to which the Church in any era is engaged or disengaged with the events of human history. Chenu tended to use the term 'Chrétienté' (upper case) for the first type: the 'Christendom' Church compromised by its allegiances to a particular historical period or political establishment. He only used 'Chrétienté' in relation to the second type to signify a dramatic shift from the established 'Chrétienté' that modified the broader understanding of Christianity, usually distinguished by an adjective like 'nouvelle' or 'missionaire'. But as often, Chenu can be flexible by using the term 'Chrétienté' also in a favourable sense as in 'les éléments qui, dans l'Église, relèvent d'une Chrétienté: Christianitas, le mot est désormais chargé d'un sens concret, avec ses éléments cosmique, ethnique, culturel, politique.'[4] Later in life, Chenu described his use of 'Chrétienté' as encompassing:

> La Chrétienté était alors très critiquée, et je n'ai pas toujours vu très clair à ce sujet ... Cela veut dire l'Église en tant qu'elle trouve son asiette dans le temporal ... C'est de l'idéalisme évidemment: toujours l'Église impliquera une Chrétienté. Je me suis toujours opposé à ceux qui rêvaient d'une Église pure, d'une foi pure, sans aucun engagement temporel. J'admets qu'il y aura toujours une Chrétienté, mais je relativise, je dis qu'elle changera. En l'an 2000, il y aura la même Église, mais la Chrétienté sera tout autre.[5]

---

3. Chenu, 'Présentation' in *La Parole de Dieu II*, 10.
4. *La Théologie au douzième siecle*, 269, and the counter in note 2: 'Ni saint François ni saint Dominique ne figurent au dossier de la «Chrétienté».'
5. *Un théologien en liberté*, 84. See 'Chrétienté' in *Dimension nouvelle de la Chrétienté* (Paris: Cerf, 1937), 6–7, 18–19, 25–27, 30–31.

Noting the absence of a clear definition of 'Chrétienté' by Chenu, Congar offered: 'Il semble qu'il entende par là la forme historique et concrète qui prend le christianisme.'[6] In a more recent study by Jean-Pierre Jossua OP, the range of Chenu's usage is surveyed and assessed for indicating also the end of Christianity.[7]

Characteristic of Chenu's theology of Church is his recovery of the Greek Fathers' doctrine of 'l'économie chrétienne'. Primarily its spatial and temporal register resisted the atemporality of 'modern scholasticism'. For Chenu, the differences of Greek theology compared with Latin theology provided the best evidence for the Western Church's own doctrinal development since the Great Schism, and thereby underscored the under-acknowledged diversity of theologies within Catholicism. Chenu first employed the concept 'l'économie du christianisme' in 'Les yeux de la foi'.[8] He used 'une *économie*, une triple économie' to encompass the order of the world as an 'Économie créatrice et gubernatrice [. . .] Économie de l'incarnation et de la rédemption [. . .] Économie enfin des sacrements et du sacrifice'.[9] Another early use in relation to ecclesiology appeared in 'Classes et Corps mystique du Christ' (1940) where Chenu declared that the radical plan of Christ incorporated in human nature is what defines

---

6. Congar, *Bilan de la théologie du XXe siècle*, 783. Congar observed that 'Chrétienté' 'significantly' appeared more in Chenu's articles in the second volume of *La Parole de Dieu: L'Évangile dans le Temps*—than in volume one subtitled *La Foi dans intelligence*. This would reflect the shift in Chenu's ministry after his removal from *Le Saulchoir*, but also highlighted the early treatment of 'Chrétienté' in 'Dimension nouvelle de la Chrétienté', in *Vie Intellectuelle*, LIII (1937): 325–351.
7. Jean-Pierre Jossua OP, 'Fin de la Chrétienté ou nouvelle Chrétienté, selon M-D Chenu', in *Cristianesimo nella storia* 26/3 (2005): 769–80.
8. 'Les yeux de la foi' (1932), in *La Parole de Dieu I: La Foi dans intelligence* (Paris: Cerf, 1964), 21–27, 21.
9. 'Position de la théologie' (1935) in *La Parole de Dieu I: La Foi dans intelligence* (Paris: Cerf, 1964), 115–138, 128–131. Chenu did not refer to 'l'économie chrétienne' in his seminal 'Dimension nouvelle de la Chrétienté' (1937) although he did use 'une création continue' and 'L'Incarnation continue' in a similar sense.

'*l'économie de la vie divine donnée à l'humanité dans un Dieu incarné*'.¹⁰ His own clearest definition of 'l'économie chrétienne' emphasises the redemptive reality for humanity:

> Le christianisme est une économie de salut: telle se présente de fait et en vérité la Révélation, au sens total. Non pas seulement un enseignement de vérités, mais, grâce à cet enseignement, la transmission de la vie divine à l'humanité selon les étapes disposées par Dieu.¹¹

The anthropological stance in both these terms derives from Chenu's privileging of the Incarnation as revealing the divine destiny of humanity within the historical location of human existence. This in turn represented a shift from the theological portrayal of Church as a repository of truths to an incarnationally understood 'body' of human lives.

Anthropological condition of faith

Fundamental to the anthropological and incarnational direction of Chenu's ecclesiology was his early work on faith.¹² Chenu rejected the extrinsicist and abstract explanations of faith that separated it from the human subject. He employed the scholastic term 'homogénéité'

---

10. Chenu, 'Classes et Corps mystique du Christ' (1939) in *La Parole de Dieu I: L'Évangile dans le temps* (Paris, Cerf, 1964), 477–494, 482-3 [his italics]. Chenu previously employed the concept 'l'économie du christianisme' (60) in 'Les yeux de la foi' (1932), in *La Parole de Dieu I*, 21–27, 21; 'une *économie*, une triple économie' used to encompass the order of the world as an 'Économie créatrice et gubernatrice [...] Économie de l'incarnation et de la rédemption [...] Économie enfin des sacrements et du sacrifice' in 'Position de la théologie' (1935), 128, 130–131; and in the section on faith and history 'l'économie' is given a particularly anthropological reference, 'La formule dogmatique n'est pas un énoncé juridique extérieur à la révélation qu'elle présente; elle est incarnation dans des concepts de la Parole de Dieu. Telle est l'économie de cette parole: elle parle humainement' in *Une école de théologie*, 60 [136].
11. 'Les sacrements dans l'économie chrétienne' (1952) in *La Parole de Dieu I: La Foi dans intelligence* (Paris: Cerf, 1964), 333, 324.
12. Congar commented that it was this work that Chenu continued to draw from and return to throughout his long theological career: 'Rarement une oeuvre s'est autant dévéloppée à partir d'une perception perpétuellement reprise.' Congar, 'Le Père M.-D. Chenu', in *Bilan de la théologie du XXe siècle*, 776.

to locate the continuity in faith between revelation, the human act of faith, and the theological interpretation of these. These traits of faith recognise human intelligibility and social cohesion as integral to faith. So, faith is not a layer of superstructure added to humanity, rather it is made incarnate in our human being, 'notre foi soit toujours HUMAINE':

> Mais cette «foi» ne s'accomplit pas par une espèce de transfert dans un inhumaine au-dèla de l'esprit; sans que sa communion à la Parole de Dieu en soit distendue, elle se réalise dans une incarnation savoureuse de sa lumière dans le tissus de l'âme, et jusque dans les propositions qui la conceptualisent selon l'humaine condition.[13]

Faith is situated as a historical and social reality and therefore constitutes, through these anthropological dimensions, the social and historical meaning of Church.

> Plus le chrétien est engagé, plus il éprouve les conditionnements individuels et collectifs de sa foi, soit dans sa croissance intérieure, soit dans son expression extérieure, soit dans sa puissance de témoignage.[14]

Chenu's ecclesiology does not only reflect the Incarnational concerns of all his theology, it is through this theology of faith that an anthropology is proposed. The human is made for faith, already incorporating the unity of creation and Incarnation, and aiming at the completion in history of human destiny through the preparatory society of Church, despite its weaknesses and 'la tentation de dissocier lumière et objet, intuition et notion, individu et société, expérience et tradition'.[15]

'Dimension nouvelle de la Chrétienté'

Armed with this anthropological understanding, Chenu responded to the ecclesial challenges of the inter-War period with a fresh apprecia-

---

13. Chenu, 'Vérité et liberté dans la foi du croyant' (1959), 357.
14. 'Vérité et liberté', 358.
15. 'L'unité de la foi', 17.

tion of faith's social and historical resilience. One key article emerged in 1937, *Dimension nouvelle de la Chrétienté*, which was republished in pamphlet form and acted as an ecclesial manifesto for the 'specialist movements' of Catholic Action.

Chenu foreshadowed much of the ecclesiological agenda of Vatican II and its aftermath in this article addressed to the chaplains of the Young Christian Workers (JOC).[16] He called attention to the long overlooked but essential mission status of the Church, anticipating 'l'Église en état de mission',[17] and outlined the important role of the laity then insufficiently acknowledged either doctrinally or officially. Within the context of widespread crisis in belief, and growth in atheistic unbelief, Chenu pointed to the inadequacy of the parish structure for serving contemporary ecclesial and social needs in contrast to the 'world of work' as 'the privileged locus of the Incarnation'.[18] He identified the anthropological change which necessitated this new ecclesiology as the alternative to the traditional milieux of family, town, and parish brought on by the 'socialisation' or social commitment of urbanisation and industrialisation.[19] There was an immediacy and freshness for ecclesial thinking in the 'milieu' consciousness presented by the JOC activists, which Chenu recognised as a new way of being Church. These new human experiences of 'mission' required a different theology of Church and the human person; they reached beyond previous pastoral conclusions that these modern circumstances were exceptional and passing human conditions. Chenu found in this new ecclesiology a more anthropologically aware dimension to the Church. The Church was being called not only to promote a more accessible type of Christianity, but to recognise the theandric unity in Christ suffusing and changing all things, continuing the Incarnation in unlikely parts of society where the light

---

16. 'Dimension nouvelle de la Chrétienté' (1937).
17. 'État de mission' was first employed by Mission de France, then taken up by Cardinal Suhard and the General Assembly of the French Bishops in 1961. Chenu, 'L'Afrique au Concile' (1963) in *La Parole de Dieu II: L'Évangile dans le temps* (Paris: Cerf, 1964), 647–653, 653; also 'L'Église en état de mission' (1958) in *La Parole de Dieu II: L'Évangile dans le temps* (Paris: Cerf, 1964), 237–240.
18. *Dimension nouvelle de la Chrétienté* (1937 reprint), 20.
19. See the section: 'Le developpement de la socialisaation' in 'Dimension nouvelle de la Chrétienté', in *La Parole de Dieu II: L'Évangile dans le temps*, 89–91 [*this subtitle does not appear in the 1938 published version.*] and what Chenu terms 'cette immense aspiration fraternelle', 'Classes et Corps mystique du Christ', 489, 491.

of the Gospel seemed long extinguished. This mission re-aligned the Church eschatologically and anthropologically.

> Chrétienté nouvelle, non pas autre, mais la même, l'unique royaume de Dieu dans l'unique Église, s'incarnant au cours de l'histoire, dans les divers régimes temporels de la société humaine. Chrétienté nouvelle, parce que le ferment qui fait lever la pâte est toujours neuf et frais; nouvelle, parce que la vraie conservation est une création continue; nouvelle, parce que, par et dans l'esprit, elle est «contemporaine» de toutes les générations, royaume de Dieu toujours jeune dans une humanité toujours renouvelée.[20]

This treatise marks Chenu's earliest incorporation of contemporary human phenomena as data for theological reflection. It began with Chenu posing the question to his master Père Sertillanges, whether the current onslaught of events (the economic and political disturbances of 1936 in France and internationally) signalled the approach of the end of the world. Had Christ secretly begun the reign of God on earth?[21] The answer came citing the contemporary writer François Mauriac and insisted otherwise: 'Nous sommes peut-être des premiers chrétiens'. From this, the article developed both its theme and method: a more anthropological reading of these human and ecclesial events for signs of the promised Kingdom, and immediate opportunities to discover new dimensions in Christianity through the understanding it revealed.[22] So *Dimension nouvelle de la Chrétienté*, like *Une école de théologie: le Saulchoir*,[23] presented Chenu's earliest examination of contemporary events as 'signs' of the Kingdom of God and inaugurated his dialectic of juxtaposing the inadequacies of the Church to the demands of social realities, as later employed in *Pour une théolo-*

---

20. *Dimension nouvelle*, 7.
21. In a later memoir Chenu listed these as: the Spanish Civil War, the Italian invasion of Ethiopia, the disturbances of the French strikes and factory sit-ins of 1936, and Le Front Populaire. de la Brosse, editor, *Le Père Chenu*, 71.
22. Chenu cited Sertillanges: 'Oui, l'Évangile est maintenant prêché à tous les peuples, mais c'est la surface de son expansion, cela; le monde a d'autres dimensions.' *Dimension nouvelle*, 5–6. Chenu later repeated this conversation/question form for the opening of 'Le devenir social' in Chenu, *Pour une théologie du travail* (Paris: Seuil 1955), 69–71.
23. *Une école de théologie: le Saulchoir*, 142–3.

gie du travail. A Church lacking either imagination about the future or an openness to change was ill-equipped to respond to the new dimensions of the world. These were land distribution adequate for a proliferating humanity on a planet shrinking from exploitation, the discoveries and inventions that completely transformed human life in the first half of the century, and the speed of change.[24] This inventory revealed the anthropological depth of Chenu's view of the world, and also anticipated the anthropological shift in the 'urgent issues' section of Vatican II's *Gaudium et spes*.[25]

Whether it is uniquely prophetic or merely current Depression and pre-War critical thinking, as illustrated in the philosophers Mounier and Maritain,[26] Chenu makes an innovative application to theology in contrast to the 'modern scholasticism' of his time. The basis of the JOC 'review of life' method for their meetings was an evaluation of contemporary human events; what Chenu did was shift this element into a formal theological conversation as reading 'les signes des temps'. Hence Chenu saw Thomist analysis in a methodological continuity with this privileging of contemporary issues in theological reflection.[27] Thus a pastoral technique for laity was deployed into a theological and anthropological dialectic, to provide a theological forum for the collective experience of the movements *la Mission de France* and *les prêtres-ouvriers*. The JOC method broke open the clerical and academic monopoly of theology, and Chenu's application of it questioned the doctrinal credentials of the Church's mentality of apparent avoidance of engagement with contemporary politics. Refraining from an abstract redefinition of the Church, Chenu instead posed a supplementary question: 'Quelle dilatation de

---

24. *Dimension nouvelle*, 6–7.
25. *Gaudium et Spes* (Part II), 46.
26. Jacques Maritain, *Humanisme intégral* (Paris: Aubier, 1936) chapter VI, 55. Chenu's *Dimension nouvelle de la Chrétienté* takes its title from this work of Maritain.
27. Chenu cited the topical or contemporary component in the medieval *disputatio*: 'Dispute «générale», l'appelait-on, où les questions les plus variées, les plus disparates, depuis les puis hautes spéculations métaphysiques jusqu'aux menus problèmes de la vie quotidienne, publique ou privée, étaient abordées'; 'l'intérêt de ces disputes est, cette fois, moins dans l'ampleur de l'exposé que dans l'incidence, dans l'actualité des questions et réponses.' Chenu, *Introduction à l'étude de Saint Thomas d'Aquin* (Montreal/Paris: Publications de l'Institut d'études médiévales XI Institut d'études médiévales/Vrin, 1950), 77–8.

l'homme s'est faite, qui requiert comme une nouvelle incarnation, en notre humanité du XXe siècle?'[28] At issue was more than a new pastoral approach or the relativist reduction of the Church to current social concerns, but the integrity of doctrine.[29]

'La Loi de l'Incarnation'

For Chenu, the Church as the embodiment of the risen Christ, 'l'Église, corps du Christ, incarnée, incorporée en humanité', continues the Incarnation in the world today.[30] Chenu insisted on the Church's situation *within* human history; this is where the Incarnation is dynamically played out, bringing humanity to its ever-expanding fuller consciousness. Chenu found in the Pauline image of 'the Body of Christ' more than a metahistorical identity, but the contemporary, temporal, and spatial analogue of a human body in this world.[31] Again, Chenu's principle is the Incarnation and what happens for humanity in the continuing event and relationship of the Incarnation within the world. Here Chenu referred to historical human reality, and only in more general terms to the whole of creation.[32] Therefore 'the Body of Christ' did not merely provide an accessible image for the hierarchical structure of the contemporary 'Church Militant', such as the revival of the term in the twentieth century Catholic Church tended to promote; rather, it was in this doctrine that Chenu found meaning for the growth of lay apostolates:

---

28. *Dimension nouvelle*, 8, and the heading '*Le monde du travail, lieu priviligié de l'Incarnation*'. in the republished 'Dimension nouvelle' in *La Parole de Dieu II*, 98.
29. 'Plus qu'une erreur de tactique: une erreur de structure, car c'était une erreur de doctrine. C'était dresser la psychologie religieuse de ces hommes contre la matière même, et la plus exigeante, de leur existence, comme si la vie chrétienne était hétérogène au contenu laborieux de leur vie humaine et ne pouvait subsister qu'en se barricadant contre ce labeur, incapable de rédemption et de joyeuse sainteté. Péché contre le réalisme de l'Incarnation.' *Dimension nouvelle*, 18.
30. *Dimension nouvelle*, 11.
31. This is further developed in 'Corps de l'Église et structures sociales' (1948) in *La Parole de Dieu II: L'Évangile dans le temps* (Paris: Cerf, 1964), 159–169, 160–161.
32. Later, this became further articulated by Chenu as the creation, in environmental and planetary terms in 'L'humanisation de la terre, dimension constitutive de l'évangile', in *Lumière* 33 (décembre 1984): 87–90; and 'Création et Histoire', in AA Maurer et al, editors, *St Thomas Aquinas 1274–1974 Commemorative Studies*, volume II (Toronto: Pontifical Institute of Medieval Studies, 1974), 391–399.

> le sol du Corps mystique, non pas agrégat d'individus, mais communauté des hommes au sens le plus fort [. . .] C'est l'incorporation mystique du Christ dans la vie communautaire des hommes.³³

The 'mystical body' is now incorporated by and in these lay Christians witnessing and proclaiming within their work and social milieux the Gospel that has brought them together in these new apostolates, and, in turn, brings together all of humanity in Christ. This reading of 'the Body of Christ' marked an anthropological shift in the understanding and the practice of the Church.

> Si telle est la loi de l'Incarnation dans le Christ, telle est aussi la loi d'incarnation de la vie divine, au cours des siècles, dans l'Église du Christ. C'est tout l'homme selon toutes ses ressources et avec toutes ses oeuvres, qui est assumé par la grâce.³⁴

'The Body of Christ', then, was portrayed as a complex image of the Incarnation and as Christ's continuing presence in the Church, which Chenu showed, requires a more complex, further elaboration and articulation in each new historical reality.³⁵ In his use of the term 'the Body of Christ', there is a deliberate Christology, not a figure for the hierarchical Church. This curbed the appropriation of the image to legitimate the sacral segregation and elevation of the Church and the clergy. The emphasis is Incarnational: Chenu does not merely offer an exclusive focus on Christ as the divine head of the body, but sees the

---

33. Chenu, from an address at the *Semaine sociale* de Rouen in 1938 cited in Olivier de la Brosse, editor, *Le Père Chenu: la liberté dans la foi* (Paris: Cerf, 1969), 80–81.
34. *Dimension nouvelle*, 11.
35. Here Chenu could be seen to be reflecting the idea of 'complex bodies' elaborated by Otto Gierke, *Political Theories of the Middle Ages* (Cambridge: Cambridge University Press, 1987), 22ff, as developed by John Milbank, *The Word Made Strange: Theology, Language, Culture* (Oxford: Blackwell, 1997), chapter 12 'On Complex Space', 268–285. Re 'complex space', Chenu refers to the term reporting on a discussion with a German priest-professor of theology: 'Il me montra comment, à chaque fois, le chrétien se trouvait en quelque sorte bloqué dans une espèce de complexe d'infériorité, d'impuissance mentale.' 'La Foi en Chrétienté' (1944) in *La Parole de Dieu II: L'Évangile dans le temps* (Paris: Cerf, 1964), 109–132, 131.

Incarnation as enfleshing 'the body of Christ' into a more socialised humanity. For Chenu, the reality of the Incarnation demands the gathering and divine incorporation of all humanity into 'the body of Christ': 'le Christ, homme-Dieu, est la «tête» de ce corps immense d'une humanité née à vie nouvelle.'[36]

In this article, Chenu provided the clearest exposition of his 'loi de l'Incarnation', yet he also demonstrated there the varied meanings and uses of *Incarnation* and *incarnation* that he employs to break open the concept of 'l'Incarnation continue'.[37] Chenu usually distinguished between *Incarnation* and *incarnation*, with the latter referring to the 'ongoing Incarnation' expounded by Möhler. The Incarnation of Christ continues in the life of the Church and its mission to bring humanity to its realisation in 'divinisation' or union with God in Christ.

> Mystère de Dieu. Et mystère de l'homme. Mais le Christ a relié à jamais en lui Dieu et l'homme; il les a unis parfaitement en sa personne, il les unit depuis, au jour le jour, dans son Corps mystique, Incarnation continue, dans les générations, à travers les âges de l'histoire.[38]

and

> Puisque un bien humain est engagée, un bien humain de très haute qualité et d'immense extension, puisque l'humanité prend là de nouvelles dimensions, il faut que la vie divine en fasse sa matière. Il faut que l'incarnation du Christ continue.[39]

Another application of this sense occurred in Chenu's use of 'incarnation' as a theological equivalent of the Annales' historical '*mouvement de longue durée*', to indicate human participation in the continuing becoming of the Incarnation as a progress towards human divinisation: 'Voici maintenant le *fait* chrétien. Dieu s'est fait homme,

---

36. *Dimension nouvelle*, 11.
37. 'Puisque un bien humain est engagé, un bien humain de très haute qualité et d'immense extension, puisque l'humanité prend là de nouvelles dimensions, il faut que la vie divine en fasse sa matière. Il faut que l'incarnation du Christ continue.' *Dimension nouvelle*, 15.
38. *Dimension nouvelle*, 30.
39. *Dimension nouvelle*, 15.

et, à partir de cette in-carnation, l'homme vit divinement.'⁴⁰ More fully he elaborated that:

> Comme le monde lui-même, la voici qui prend une nouvelle dimension, à la mesure de cette humanité en laquelle elle s'incarne. Car l'Incarnation de Dieu, dont elle est le signe et le mystère à la fois, ne s'est pas faite une fois pour toutes dans un coin de Judée; elle dure toujours, elle vaut, toujours, elle vaut partout, et tout ce qui échapperait à son emprise dans l'homme, et par l'homme, dans ce monde distendu et magnifique, retomberait à sa misère: la redemption du monde serait pour autant manquée.⁴¹

This 'continuing Incarnation' is not cancelled out by the consequences of sin, even while the power of sin in the world is significant for Chenu's anthropology. 'Continuing Incarnation' occurs both through the Church and as the destiny of humanity promoted by the Holy Spirit through the Church:

> Car voici précisément la loi de cette incarnation qu'inaugura et que réalise la présence de l'Esprit dans l'humanité: Si Dieu s'incarne pour diviniser l'homme, il faut qu'il prenne *tout* dans l'homme, du haut en bas de sa nature.⁴²

It is important to remember that Chenu was not concerned here to develop an innovative theology, but rather to find in established doctrine the coherence of these pastoral, and for him theological, realities with the Tradition of the Church. The reduction of Catholic theology to 'modern scholasticism' required that Chenu's theology operated within these constraints. He worked from a dynamic understanding of the Incarnation and its historical reality to show how the revival of the doctrine of 'the body of Christ' tallied with this new practical articulation of gospel witness: initially through the lay-apostolate of Catholic Action and eventually the worker-priests.

The innovative 'apostolat du milieu par le milieu' practised by the JOC movements, but not by all Catholic Action, was a fresh approach to evangelisation. It incarnated the life of grace within people's social

---

40. *Dimension nouvelle*, 10.
41. *Dimension nouvelle*, 7.
42. Chenu, *Semaine sociale* de Rouen in 1938 cited in Brosse, 80.

milieux rather than through separatist lay associations that withdrew into the ascetic culture of the 'apostolate of prayer' and charitable works.[43] Chenu saw this apostolic witness freeing the Church from a position of 'un christianisme d'émigrés, coupés de la vie, de sa réalité quotidienne, de ses états, de ses classes'.[44] Mass socialisation and the class consciousness initiated through industrialised labour had disrupted all social relations, with implications for parishes as well as families. Chenu paralleled the more obvious pressures from new social and economic demands on the family, the cell of society, with those confronting the local parish, the basic cell of the Church. The parish with its geographic stability and temporal regularity had been an excellent spiritual space for village-based families, but Chenu noted that neither the family nor parish could function any longer as the exclusive domains for human interaction, with each other and with God. He argued that parishes kept Christianity on the margins of modern life, accessible only to the upright bourgeois or rural peasantry. The power of the Incarnation, working within the new lay apostolates, had raised up an appropriate ecclesial form for penetrating modern human situations. Again, belief in the doctrine of the Incarnation and its theological openness to humanity was at issue: not whether Christianity could be made relevant to modern humanity, but how the Church could revise its narrow theological anthropology in terms of the Incarnation. Was all humanity included in this continuing Incarnation, or only churchgoers? Chenu, insisting on the universality of the Gospel, declared that nothing is foreign to Christian life: human civilisation in its entirety is the domain of Christianity because of the Incarnation.[45]

Despite the still predominantly rural profile of the French population before the end of the German Occupation, a working class had concentrated in the industrial cities which was predominantly atheistic, judged to be aesthetically coarse and uneducated, and hostile to the Church. The denial of the pastoral worthiness of these working classes meant the abandonment of an entire class of people by an elitist Church. Chenu declared that the negative judgement on this new missionary situation amounted to docetism. It was characteristic of

---

43. *Dimension nouvelle*, 21, 23.
44. *Dimension nouvelle*, 17–18.
45. *Dimension nouvelle*, 18.

Chenu to employ Christological heresies to label the effects on the Church of a spiritual withdrawal from its evangelical duty. For him this was compromising the Incarnation. While his use here is pejorative, Chenu intended more to jolt than to condemn, since elsewhere he described heresies as merely inadequate choices.[46] Heretical labels are also a reminder that change has happened before in the Church and that the Church's humanity means it is always historically bound and modifiable.[47] In a reference to his historical study of the social and cultural renaissance of the middle ages, Chenu equated the new 'milieux' with the emerging autonomy of medieval towns that shifted the missionary task of the Church from rural cosmology to urban humanism.[48] Rather than being profane space outside the Church's sphere, modern human working places, like factories, docksides, and offices had the potential shown by the mendicants' missions in the medieval towns. They provided the context for human gathering and solidarity, as had the guilds and eucharistic confraternities, the '*communautés de frères*' that are the truest form of the Church.[49] The apostolate of the 'milieux' also introduced the concept of 'the church of the poor'.[50] The Incarnation is not selective: the humanity it embraces particularly includes those who are deprived and excluded. Returning to his initial inquiry about the imminent Kingdom of God, he found in Jesus' announcement in Luke 4:18—'*Pauperes evangelizantur*'—that 'l'apostolat du milieu par le milieu' of the poor was the sign of the coming Kingdom.[51]

---

46. 'ces choix (*airêsis*, dit le mot grec) sont effet normal d'une foi avide de saisir son objet, dans une investigation toujours inadéquate, mais dans un appétit qui est le bon signe de la santé.' 'Vérité et liberté', 344. Chenu returned to this theme of the value of heresies for refining the communal understanding of the church in 'Orthodoxie et hérésie: le point de vue de théologien' (1960), in *La Parole de Dieu I: La Foi dans intelligence* (Paris: Cerf, 1964), 69–74.
47. This is the subject of 'Vérité et liberté dans la foi du croyant' (1959).
48. Chenu, 'Le réveil évangélique', *La théologie au douzième siècle* (Paris: Librairie Philosophique J Vrin, 1957), 255–256.
49. Brosse, *Le Père Chenu: la liberté dans la foi*, 82, also 'La Chrétienté est une fraternité.' in Brosse, 79; Chenu directly linked industrial socialisation with the medieval guilds in 'Laïcs en Chrétienté (1945) in *La Parole de Dieu II: L'Évangile dans le temps* (Paris: Cerf, 1964), 71–83.
50. Chenu, 'La Fin de l'ère constantinienne' (1961) in *La Parole de Dieu II: L'Évangile dans le temps* (Paris: Cerf, 1964), 17–36, 35–36.
51. *Dimension nouvelle de la Chrétienté*, 28–9.

As Catholicism became defensive and protective of its 'spiritual' domain, the apostolate became reserved to priests and to their administration of the sacraments: a cultic appropriation according to Chenu that had blocked off Christianity from its anthropological sources and purpose. The Incarnation demands the valuing of all that is human; it is the new creation encompassing all created beings, and salvation for all comes through the Incarnation.[52] The apostolic awakening of the laity, in contrast to this clericalism, was not merely an evangelising tactic, through its activism within wider humanity ('action de milieu'), the laity articulated further the ecclesial reality of the doctrine of Incarnation. 'C'est la vie divine assumant sans déchet aucun *toute* la vie humaine. Incarnation continuée, dans le corps mystique du Christ.'[53] Rather than the official Catholic Action demarcation of the sacred sphere as the domain of priests while the secular was the domain of the laity (because it was unable to be reached by the traditional Church), Chenu proposed a mixture of apostolic work between parishes and 'les oeuvres spécialisées' that included 'les chicanes de frontières'.[54] In the later disputes over the ministry of the worker-priests, this mixture became particularly important when a distinction of apostolates was used as the argument against priests ministering outside traditional ecclesial domains.[55] Again, the incarnational basis and object of Chenu's understanding of these ecclesial movements as a 'new dimension of Christianity' disallowed any divisions that would exclude or compromise the unity of the Incarnation and universal mission of the Church: 'par-dessus l'abîme des absences et les murs de séparation'.[56]

For Chenu this 'new dimension of Christianity' was forming a Church more directed by the mystery of the Incarnation and more conscious of its anthropological mediation. Chenu highlighted the theological register of 'présence', the JOCist catchcry to describe their

---

52. *Dimension nouvelle de la Chrétienté*, 7.
53. *Dimension nouvelle*, 18.
54. 'La paroisse est à l'apostolat en Chrétienté ce que la famille est à la vie en société', 14, 24.
55. Brosse, *Le Père Chenu*, 124. The implications of this distinction also reappear in Chenu's later objection to 'consecratio mundi' in Vatican II's *Gaudium et spes*. Chenu, '«Consecratio mundi»', in *Nouvelle Revue Théologique* 86 (1964): 608–18.
56. 'Le sacerdoce des prêtres-ouvriers' (1954) in *La Parole de Dieu II: L'Évangile dans le temps* (Paris: Cerf, 1964), 275–281, 280.

preference for being in 'les milieux sociaux' rather than evangelising people from outside the industrial context. It was through their 'présence' as co-workers that activists made the Gospel known without assuming the 'priestliness' of authority and sacral separation. 'Présence' in these milieux did not dispense with the ministering of the sacraments; rather, it found sacramental content in these profane situations. Again 'présence' resonated with further anthropological implications of the Incarnation: it echoed a eucharistic character, presence, and communion in the world through the unity of spirit and matter. The incarnational as anthropological was thereby not reserved only to sacramental adoration in a prescribed sacred space. 'Présence' also meant a politically conscious activism that walked a fine line between alignment with radical ideology and missionary outreach. Its theological truth was found in not limiting the range of the Incarnation to familiar ecclesial locations but in engagement with all human frailty:

> L'Église ne se construit vraiment que dans des communautés humaines dont elle a discerné, adopté, aimé, quitte à les purifier de leurs faiblesses, les lois intérieurs, les aspirations, les droits, les coutumes, les espérances [. . .] C'est sans doute par la manière dont est définie et réalisée cette «politique» apostolique, que se distingue, aussi bien en Occident que dans les autres continents, une Église missionaire d'un Chrétienté établie dans ses pouvoirs terrestres et ses pressions sociales.[57]

Chenu also recognised that the practice of 'présence' checked abstract formalism and uncritical universalism: 'Ainsi est-il présent à son temps: c'est la loi même de son savoir.'[58] 'Présence' is not formal teaching, 'un «enseignement» (didaché)', nor a sacrament, but most of all it is not a passive 'being there' type of voyeurism: 'C'est la première expression, souvent silencieuse en mots, mais toujours en acte, d'une vraie évangélisation, et du visage visible de l'Église.'[59]

The ecclesiology outlined in *Dimension nouvelle de la Chrétienté* coincided with Chenu's censured *Une école de théologie: le Saulchoir*

---

57. 'Communautés humaines et présence missionaire' (1957) in *La Parole de Dieu II: L'Évangile dans le temps* (Paris: Cerf, 1964), 261–264, 262–263.
58. *Dimension nouvelle de la Chrétienté*, 31.
59. 'Le sacerdoce des prêtres-ouvriers', 280.

and contains much of the same challenge to the separatist elitism and atemporality of the wider Catholic Church. More radically the *Dimension nouvelle* article provided a theological warrant for a more anthropological perspective on the Church and the need for its abandonment of a 'siege mentality' in relation to the world. Extraordinarily, despite its overt challenge to the traditional parish organisation of the Church and its articulation of a wider role for the laity in Church life and evangelisation, there was little official reaction to its innovation. This is some indication of the insularity of Catholic theological discourse at this time, since such an ecclesially significant manifesto of Church reform was so overlooked, while the internally addressed reform curriculum of *Une école de théologie: le Saulchoir* drew the condemnation it did, even to being put on the Index of Forbidden Books. This provocative and widely circulated throughout France ecclesiology for the laity was to have more significant implications for the universal Church.

Later pre-Vatican II ecclesiological writing

Despite Chenu being silenced again and exiled from Paris in 1954 following the condemnation of the worker-priests, ecclesial issues continued to appear in Chenu's writings. These include elaborations of the themes about the nature of the Church presented in *Dimension nouvelle de la Chrétienté*, and observations on the Church as mission, Church engagement in the world, the role of theology and authority in the Church, the sacraments, and the priesthood. The earlier works were written either for or in defence of the lay apostolate and worker-priests, while the later works focused on the possibilities offered by the forthcoming Second Vatican Council.

Mission and reform

By the end of the World War II in 1944, when Chenu proposed the *Mission de France* as 'une réforme des structures cléricales et apostoliques', the calls for a new articulation of Christianity were more widely accepted. To signify further radical change, Chenu used 'mission' with its corollary meaning of leaving behind, instead of his preferred term 'ré-formation' because it was compromised by association with the Protestant Reformation. Reform as 'mission' was limited by the Church to the challenge of new territory to Christianise, but after industrialisation, mission was no longer in some far-flung corner of the world but at home in modern France. 'Le retour à l'Évangile, c'est la libération des sociétés établies, des plus pieux conformismes, pour une promotion spirituelle pure de ces ressources humaines toutes neuves.'[60] From Chenu's viewpoint, 'le retour à l'Évangile et mission' is a double challenge from and for the Church. The need for reform in the Church is argued more directly in his study of two types of reform, moral and institutional, or apostolic.[61] The moral reforms of Gregory VII, feudal and authoritarian, and those of the canons regular to do with interior piety and simplicity of life, are contrasted with the thoroughgoing institutional reforms of the apostolic movements of Saints Francis and Dominic, and that of Savonarola and the Reformation. Chenu assessed institutional or, his preferred term, apostolic reforms as more significant and responsive to the call of the Gospel, and judged the Counter-Reformation as failing sufficiently to implement structural reform.

His criteria were social and anthropological: the ability to make the Gospel accessible to the collective consciousness of new generations and responding to the Spirit re-creating 'the Body of Christ', which shares the historical reality of humans. Carefully reiterating the received doctrine of the changelessness of the Church, more openly Chenu also expressed his historical suspicion of piety's conservatism and of the tendency for theology and faith to be equated with or reduced to morality, themes discussed in his later theology of work and in La 'doctrine sociale' de l'Église comme idéologie.[62]

Church as historical and social

In 1948 in 'Corps de l'Église et structures sociales', Chenu detailed his understanding of the nature of the Church: as necessarily engaged

---

60. 'La Foi en Chrétienté' (1944), in *La Parole de Dieu II: L'Évangile dans le temps* (Paris: Cerf, 1964), 109–131, 126.
61. 'Réformes de structure en Chrétienté' (1946) in *La Parole de Dieu II: L'Évangile dans le temps* (Paris: Cerf, 1964), 37–53.
62. 'Les «réformes» n'y sont plus seulement alors des purifications morales ou de bienfaissantes réparations; elles sont, par un retour à l'Évangile, l'avènement d'une nouvelle Chrétienté, dans l'unité historique, géographique, spirituelle d'une Église une, sainte et catholique.' 'Réformes de structure en Chrétienté', 53.

with 'la crise des structures de la société humaine', which demands 'almost brutal questioning' of the behaviour of its inner organisation and its practical activity.[63] Chenu deemed such historical demands a happy 'conjonction' or watershed to awaken the Church's understanding of the Christian economy. The Church is a mystery, but a mystery in history, through Christ's accomplishing the divine economy in humanity.

> Par cette communion s'accomplit l'opération paradoxale qui nous rend, selon le mot fameux, les contemporains du Christ, par une foi qui n'est aucunement la visibilité historique et psychologique d'une expérience religieuse, mais le témoignage de Dieu en nous.[64]

Because the Church has a body (namely humanity), the historical location of this communion becomes a 'sacred history'. So the Church is 'ce super-sacrement',[65] not in past events which we recall, but through the celebration of the mysteries of Christ's death and new life, the entry of God into time is proclaimed, by gathering up all that is created in the Incarnation: 'c'est la transformation du monde, la divinisation de l'homme dans la transformation de l'univers. L'économie du salut est engagée dans l'histoire'.[66] Therefore, while acknowledging that salvation is personal, Chenu insisted it can only be obtained through the mediation of a human community, where human solidarity is equated with fraternal love in Christ.[67] The Church finds its internal coherence, its organisation, its mission, not by opposition to contemporary society, however hostile, but by revealing those values contained within society that are recognisably disponable to grace.[68] Chenu distingushed such recognition from a moralistic separating out of the good, as the Church's role is to embrace all humanity in

---

63. 'Corps de l'Église et structures sociales', 159.
64. 'Corps de l'Église', 160.
65. Chenu noted that mystery and sacrament are cognates in Christianity.
66. The debt to Ireneaus and his doctrine of recapitulation in Christ is clear. 'Corps de l'Église', 161.
67. This understanding was developed further by his pupil Schillebeeckx in his slogan: 'no salvation outside the world'. Edward Schillebeeckx, *Church: The Human Story of God* (London: SCM, 1990), xvii–xix, 5–15.
68. Chenu saw a close equation between grace and nature already anticipated in humanity, but only fully realised eschatologically. 'Corps de l'Église', 161.

all times and places.⁶⁹ An anthropological shift is evident in Chenu's re-location of the Church from the margins of human society: '*Les structures de la vie humaine, dans cette économie d'incarnation, seront donc les substructures de la vie divine, dans les communautés comme dans les individus*.'⁷⁰

Beyond 'spiritualisme' or theocracy

Chenu judged that this essential engagement of the Church with the world had been compromised by its theocratic predecessor, the uncritical correlation of the Church with existing political structures.⁷¹ Heeding Maritain's call for 'attention évangélique à la réalité humaine', Chenu attributed this surrender of the Church's *raison d'être* as much to its inability to perceive incarnational grace operating in increasingly autonomous human affairs as to the inevitability of its human sinfulness.⁷² He insisted that the modern reaction, since the Renaissance, of a spiritual schism between Church and culture did not avoid the errors of the 'Constantinian era' Christianity either.⁷³ Instead it created its own problems. As the autonomy of knowledge and civilisation developed, making the world profane, there occurred a corresponding 'spiritualisation' of the Church, as evidenced by Pius XII's defining the Church, in the midst of the revolutionary twentieth century, exclusively with reference to mystical reality and transcen-

---

69. 'Corps de l'Église', 162.
70. 'Corps de l'Église', 161.
71. In 'La Fin de l'ère constantinienne' (1961), Chenu examined the abdication of the Gospel to political alignment by the church, which was, he concluded, a cultural, political, and religious 'mutation' of Christianity that fused spiritual and temporal powers. That reduced the church to a society of its own, ruling like other monarchies before the loss of the Papal States and in isolation after their loss. It also imperially defined humanity in abstract terms of *nature* and *person* disregarding any different conditions of geography, race, 'milieu', and education. This fixed the church in a theocratic socio-economic accommodation to the established order, equating this with divine will. 'La Fin de l'ère constantinienne' (1961) in *La Parole de Dieu II*, 20–29.
72. 'Corps de l'Église', 162.
73. In contrast to the medieval church: 'La Chrétienté médiévale reste une authentique incarnation, parce que précisément elle prenait corps dans l'histoire.' 'Corps de l'Église', 165.

dence.⁷⁴ Again, Chenu detected here a failure to believe in the unity of the Incarnation and in its reality outside the Church's inner life, a failure due to 'ce faux aristocratisme de l'esprit'.⁷⁵ Despite this, he proposes that the rise in the consciousness of the laity, whose insertion of the Church in the world witnesses to 'the declericalisation of grace', also signals the advent of a new concept for the Church—'Chrétienté profane'.

> Plus la Chrétienté est profane, plus l'Église assure la primauté du spirituel; et cette spiritualisation, si paradoxal, que ce soit, est la condition même de son incarnation.⁷⁶

Chenu insisted that by relinquishing its imposition of the sacral on earthly things, paradoxically the Church finds both its own meaning and the Incarnation as continuous in history, in the very things of the world that the Church then did not consecrate but could identify as participating in the Christian economy. Chenu admitted the irony and incoherence of this sudden optimistic leap recasting the 'spiritualisme' of the Church, but insisted that it is only the full incorporation of the Church in the world that will promote its essential transcendent mission.

> La prise en charge spirituelle n'en est certes pas diminuée; mais elle s'accomplit une assomption des rouages humains eux-mêmes: plus la grâce est grâce d'incarnation, plus elle saisit par sa pureté même la totalité de l'homme, selon la tonalité de la nature humaine, sans confusion ni mélange, sans réduction ni détournement. L'unité spirituelle nature-grâce sera d'autant mieux réalisée que sera respectée la distinction: autonomie structurale et technique de la nature, transcendance de la grâce.⁷⁷

---

74. Chenu, 'La Royauté du Christ', in *Vie Spirituelle* (octobre 1959): 325–335. 'Les pauvres, les petits, les non-politiques, sont les témoins privilégiés—et redoutables—de la puissance spirituelle du Christ', 333; 'la distinction du temporel et du spirituel . . . ne réduit nullement l'universalisme de la Royauté du Christ', 335.
75. 'Corps de l'Église', 163.
76. 'Corps de l'Église', 167.
77. 'Corps de l'Église', 169.

So Chenu found continuity between the mass secularisation of modern society and the triumph of the Incarnation, despite their apparent present rupture. He developed this into a fuller embrace by the Church of the Incarnational significance of secularisation in a prototype of Metz's *Theology of the World*.[78] Chenu considered how the Church discerns the difference between theocratic appropriation and evangelical openness to the world before the Council began in 1961. He cited four factors that reduce the errors of the Constantinian era and give hope for 'une nouvelle Chrétienté': constant re-awakening to the Gospel, giving primacy to the Word of God, understanding the Church as mission, and recognising the poor's privileged reception of the Word of God.[79] All of these marked out an anthropological shift that, for Chenu, required of the Church constant re-location into the material and spiritual reality of human lives, an engagement that does not bring the gospel to but finds grace within 'la jonction subtile et ambiguë de l'esperance du Royaume de Dieu et des espoirs terrestres en un monde fraternel'.[80]

Chenu's theological evaluation of socio-economic classes was an earlier example of where he drew out the implications of the ecclesial conflict between flight from the world or recognition of the divine life in human affairs.[81] Written in 1939, 'Classes et Corps mystique du Christ' sought a point of contact between Christianity and these influential human associations where the values of class appeared to displace the Incarnation's revelation of the Gospel of salvation overcoming all distinctions, including race, gender, and class. Chenu avoided a mere Christianising of any socio-economic phenomenon or an alternative idealising of class solidarity while ignoring its oppressive and divisive realities. He based his theology, unusually for the time, on a study of economic, sociological, political, and moral analyses of class. Yet he admitted also to privileging as data a single

---

78. Johannes B Metz, *Zur theologie der Welt* (Mainz: Matthias-Grünewald-Verlag, 1968).
79. 'La Fin de l'ère constantinienne', 29–36. Re the poor: 'Les pauvres, précisement parce qu'ils vivent dans l'insécurité économique, culturelle, spirituelle, mettent perpétuellement en cause l'ordre dans lequel s'est installée la Chrétienté; leur espérance même met en cause et cet ordre et cette Chrétienté', 'Corps de l'Église', 35.
80. 'Corps de l'Église', 35.
81. 'Classes et Corps mystique du Christ' (1940) in *La Parole de Dieu II: L'Évangile dans le temps* (Paris: Cerf, 1964), 477–494.

human experience: the observation of the class-transcending mutuality of a particular encounter between two women. It persuaded him to recognise that even the divisions of social class were not impervious to fraternal communion: 'divine fraternité qui ne s'évade pas en quelques expériences privilégiées, mais s'incarne au jour le jour dans les plus terrestres solidarités.'[82] The centrality of this experience to Chenu's reflection reveals the increasing anthropological shift of his ecclesiology.[83] This anthropological dimension was also evidenced in his reapplication of the scholastic principle of 'distinguer pour unir'.[84] Insisting that human autonomy does not demand rejection of the Church or divine authority, he claimed that a more communal concept of humanity actually allowed for the distinction and autonomy of groups while working to promote mutual service of needs and effective communication of material and spiritual values.[85] Hence a class-based humanity oriented beyond the narrower individual or traditional familial allegiances can extend human fraternity, and act as a locus for the community of divine life.[86] Chenu judged that the Gospel potential of these classes reached beyond their own construction from division and class warfare to challenge Christianity's surrender to a bourgeois individualism, that opted for isolated gestures of charity rather than communal action for social change. The 'désincarné' Church amounted to being 'absent à son temps' and for an historical faith this meant abandoning its purpose. 'Christianisme désincarné qui redoute la puissance terrestre de l'homme et sa destinée collective, qui ne consent pas à suivre le mouvement de l'histoire.'[87]

The question must be posed, though, whether Chenu's openness to these mass movements on the grounds of their inclusiveness is too

---

82. 'Classes et Corps mystique du Christ', 494.
83. 'Famille, profession, cité, classe, traduisent cependant et organisent une richesse native de l'homme, et toutes, à certains égards quoique à des degrés divers, sont des sociétés naturelles', 'Classes et Corps mystique du Christ', 483.
84. Also in *Dimension nouvelle de la Chrétienté*, 26.
85. 'cette conception d'un engagement communautaire progressif où la différenciation et l'autonomie des groupes jouent en faveur d'un plus ample service mutuel et d'une plus réelle communication des valeurs matérielles et spirituelles.' 'Classes et Corps', 488.
86. 'elles doivent être les milieux providentiels qui donneront un *corps* à la fraternité chrétienne', and in line with the reciprocal dynamic of the Incarnation 'elles contribueront à l'édification du «corps mystique»' 'Classes et Corps', 489.
87. 'Classes et Corps', 491.

wide, allowing any claims to brotherhood, however totalitarian? In his attempts to shake the Church out of its bourgeois class alignment and atemporal distrust of all modern or mass consciousness, there can be an over optimistic reliance on divine ability to penetrate the oppression in the industrial world. Chenu later denounced the violence, despair, economic determinism, and structural oppression that mark mass movements, but he insisted that this is the same as the sinful world that Christ came to save, by assuming all that is human, revealing good in the midst of evil and despair. He also determined that the Christian vocation is to view more than this despair and condemnation of sin in any situation, but that this must be a critical examination. Although there can be no simple equation of any human gathering with fraternity, as well there is no exception to the inclusiveness of the economy of grace, for that concession would be 'l'échec de l'Incarnation même, en laquelle tient tout le mystère de notre foi.'[88] This early theological experiment of engagement with socialisation is developed more thoroughly and critically in his later theology of work.

Theology and authority in the Church

Chenu's theology of faith underlies his understanding of ecclesial authority and the role of theology. More than a 'deposit' of propositions guarded by the Church and limited to the Church's solemn dogmatic teaching, faith acts to critique all authority and point instead to the utter transcendence of the mystery of God. This is the theme of 'Vérité et liberté dans la foi du croyant' (1959) commissioned by *Esprit* in 1957 shortly after Mounier's death and still in the shadow of *Humani generis* (1951), the encyclical that condemned 'la nouvelle théologie'. Chenu was invited by *Esprit*'s editors to explain the Vatican intransigence in a world of upheavals, such as the decolonisation precipitated by the Algerian War and the contagion of atheism and materialism, that discredited any appeals to certainty and immutability of doctrine.[89] Situating the Papal restrictions on 'la nouvelle

---

88. 'Classes et Corps', 492.
89. J-M Domenach, 'Célébration du Père Chenu', in Claude Geffré, editor, *L'Hommage différé au Père Chenu* (Paris: Cerf, 1990), 122–125, 122–3.

théologie' against the background of earlier condemnations in the history of doctrine, he portrayed truth and freedom, 'les irréductibles exigences de la transcendance du mystère', as surprising survivors of the time-bound and ideological temper of other periods in the Church's history. Chenu overturned the conventions of ecclesial debate by including his largely lay audience among those who do theology: adult believers attentive in their faith 'au niveau des problèmes posés par une humanité en marche'. This broadening of who can be designated theologian derives from Chenu's understanding of faith and the relationship of theology to faith. Theology is a human activity, an intellectual dimension of faith, so, humans do theology, not automatically, but as part of their rising consciousness of the divine life operative in the world. He equated fear of theological freedom with weakness in faith.[90] Yet Chenu accepted the need for authoritative definition and instruction as integral to faith, particularly as this makes faith communicable to each age.[91] He invoked a critical brake on dogmatic despotism by citing the subversive story of Pope Pius XI tempering an encyclical-fundamentalist with the exhortation to move on, and not keep referring to texts produced five years before.[92] Emphasising that the object of faith is truth and divine reality, not the edicts of the Church, Chenu relativised this phase in the Church's theological conservatism by stressing the human conditioning of faith: 'la foi trouve une lucidité réaliste à observer les ressources individuelles, les capacités humaines, et comme le génie particulier de ces porte-parole de Dieu dans l'Église.'[93] By drawing attention to the human situation of theology, Chenu began discriminating between the levels of meaning in faith, thereby distinguishing the degrees of assent required from believers.[94] Church teaching, like the Bible, needs critical reading and interpretation to identify the ideological sources and context of its composition, yet faith is not bound by the

---

90. 'Le croyant, conscient de sa foi, adulte dans son engagement, n'a pas peur de son intelligence'. 'Vérité et liberté dans la foi du croyant', 346–7.
91. 'parce que cette Parole trouve les moyens de parler aux hommes de ces nouveaux temps.' 'Vérité et liberté', 341.
92. 'oui, oui, avancez, il y a déjà cinq ans passés depuis la publication de ces textes.' 'Vérité et liberté', 350.
93. 'Vérité et liberté', 348.
94. Chenu referred here to Abelard's '*Sic et non*' and the original scholastic 'mise en question' as examples of such theological method. 'Vérité et liberté', 349.

limitations imposed by these conditions.[95] Chenu claimed from a Thomist anthropology an inclination to understand doctrine as open to progressive development of its content. He countered the piety of dogmatism with the assertion that it is faith that suffers when mindless obedience to authority reigns over believers rather than the free search for truth, 'car le fidèle s'avancerait dans certitude peut-être, mais dans la vacuité de l'esprit'. It is the role of the Church's doctrinal authority rather to find in 'la relativité des systèmes théologiques' the guardian of the transcendence of the Word of God.[96] In this article, Chenu privileged both the human condition of faith along with the transcendent character of its object. He reminded the Church of the reasons for its historical unwillingness to canonise any one theological approach, 'elle associe les plus grands, dans leur grave diversité', and called for a differentiation between its doctrinal and disciplinary roles.[97] Differentiating theology from doctrine, and including the laity as theologians anticipated the yet-to-be-realised reforms of Vatican II, even as it addressed the current ecclesial discomfort of *Esprit*'s critically conscious lay readership. This was a frank treatment in cautious times of theology's relationship to authority, asserting that confidence in the human that marks Chenu's ecclesiology.

Sacraments and the priesthood

Chenu viewed the liturgical revival as correcting an imbalance in the established moralistic and intellectualised Catholic theology, which had denied the anthropological dimension of sacramental life.[98] He insisted that sacramental life reinforces our understanding of the engagement of the profane and sacred within the Christian economy. In sympathy with the liturgical revival of the time, he refused the separation of pastoral from liturgical expression as exemplified in the then prevalent 're-production' theology of sacrament. With

---

95. 'La vérité de la foi n'est pas solidaire des contextes idéologique qui la présentent, et peut-être la favorisent sur la moment.' 'Vérité et liberté', 349.
96. 'Vérité et liberté', 359.
97. 'Vérité et liberté', 355.
98. 'La liturgie, présence mystérieuse de Dieu par le truchement des symboles, est le milieu vital où les puissances religieuses primitives de l'homme trouvent leur équilibre.' 'Anthropologie et liturgie' (1947) in *La Parole de Dieu I: La Foi dans intelligence* (Paris: Cerf, 1964), 309–321, 315.

reference to Aquinas' discussion on why there are seven sacraments, Chenu noted that, rather than deriving them from a typology of Revelation events, Thomas distinguished these as typical human actions, individually and collectively reflecting how human life is organised around such events.[99] Chenu's interest was that, the relationship of these sacraments to human needs and commitment was Thomas' theological insight about the incarnation of the human condition, its social nature, and its engagement with the natural world. So the sacramental order reflects the action of the Incarnation in human affairs, unifying the human and the divine, the individual with society, and the human with the natural world. Also, humanity engaged in liturgy is not divided against itself, but is a psychological and biological unity, whose self-expression through material reality links it with the symbolic through the intellectual effort of its sacramental theology, thus uniting thought and action. All of human life, individual and collective, is brought together in the sacramental combination of mystery and symbol that communicates the grace of salvation.[100]

> Ainsi la liturgie sera-t-elle essentiellement communautaire, parce qu'elle exprime dans le Corps mystique du Christ la nature essentiellement sociale de l'homme. Puisqu'elle assume les requêtes et les ressources de l'homme, de la communauté chrétienne en prière, la liturgie implique, confirme et consacre une anthropologie.[101]

For Chenu, it is not that the sacraments sacralise the ordinary events of human existence, making history sacred; rather, they form what he terms 'un immense sacramental:'[102] the mystery is recognisable in all life and realised through that sacramental participation that is the earthly continuation of the Revelation of the divine mystery.

> Les lois du sacré, que ratifie et consacre l'économie chrétienne, nous deviennent intelligibles dans la nature même de l'homme, sujet de la grâce; et les conjonctures que cet homme traverse en illustrent la portée sous nos yeux.[103]

---

99. Thomas Aquinas *Summa Theologiae*, IIIa, q. 65, a.1 cited in 'Les sacrements dans l'économie chrétienne' (1952), 332; and 'Anthropologie et liturgie', 309.
100. 'Anthropologie et liturgie', 310, 315.
101. 'Anthropologie et liturgie', 309.
102. 'Les sacrements dans l'économie chrétienne', 331.
103. 'Anthropologie et liturgie', 321.

The sacraments ensure that the Christian life is not defined only in moral terms, instead liturgy makes clear the mysterious yet visible and redemptive unity of divine and human truth that constitutes the humanity of 'the Body of Christ'. Again, Chenu registered his aversion to the reduction of Christianity to an ethical system. At the same time he avoided a mystifying alternative liturgical construction of an ideal humanity in ideal conditions.

In the aftermath of the totalitarianism and genocide of World War II, Chenu claimed for this sacramental perspective on humanity what he calls the original insight of Christianity, that the subject of grace is the autonomous person. The sacraments act to reinforce this autonomy in the face of depersonalisation and subjection by mob rule or manipulation, but not by a counter-individualism. Through the liturgical communion celebrated in the true community of the Church, the dynamic of the personal and the collective belongs to both the sacred and profane realms, through the Incarnation.[104] This continued his earlier discussions of the anthropological implications of 'the Mystical Body of Christ' in *Dimension nouvelle de la Chrétienté* and 'Classes et Corps mystique du Christ'.

Chenu welcomed a theological re-location of the sacraments in the Christian economy 'comme dimension nécessaire de la conduite humaine, y compris au plan spirituel et religieux'. The influence of Henri de Lubac's *Corpus Mysticum* is evident here.[105] To Lubac's recovery of the triple symbolic of the body of Christ in the Eucharist and the Church, Chenu added his own emphasis on the historical reality of the sacramental life, in the triple symbolism of time: past, present, and future.[106] Chenu also distinguished that there is a coherence and contingency in history whereas the temporal economy of mystery represented in sacraments is constituted by symbolic actions that retain continuity and density with historic Revelation. Chenu cited Lubac's *Histoire et Esprit* where a similar distinction is made between

---

104. 'Anthropologie et liturgie', 316–7.
105. Henri de Lubac SJ, *Corpus mysticum: l'Eucharistie et l'Église au Moyen Age*, second edition (Paris: Aubier, 1939). Chenu reviewed *Corpus mysticum* in 1945. In his 'Avant-propos' to the second edition, 9, Lubac quotes Chenu's review approvingly.
106. Chenu illustrated this through the reductionist misuse of Thomas' Corpus Christi sequence: '*O sacrum convivium, in quo . . . recolitur memoria passionis, mens impletur gratia, et futurae gloriae nobis pignus datur.*' 'Les sacrements dans l'économie chrétienne', 331.

the timeless truths of Revelation and the historical situation of the events of Revelation.[107] Through the distance in the symbol between signs and the mystery signified, mystery and history are united. Chenu's model again is the unity of the Incarnation, its 'mystère dans l'histoire, et l'histoire dans le mystère du Christ'.[108] Chenu's anthropological insistence that liturgy should reflect the ordinary actions and gathering of human lives actually highlights the symbolic distance between it and the transcendence of the mystery registered in the multi-layered meaning of the sacramental symbols. This is in contrast to a collapsed symbolic in some understandings of sacrament, which separated ritual from its material and contemporary references. Only through a metaphorical symbolic tension with an historical reality can the sacraments communicate effectively the divine continuity in the ordinariness of human lives. Hence Chenu cautioned against the redundancy of sacralising human reality, and warned how restricted a view of the Incarnation would result from a pessimistic preoccupation with morality, whether Pelagian or Augustinian.

Such a view of sacramentality, beyond the limited understanding of the sacraments as seven forms of 're-production' of the transcendent mystery for a human audience, both informed and was affected by the challenges posed by the experience of the worker-priests in the 'de-christianised' context of their apostolate to the working world. Chenu defined a new understanding of priesthood in 'Le sacerdoce des prêtres-ouvriers', published within months of the suppression of the worker-priest movement in 1954. Based on the 'présence' and 'mission' understanding of the apostolate developed in his earlier works, Chenu responded to the charge that the priesthood of the worker-priests was a reductionism of the sacrament of ordained priesthood. Traditionally what is deemed essential to the priesthood is prayerful adoration, celebration of the sacrifice of the mass, ministering the sacraments, catechesis and pastoral ministry. Chenu questioned the segmentation and disconnection of these from their foundation and principle, witness to the faith of the Church. Because sacraments are more accurately described as sacraments *of faith*, the sacraments are emptied of their human and Christian content when they lose this

---

107. Henri de Lubac SJ *Histoire et Esprit* (Paris: Aubier, 1950), 380; cited in 'Les sacrements dans l'économie chrétienne', 325.
108. 'Les sacrements dans l'économie chrétienne', 325.

common purpose. Therefore, the priesthood's prime function as sacrament is to witness to the faith and the mystery of Christ in the non-Christian world, 'de donner aux hommes la Parole de Dieu, là même où les hommes la peuvent entendre, là même où ils sont'.[109] As in the various ministries exercised in the missionary areas of the world, Chenu claimed that the act of evangelisation is not peripheral to the function of priesthood. Instead of condemning the worker-priests' method of ministry as discounting and secularising the priesthood, Chenu insisted theirs was the fullest expression of the sacrament.

> Le sacerdoce ne se définit pas seulement par sa fonction de continuer sacramentellement le Mystère du Christ dans des communautés constituées; il a aussi la fonction, la mission d'évangéliser les Gentils.[110]

In a 1947 *Semaine sociale* session on 'Essor ou déclin de l'Église', Chenu described the priestly function as the transmission of faith, hope, and love through the sacramental order.[111] This prioritising of witness to the faith also heightened the complementary understanding of the lay apostolate as an expression of the baptismal charism of the priesthood belonging to all believers. Those recalling the effect on lay-workers of Chenu's teaching report that many of them felt for the first time as if they were truly members of the Church, and in their own way, like the priest, had been chosen by the Holy Spirit to take part in the priesthood of Christ in the world.[112] Chenu recognised that the spirituality of 'présence' and engagement with the working world by priests and laity was superseding the traditional ecclesial format of 'les structures de conquête, la computation des présences, et même la participation aux sacrements'. This renewal in the understanding of priesthood also reformed the ecclesial role of the laity, later recognised by Vatican II, but already described by Chenu in 1947: 'la place qui convient à chacun selon ce qu'il est (prêtre ou laïc,

---

109. 'Le sacerdoce des prêtres-ouvriers', 276.
110. 'Le sacerdoce des prêtres-ouvriers', 279.
111. Cited in Robert Wattebled, *Stratégies Catholiques en monde ouvrier dans la France d'après-guerre* (Paris: Les Éditions Ouvrières, 1990), 129.
112. Cited in Maurice A Barth, 'MD Chenu', in *Tendenzen der Theologie im 20. Jahrhundert*, edited by HJ Schulz (Stuttgart: Kreuz-Verlag Stuttgart und Walter-Verlag Olten, 1966), 412.

baptisé ou non) et ses possibilités d'engagement pour construire la cité de dieu dans sa double phase, terrestre et céleste.'[113]

With this re-instatement of the gospel proclamation as the common end of priestly and lay Christian life, Chenu sought a collective mission of the Church that transcended the clericalisation that had isolated it from effective mission in the contemporay world. While the need for this was practical, Chenu also recognised its doctrinal significance and enlarged the compass of the concept of 'the Body of Christ' to include, first, all members of Christ's Church in its mission by means of their shared baptism, and then, following Thomas, all humanity by means of their shared humanity with Christ.[114] This led to the eschatological inclusivity of *Lumen gentium*'s anthropology where the phrase 'people of God' potentially carries the meaning of including all people.

Conclusion

Chenu's pre-Vatican II ecclesiology began as a pastorally led outreach, which he recognised as shedding the sectional, 'une espèce de pudeur religieuse', and spiritual bourgeois religiosity.[115] Chenu's insistence on the Church's historical condition relativised the existing forms of the Church and the origins of their doctrinal warrants. This historicity enabled the Church to differentiate what really is changeless—not its Tradition, but its object and the object of faith, God and the Revelation of the continuing mystery of the Incarnation. Directing the Church towards the modern world and its evangelisation, his ecclesiology assumed more anthropological concreteness. Chenu's ecclesiology envisaged the recovery of the Church's missionary character, first, by turning the Church inside out and ending its confinement to a familial and complacent spiritual hearth. Then, he re-located the Church in the current world among those humans apparently abandoned by the Church. This connection of history and place situated the Church not within 'the world', some space extrinsic to it, but within the changing human reality with which it is intrinsically

---

113. Cited in Robert Wattebled, 129.
114. Thomas Aquinas *Summa theologiae* III. q.8. a.3.
115. Chenu, '«Spiritualisme» et sociologie' (1961) in *La Parole de Dieu. II. Évangile dans le temps* (Paris: Cerf, 1964), 437–445, 444.

engaged, because the Church exists to witness every-where to God's love and truth. After the Second Vatican Council, Chenu captured this in his slogan: 'Le Mystère est dans l'histoire. L'Église est dans le monde.'[116] The Church Chenu saw emerging anticipated the ecclesiological reforms of the Second Vatican Council with *Gaudium et spes* proclaiming the Church's situation in the modern world and *Lumen gentium*, issuing its confirmation of universal call to human holiness.

---

116. Chenu, 'Histoire du salut et historicité de l'homme' (1968), 26.

Chapter 4
Anthropological Shift of Vatican II Ecclesiology

'Si ce monde s'humanise, cette humanisation est d'avance le support de la divinisation par une incarnation continue de l'Église corps du Christ.' Chenu, 'Un Concile à la dimension du monde', *La Parole de Dieu II. L'Évangile dans le temps* (1962) (Paris: Cerf, 1964), 633–37 634.

Roman Catholic ecclesiology was dramatically changed by the Second Vatican Council (1962–64) with many of the reforms either influenced by Chenu and his colleague Congar, or consonant with his openness to the historical situation of the Church and the need for reform of its engagement with the contemporary world. In this chapter, Chenu's participation in the anthropological shift of the Church's reforms will be examined with particular emphasis on the role of the Church in the modern world.

A Council called

For Chenu and his contemporaries, the accession of Pope John XXIII in 1959 held out little hope of changing the official Church under which they had been repeatedly condemned under his predecessor, Pope Pius XII. To the wider Catholic world, Guiseppe Roncalli was an unknown Vatican diplomat. To the French Dominicans, he had been the Vatican's nuncio in Paris immediately before the condemnation of the worker-priests, whose role, whether complicit in this or merely passive, remained undisclosed.[1] When as Pope he called the Second Vatican Council (1959), their curiosity was raised, but the Dominican theologians' concern was not relieved by the Curia's monopoly of the processes that created the disappointing schema for the Council's preparatory Commissions.[2] These bodies withheld detailed information, even from the officially appointed Council theologians like Congar and Lubac, and confusion resulted from the Pope's contradictory decrees which Chenu observed to Karl Rahner: 'Le Concile devient une opération de police intellectuelle, dans les murs clos de l'École.'[3] Despite Chenu's theological sympathy with the announcement of a conciliar *aggiornamento*, he did not publish on the Council until 1961, again invited by *Esprit*.[4]

---

1. Étienne Fouilloux, 'The Antepreparatory Phase, the Slow Emergence from Inertia (January 1959—October 1962)' in Giuseppe Alberigo and Joseph A. Komonchak (eds.), *History of Vatican II. Volume I* (Maryknoll/Leuven: Orbis/Peeters, 1995), 54–156 (90). Political details, secular or ecclesial, are absent from John XXIII's Paris diary, *Mission to France,* and his *Journey of a Soul*. Peter Hebblethwaite's biography failed to unearth Roncalli's attitude to the worker-priests or to the general condemnation of 'nouvelle théologie' in *Humani generis*, except that 'Roncalli was not directly involved in the purge.' *John XXIII. The Pope of the Council* (London, DLT, 1984), 227–230.
2. Pope John XXIII first announced the Council to a stunned Curia on 25 January 1959.
3. On this Chenu wrote to Karl Rahner: 'Les deux premières "constitutions", émanant de la Commission théologique (card. Ottaviani) ont provoqué en moi affliction et regret. Je me permets de vous faire part de cette émotion.—L'ensemble de ces textes est inspiré et rédigé dans une perspective strictement "intellectualiste" (au sens péjoratif du mot), c'est-à-dire qu'ils font prévaloir sur la Parole de Dieu les analyses et les critiques scholastiques. [. . .]—Ainsi ces textes condamnent des "opinions" théologiques, libres dans l'Église, au détriment de la transcendence de la foi, au détriment de la nécessaire recherche de l'*intellectus fidei* [. . .] Triste et hargneuse mesquinerie de l'esprit!' Letter 4 septembre 1962, Archives de Saulchoir, Paris, Fonds Chenu, *Concile Vatican II*. Cited in Chenu, *Notes quotidiennes au Concile: Journal de Vatican II 1962–1963*, edited Alberto Melloni (Paris: Les Éditions du Cerf, 1995), 57, n 1.
4. Chenu summarised favourably the Pope's main themes in 'Un Pontificat entre dans l'histoire' (1963) in *La Parole de Dieu II: L'Évangile dans le temps* (Paris: Cerf, 1964), 189–198, 192, but showed some caution about the excess in using the epithet 'Génie' for John XXIII, preferring instead to speak of his 'instinct'. Presumably Chenu recognised 'the instincts of an historian' as noted by Joseph A. Komonchak, 'The Struggle for the Council during the Preparation of Vatican II (1960–1962)' in *History of Vatican II. Volume I*, 167–366, 167.

The article 'Vie conciliaire de l'Église et sociologie de la Foi' focused on faith, but this time Chenu explored how a Council added sociological dimensions to the faith.[5] He called for a more exact theology of faith which could confront extrinsicist appeals to the Holy Spirit used to justify turgid ('dithyrambique') expositions of doctrine that blocked any consideration of the place of human affairs in faith. He charged the Council's preparatory schemas with such faith-less obscurantism. In contrast to this narrowing of the meaning of faith and dismissal of 'conjonctures économico-sociales', Chenu proposed broadening the perspective on faith to include 'les procédés du savoir collectif, que tout sociologique peut observer dans les sociétés humaines'.[6] Chenu was careful to distinguish here between the sociology of accidents, like data on participants, their origins, their education, etc, and the implications of these for the direction of a Council, and the 'communion' of thought and social awareness that exponentially combines in the meeting and the dynamic of a Council as a collective phenomenon. As faith acts in a person according to the requirements of human understanding, so, as each person engages with others in the human community of Church, faith operates expansively according to the ways humans collectively communicate

---

5. Chenu proposed that the Council cast a social context for faith which he aligned with the psychological unity of Thomas' law of human knowledge in *Summa theologiae* IIa IIae q.1 art. 2. 'Si donc aujourd'hui, sous la convergence de conjonctures sociales et de réflexions pastorales, on discerne, on analyse, on classe les facteurs collectifs de la foi, assentiment strictement personnel, mais intérieurement tenu dans la communauté ecclésiale et conditionné en sous-oeuvre par les phénomènes sociaux'. 'Position théologique de la sociologie religieuse' (1950) in *La Parole de Dieu I: La Foi dans intelligence* (Paris: Cerf, 1964), 59–62, 61.

6. This sociological awareness reflected the influence of the social agenda of the *Annales* school on Chenu, who judged such inclusion is required in order to 'mettre en valeur les aspects *sociologiques* qu'en générale ni la théologie ni l'histoire ne suscitent, et qui, en vérité, donnent au phénomène historique, fût-il sacré, ses plus grandes dimensions, sinon sa totalité. Aussi bien, dans la religion, dans l'Église, comme dans le monde profane, les réalités sociales sont fondamentales'. 'Vie conciliaire de l'Église et sociologie de la Foi' (1961) in *La Parole de Dieu I. La Foi dans intelligence* (Paris: Cerf, 1964), 371–383, 371.

and seek understanding.[7] For Chenu, 'les causes secondes, les sociales comme les individuelles, sont composantes mêmes de cette action de l'Esprit'.[8] He envisaged the promise of Christ's presence when one or more are gathered as applying in a broader anthropological openness to the 'humanité de l'Esprit', co-operating in the Church. He cited as a tangible example the otherwise imperceptible interplay that dramatically advances deliberative gatherings, from where they would tentatively remain without such communion. Chenu continued to criticise tendencies to downplay the human factor in doctrine as 'monophysite' denial of the Incarnation. Vatican II presented as 'la taille du Concile de Chalcédoine' in its significance and further clarification of the implication of the Incarnation, that the continuing of the Incarnation requires the Church be *in* the world.[9] For Chenu, this world consciousness entailed more than geographical expansion. Vatican II's preparatory call to the local churches to register their *vota* or desires for the forthcoming Council presented the reluctant Curia with an unprecedented poll of the issues facing the Catholic world (over 2,000 documents), which allowed the local bishops across the world to overthrow the narrow agenda of the Curia.[10] No longer could papal rule alone define the Church's authority, instead a 'Catholicity' that was signified by collegiality was needed.[11]

Besides the projected completion of the First Vatican Council's programme advocated by the Roman authorities, Chenu hoped for a conciliar movement towards more congruent reform and commitment of the Church to positive engagement 'à la mesure du monde,

---

7. De même que la foi d'un individu se structure et s'énonce selon les lois de la psychologie individuelle de l'intelligence, de même la foi d'un concile s'élabore, se construit, se formule, selon les lois de la sociologie de l'esprit. 'Vie conciliaire de l'Église et sociologie de la Foi', 372.
8. 'Vie conciliaire de l'Église et sociologie de la Foi', 372.
9. Their difference lies in the inductive method used to develop *Gaudium et spes* at Vatican II. *Un théologien en liberté: Jacques Duquesne interroge le Père Chenu* (Paris: Le Centurion, 1975), 184.
10. 'Vie conciliaire de l'Église', 376. See É Fouilloux, 'The Antepreparatory Phase: the Slow Emergence from Inertia (January 1959—October 1962)' in *History of Vatican II. Volume I*, 55-153 (97-126) and Thomas F Stransky SJ, 'The Foundation of the Secretariat for Promoting Christian Unity', in Alberic Stacpole OSB, editor, *Vatican II by those who were there* (London: Geoffrey Chapman, 1986), 62-87.
11. 'Vie conciliaire de l'Église', 375-6.

de ce monde admirable et terrible'. He imaged this as the planting of 'véritables laboratoires de l'Évangile dans le monde'.[12] His provocative rather than programmatic proposals concerning Church relations with the world became Chenu's key criterion for judging the efficacy of the Council's agenda and its later implementation. Chenu paralleled claims for self-determination and decolonisation in the wider world to the challenges to the Church's disjunction with the contemporary world. While resisting an historical determinism, Chenu saw this process as historically conditioned, so the capacity of the faith of the community to engage in its historical and social reality is the measure of its faithfulness to the Incarnational revelation: 'Car Dieu parle *aujourd'hui*; et cela ne se peut faire que si son Église est présente au monde.'[13]

Vatican II: a different 'présence'

Chenu's involvement in the Council was peripheral, but not inconsequential. Judged 'un peu suspect' he was not rehabilitated as a *peritus* or official theological adviser unlike Congar, Schillebeeckx, Lubac, and Rahner. He only gained entry to the Council as the theologian of his former student, the francophone Madagascan Bishop, Claude Rolland.[14] Chenu spent most of the sessions outside. His 'présence' was limited to consulting and advising the Eastern-rite bishops, third-world bishops, and theologians, other recently suspect theologians, while giving strategic inputs on schema topics to some interested bishops.[15] Congar wryly observed Chenu's peripatetic activity in his

---

12. 'Vie conciliaire de l'Église', 381.
13. 'Vie conciliaire de l'Église', 383.
14. Bishop Rolland was educated at the Dominican studium Le Saulchoir in Belgium. His invitation (2 April 1962) to Chenu opened with: 'J'étais du groupe de "noirs" que formaient les scholastiques missionnaires de la Salette pendant les années 1930-38'. *Notes quotidiennes au Concile*, 65, n 2.
15. Chenu's diary recorded meetings with, naturally, Congar and Schillebeeckx, also the French Jesuits Lubac, Daniélou, Rondet, Lyonnet, the Belgian sociologist Houtart, and the Germans Rahner, Grillmeier, and Häring. Alberto Melloni notes that Chenu did not mix with the more powerful theologians of the Council, that he ignored Ratzinger and made little contact with Küng, and Philips. 'Introduction: Les journaux privés dans l'histoire de Vatican II', *Notes quotidiennes au Concile*, 7-54, 50.

diary entry: 'Dans l'après-midi, bonne visite du P. Chenu, qui voit beaucoup de monde: journalistes, évêques africains, etc.'[16]

'The Message to the World' from the Bishops of the Council was Chenu's initial and most significant intervention.[17] Conceived with Congar to counter the inwardness of the prepared Council schemas, Chenu composed a text that amplified the themes of Pope John XXIII's allocutions and significantly addressed *all* the people of the world, Catholics, other believers, unbelievers. It was this emphasis on communicating beyond the Catholic world that made Chenu's original text deliberately not 'doctrinal' in the apologetic sense, so that even Congar found it too sociological. Yet the idea was adopted by the assembly of Bishops, after the text was modified (doused in holy water according to Chenu). It was accepted even by traditionalist elements of the Council, like Archbishop Lefebvre. Chenu judged that while it had a lasting effect on the Council's direction, it hardly touched the wider world due to its final clerical tone. Yet its citation by Pope Paul VI in his opening address of the second session legitimated the concept of *dialogue*, one of the key words of the Council according to Chenu, and its themes anticipate those of the final Pastoral Constitution of the Council, *Gaudium et spes*.[18] 'The Message to the World' brought to the ecclesial foreground Chenu's preoccupation with the Church's relationship with the world, and more specifically a commitment to the world as the locus of the Gospel. In his version that reclaimed the radicality of the original draft, Chenu asserted the presence of the Gospel in the world, usually independent of the Church's influence and despite the Church's dislocation from the human suffering of starvation, slavery, racism, and war. He argued that human values

---

16. Yves Congar, *Mon journal du Concile* [Paris, Archives du Saulchoir since published as *Mon Journal du Concile* (Paris: Cerf, 2002)] (18 October 1962), cited in *Notes quotidiennes au Concile*, 73; much later he recalled: 'le P Chenu voyait beaucoup de monde; il allait tous les jours à la salle de presse. Il commentait les texte et les événements, de sorte qu'il a ainsi contribué à une formation de l'opinion. Congar, 'Hommage au Père M.-D. Chenu', in *Revue des sciences philosophiques et théologiques*, 75/3 (1991): 361–2, 362.
17. Chenu, 'Le Message au Monde des Pères Conciliaires (20 octobre 1962)', in Yves M-J Congar OP, and M Peuchmard OP, editors, *L'Église dans le monde de ce temps—réflexions et perspectives*, Unam Sanctam 65c: tome III (Paris: Cerf, 1967), 191–193.
18. *Un théologien en liberté*, 177–9.

and efforts for peace, promotion of the poor, justice and community participate in the proclamation of the Gospel like 'les pierres d'attente', 'toothing-stones', a figurative term employed by Chenu to evoke features that are in readiness for future construction or awaiting completion: 'ces suprêmes biens humains sont comme des «pierres d'attente» pour la construction du Royaume de Dieu'.[19] Chenu was concerned to recognise in the world both the 'hope and anguish' of human struggle, but not merely as a pastoral strategy for the Church. He aimed to trace the reality of the Incarnation, the humanising of the world, by drawing out the Gospel already there, waiting to be activated through the valuing of human good. For Chenu, such engagement in the human situation is not Lubac's Christian baptism of Prometheus, nor even Mackinnon's rightly wary requirement that Prometheus should welcome the metanoia of the cross and resurrection, dying to the 'old man'.[20] Chenu delineated something more preliminary: not that the Church decides that Prometheus, the modern self-confident, autonomous world, can be baptised or is ready to be baptised, but that the Church must be there within this world to be near enough to respond *when* Prometheus wants or seeks to be baptised.[21]

Chenu's next intervention in the Council came from his determination to correct the neglect in all the Council's schemas of the theology of the Eastern Churches in union with Rome. It is some indication of the Roman theology's blockade of the *ressourcement* theologians, like Lubac, Congar, and Daniélou, that the debt to the early Eastern Fathers, unearthed by their scholarship, could be so ignored. He composed a response to the schema on the Church for the Melkite Bishop Georges Hakim that stressed the Patristic riches of the East, the doctrine of the economy of the mystery of Christ

---

19. Chenu, 'Le message du Concile au monde', in *La Parole de Dieu. II. La Foi dans intelligence* (Paris: Cerf, 1964), 639–645, 644. Chenu's concept of 'les pierres d'attente' or 'toothing stones' was described further in 'Les Communautés naturelles, pierres d'attente de cellules d'Église (1964)' in *Peuple de Dieu dans le monde* (Paris: Cerf, 1966), 129–43.
20. Donald MacKinnon, 'The Future of Man' (1967) in *Explorations in Theology 5* (London: SCM, 1979), 1–10, 3–4.
21. Chenu began with Lubac's distinction, that Christianity has not 'le caprice de quelque Jupiter écrasant Prométhée', then he concluded: 'L'*homo artifex* est vraiment un homme, et donc un lieu de la grâce.' 'Une Constitution Pastorale de l'Église' (1965) in *Peuple de Dieu dans le monde* (Paris: Cerf, 1966), 11–33.

unfolding in history, the definition of humanity as *imago Dei* in contrast to the abstract neo-scholastic theology of nature and grace, and its broader theology of the paschal mystery, rather than Western theology's emphasis on satisfaction for sin.[22] The economy of salvation and the *imago Dei* anthropology already featured in Chenu's ecclesiology, and his positive anthropology already reflected the resurrection more than atonement. Again, the trajectory of Chenu's ecclesiology was to engage with the world: in this case a wider theological world and faith experience beyond Latin Catholicism.[23] Exclusion of these Churches constricted the claim to Catholicity by the Council, whereas acknowledging them not only broadened the meaning of Catholic, but also engaged the modern world with a wider theological understanding of its humanity. The embodied Incarnational focus of Eastern theology compensated for the narrow reading of the Latin tradition that had shrivelled its Patristic roots. Chenu's Eastern ecumenism also avoided a universalist monocultural worldview looking exclusively from Rome; other perspectives were available to the Church from different locations with different histories and other views of humanity.

As Chenu was to reflect later, *aggiornamento* signalled for him 'faire entrer l'Église jour par jour dans le mouvement du monde et de l'histoire.'[24] So the world came to represent more clearly the focus and future of the Church in his theology. Some idea of what constitutes the world for Chenu and what is at stake in this negotiation with modernity can be gathered from his theological observations on the two Constitutions on the Church, *Lumen gentium* and *Gaudium et spes*. For Chenu, the pastoral designation, inductive method and overall incorporation of many of Chenu's preconciliar theological proposals, among those of other theologians of '*la nouvelle théologie*', announced the 'originalité sensationnelle' of *Gaudium et spes*. A number of commentators attribute much of

---

22. Chenu, *Notes quotidiennes au Concile*, 107–109.
23. Chenu acknowledged the influence of Karl Barth's *Christengemeinde und Bürgergemeinde* (Munich, 1946), 36: 'dans la théologie de Pères grecs, sinon des latins, peu sensibles, dans leur psychologisme, à un engagement cosmique de l'homme.' 'Une Constitution Pastorale de l'Église', 20, n 4.
24. *Un théologien en liberté: Jacques Duquesne interroge le Père Chenu*, 174.

this Pastoral Constitution to Chenu, but he was neither a member of the commission of Schema XIII nor did he meet with its membership. Rosemary Goldie, a lay activist and one of the few women participants on the central commission for Schema XIII, never met Chenu and was only aware of his influence 'in the ongoing debate up to 1965 about the *'consecratio mundi'* theme.'[25] In a note recognising Chenu's hidden role, Roberto Tucci SJ, who was a member of the sub-commission on culture, observed that Chenu's talk 'Une Constitution pastorale de l'Église', where he defended the appropriateness of the name and sense of the document as pastoral had important repercussions for its acceptance by the Bishops in the second debate in 1965.[26]

The Pastoral Constitution had emerged in response to the early call of Cardinals Suenens, Montini, Lercaro, and Frings for an *ad extra* dimension to the Council, Chenu noted, and like 'The Message to the World' was addressed to all humanity, not merely the faithful.[27] Chenu was sympathetic to the strategic nature of Suenen's corrective while he warned against implications for the nature of the Church that separated the *ad intra* concerns from that of the *ad extra*

---

25. 'I never met Fr Chenu. Not surprising, since—not being an official "peritus", but a "private" theologian—he took no part in official commission work, even for "Gaudium et Spes". Rosemary Goldie, personal correspondence, 6 January 1997. Miss Goldie is French-speaking so this was not an outcome of the segregation of language groups, but her entry to the conferences held by Bishops and clerical theologians would have been restricted. Yet, given her prominence, especially within the pre-conciliar Office for the Apostolate of the Laity, it is surprising that Chenu did not make her acquaintance. This gives some indication of to what degree he was alienated from the officials in Rome.
26. He identifies Chenu's contribution further: 'Notons en passant que cette intervention, comme tant autres précédentes du même auteur, sont d'autant plus appréciables, si l'on considère que, à la surprise générale, il n'avait pas été désigné parmi les experts du Concile et pas même parmi les experts officiels de la Commission mixte, quoique indirectement par ses écrits et ses consultations privées, il eût exercé une influence notable sur la rédaction du Schéma XIII'. Roberto Tucci SJ, 'Introduction historique et doctrinale: Ferments rénovateurs durant la Troisième Session Conciliaire (14 septembre—21 novembre 1964)' in Congar and Peuchmard, *L'Église dans le monde de ce temps*, 73–127, 102, n 97.
27. 'Une Constitution Pastorale de l'Église', 12.

mission.[28] Chenu regarded the call for a new articulation of the Church's engagement in the world and to broadening its pastoral dimension as an echo of its true nature: 'par la logique interne d'une prise de conscience, l'Église, se cherchant elle-même, cherche le monde, pour être elle-même.'[29] The recognition of the historical and anthropological particularity of faith, of the Church itself, and its theology was intrinsic to its existence and not only a response to an external exigency. Chenu believed that to avoid the dichotomising of faith and the world and constituting the church as inhabiting an exclusive spiritual realm required that the church respond to Christ's call to engage 'dans le monde et dans l'histoire'.[30] So he used the term 'l'homme-dans-le-monde' (rather than the existentialist 'être-dans-le-monde', which, though, it is important to note he did not oppose),[31] to indicate a humanity which is social and made of the same stuff as the rest of creation. The distinction between the world and the Church cannot therefore be absolute because that would require the church to deny its historical and human reality. Thereby, humanity would be abandoned to a world constructed on Cartesian individuality and modernity's historical determinism.

> Si la présence au monde, au monde de ce temps (condi*tiones nostri temporis*), est de la nature même de l'Église, si la Parole de Dieu, dont elle est le témoin et le garant, parle aujourd'hui, jour après jour, dans la succession du temps, il ne s'agit pas seulement de conséquences pratiques que le pasteur tire de la décision du docteur; *exister* aujourd'hui (*dasein*) est de

---

28. 'Une Constitution Pastorale de l'Église', 16–17. This concern was earlier discussed by Chenu in the section 'Pastorale ou doctrinale?' in 'Un Concile «Pastorale»', *La Parole de Dieu II. L'Évangile dans le temps* (Paris: Cerf, 1963), 655–72, 658–661: 'Certains proposèrent, par manière de conciliation, la rédaction de doubles schémas, l'un pour la vérité des doctrines, à l'usage des clercs, l'autre pour les applications pratiques, à l'usage des fidèles. Mais c'était durcir encore un dualisme auquel spontanément répugnaient des hommes dont la pastoration était nourrie de l'instinct de la Parole de Dieu à porter au monde', 661.
29. 'Une Constitution Pastorale de l'Église', 12.
30. 'Une Constitution Pastorale de l'Église', 13.
31. Chenu's source here was Merleau-Ponty rather than Heidegger, even though he did use the German: '*dasein*'. Chenu cited Merleau-Ponty in reference to: 'c'est la consubstantialité de la matière et de l'esprit. «Être au monde à travers un corps.»' Merleau-Ponty, *Phénoménologie de la perception* (Paris: Gallimard, 1945), 357 in 'Une Constitution Pastorale', 22 and n 7.

l'essence même de l'Église. L'acte de pastoration n'est pas livré à un pieux opportunisme de circonstance: il est l'Église en acte, lieu théologique de la Parole de Dieu, dans la communauté hiérarchique . . . La théologie est par définition pastorale, réflexion organique sur l'Église en acte de salut, au point d'impact de son action dans le monde, à un moment donné de l'histoire.[32]

At the same time, Chenu was cautious about an over theocratic definition of the Church's engagement in the world. His argument rested on a Christian anthropology where the humanity identified is not 'abstraite, intemporelle et acosmique' but shares in the consubstantiality of the Incarnation. As such it is modifiable in response to the new psychological, economic, social, and political understandings of humanity, while still constituted by the interior truth, of grace built on nature.[33] Chenu was not advocating a capitulation by the Church to the world as it is, as the world needs redemption: 'La construction du monde est réintegrée dans l'économie du salut. Par et dans l'homme, la grâce est chez elle dans le monde, corps agrandi de l'homme.'[34] Chenu's argument was with an interiorising of faith that promoted a 'dualisme psychologique, qui aboutissaità une à une dépréciation tant au corps que de la présence au «monde» matériel'. He insisted that 'une foi réaliste en l'Incarnation conduit à la résurrection de la chair, à l'instauration de cieux nouveaux et de terres nouvelles.'[35]

Signs of the times

Chenu had long invoked the prophetic value of events as theological data in which the presence of the Word of God in the course of history could be detected. His *Une école de théologie: le Saulchoir* (1937) outlined a number of '«lieux» théologiques' which were revelatory when the Church was 'présent à son temps'.[36] The appearance of the concept of 'the signs of the times' in recent ecclesiology was attributed

---

32. 'Une Constitution Pastorale', 16–17.
33. 'Une Constitution Pastorale', 18–27.
34. 'Une Constitution Pastorale', 23.
35. 'Une Constitution Pastorale', 23.
36. *Une école de théologie: le Saulchoir*, 142; and also *Dimension nouvelle de la Chrétienté* (1937) and *Pour une théologie du travail* (1955).

to Chenu, but there is no evidence of a direct influence on Pope John XXIII who introduced it in his bull of convocation for the Council, *Humanae salutis* (1961) and then developed the concept as the basis for his encyclical to the world, *Pacem in terris* (1963). In the early days of Vatican II, Chenu was very concerned that the Curial blocking was leading the bishops to repeat Vatican I by not responding to the calls of contemporary concerns.[37] Similarly, he reported on a meeting with Daniélou where they concurred that the doctrinal schemata lacked 'de tout sens des appels de ce temps', despite John XXIII's lively protest against the pessimists attached to the past.[38] Chenu's theological reflection on 'the signs of the times' presented a practised use of this methodology as well as a discussion of the reception of the term. This is one of his more theologically substantiated writings, in which he situated 'the signs of the times' within the vocabulary of Vatican II, while he explored its meaning within the competing context of neo-scholastic suspicion. He also noted Protestant unease at the warrant being claimed for 'the signs of the times' by the ecclesial appropriation of the biblical concept out of its context, and the challenges it posed for the deficient understanding of secularisation and impoverished theological anthropology.[39] History and the world figure as the object of the crucial mediation that the events read as signs embody. Examples repeatedly cited by Chenu since his list in *Une école de théologie: le Saulchoir* included: increasing human socialisation due to the civilisation of work, the rise of the working classes, the entry of women into public life, and the emancipation of colonised peoples.[40] Discernment of 'the signs of the times' required some distinguishing between random apparently extraneous human events and those

---

37. *Notes quotidiennes au Concile*, 67.
38. *Notes quotidiennes au Concile*, 68, 65.
39. 'Les Signes des temps', in Congar and Peuchmard, *L'Église dans le monde de ce temps*, 205–225.
40. 'Les Signes des temps', 206. The list in *Une école de théologie: le Saulchoir* was: missionary expansion that was promoting the autonomy and adulthood of the (otherwise) colonised peoples, more recognition of the pluralism of human civilisations, the originality of the East being blocked by Latin Christianity (and historically the incursion of Islam and schisms), the ecumenical movement, socialisation of the masses and their greater presence in public life, and the militant movements in the church that were witnessing in the world that the church had become detached from (142).

indices of the mystery in history of the presence of the Kingdom of God.[41] This discernment is a dialogue, not a wholesale surrender to prioritising human history:[42]

> Efectivement, c'est l'Église en tant que «Peuple de Dieu» qu'il incombe d'ausculter, de discerner, de discerner, d'interpréter les signes des temps. Nous avons là l'immédiate application, dans le domaine du témoignage évangélique, de la doctrine générale du Concile sur l'Église peuple de Dieu (LG, II). C'est dans le registre du *sensus fidei* (*loc. cit.*, number 12) que s'inscrit le discernement des signes, selon les conditions générales de la structure hiérarchique de l'Église et de la régulation des charismes, non comme des dons «extraordinaires», mais comme des grâces données au bénéfice de la Communauté et «appropriés aux nécessités de l'Église» (*ibid*).[43]

Chenu was not naive about the difficulty of this discernment. He gave the example of the Church's resistance to the better values of the French Revolution, due to abhorrence not only at its atrocities and its long-term effects of dismembering of faith from culture and society, but because of the vested ideological accommodation of the church to the *ancien régime*.[44]

How Chenu envisaged avoiding similar accommodations to the modernity of the world is not so clearly articulated in this paper.[45] Yet he pointed out the danger of applying overriding general principles, which would atribute sign-value to anything that is deemed to be an anticipation of the Kingdom of God. Characteristically, his critique is better able to determine what cannot be allowed than what

---

41. 'Les Signes des temps', 214.
42. Chenu acknowledged that *Gaudium et Spes* 'est vigoureusement affirmé l'ambiguïté de ces signes.' 'Les Signes des temps', 218.
43. 'les impacts de l' Évangile dans les appels, les exigences, les échecs eux-mêmes de l'espérance humaine en travail.' 'Les Signes des temps', 223-4.
44. Chenu cited the French Revolution's assertion of 'la dignité de la liberté' as representing a prophetic moment unrecognised by the church because of its ambiguity, along with 'les hautes valeurs institutionnelles et culturelles de l'Empire romain', and the Galileo affair when 'l'Église ne sut pas reconnaître l'autonomie légitime de la recherche scientifique'. 'Les Signes des temps', 211.
45. Although he did consider this problem in a very early exploration of in: Chenu (published under the pseudonym 'Apostolus'), 'L'intelligence des signes', in *La Vie Spirituelle* LII/3 (1937): 183-88.

defines 'the signs of the times'. Chenu applied both the apparently modern criterion of 'le principe de l'autonomie des valeurs terrestres' (which was also affirmed in *Gaudium et spes*) and the more Hegelian 'discernement entre «mouvements de l'histoire» et «idéologies»'. To these he added the discernment of qualities evident in the present condition of humanity that present as more disponible to a theological meaning: the human person, human community, and the building up of the world.[46] Chenu detected a dialectical operation inherently active between the understanding of human events and their capacity to carry the message of the Gospel. He employed a distinctly bodily description of this attentiveness to 'the signs of the times', 'l'auscultation': not a Rahnerian 'hearer of the Word' but one who waits obediently (listening) like a servant at the door. The emphasis in this image is on the ability to discern, judge, and interpret the '«multiples langages» de notre temps', which will always be ambiguous and can never be so systematisée that the eschatological tension of the Kingdom of God is resolved.[47]

> Bien plus le monde est ambigu, et le péché y est mêlé au meilleur. . . . En vérité, l'histoire passée nous est une lumière et une rude leçon, tant pour la mésintelligence des signes ou leur confusion mal dechiffrée, que pour leur authentique efficacité.[48]

So for Chenu, 'the signs of the times' are the embodied posture of the Church as servant to the world, conditioned by the inductive method of interpretation of events and the sense of history as open to the Gospel message of salvation. It is important that the whole Church is engaged in this discernment, the whole people of God, not only its hierarchy.[49] Again, his anthropological emphasis in this ecclesiology is adamant: the Church as a whole people, not only institutionally, discerns 'the signs of the times'. Chenu detected the mystery of the Incarnation embodied in the *communio* of the Church-community.

---

46. These also figure as the themes of chapters in *Gaudium et spes* respectively: Chapter 1: nos 12–22; Chapter II: 23–32; Chapter III: 33–39 and Chapter IV: 40–45.
47. 'Les Signes des temps', 218.
48. 'Les Signes des temps', 216.
49. 'Les Signes des temps', 224.

'The signs of the times' and their consubstantial relationship with the world and history are constitutive of the Church, not a pastoral application of doctrine.

Chenu's contribution to the ecclesiology that proceeded from Vatican II is more pervasive than specifically attributable. His ecclesiology informed indirectly much of the reform agenda of Vatican II, promoted by some of the French bishops, but more significantly it also coincided with the concerns being raised across the universal Church, because both were sourced from the same inductive approach to pastoral realities. That this approach was so crucial to the reform understanding of the Council has been discussed widely,[50] and, as Chenu later identified, the use of an inductive method by John XXIII in *Pacem in Terris* (1963) distinguished future papal social teaching from that before Vatican II. He also insisted later that the failure of Catholic social doctrine to be received by Catholics as normative was due to its ideal and imposed analyses rather than the inductive methodology developed from human experience.[51]

Consecratio mundi

Chenu's contribution is perhaps most evident in the controversy produced by his objection to the use of the phrase '*consecratio mundi*' in *Lumen gentium* (number 34).[52] Chenu wrote on the subject, first

---

50. Peter Matheson, 'The Inductive Methodology of "Gaudium et Spes"', in *Australasian Catholic Record* LXIII/3 (1986): 280–93.
51. 'Ce fut là la cause de la médiocre efficacité de l'enseignement des pontifes ... cette tiédeur n'était pas la cause première de cet echec, mais la méthode elle-même, dans son irréalisme psychologique et sociologique.' Chenu, *La 'doctrine sociale' de l'Église comme idéologie* (Paris: Cerf, 1979), 63, 89. He also recognised the abandoning of inductive method under Pope John Paul II, 13.
52. The final version of *Lumen gentium* (no 34) was: 'Sic et laici, qua adoratores ubique sancte agentes, ipsum mundum Deo consecrant.' (in Latin) and 'De cette manière, les laïcs, en une sainte et universelle adoration, consacrent à Dieu le monde même.' (in French). The concept of '*consecratio mundi*' was changed to 'to consecrate the world'. See Protais Safi, 'La «consecratio mundi» et la théologie du laïcat à la veille de Vatican II' (unpublished STD thesis, Lateran Pontifical University, Rome, 1981).

in 1964 and twice in 1966, after the close of the Council.[53] At issue for him was the integrity of the lay apostolate not to be understood as a crypto-priesthood in a theocratic worldview, and the inherent goodness and autonomy of creation.[54] In the 1964 paper he surveyed the use of the term, tracing its introduction as recently as Pius XII's address to the Second World Congress of the Apostolate of the Laity in Rome (5–13 October 1957).[55] His objection to the term was that it alienates what is being consecrated from its true nature, psychology, social engagement, and free disposition.[56] Rather than consecrating the profane world because of its sinfulness, he argued that the world is profane due to its autonomy: 'La grâce ne «sacralise» pas la nature'. Chenu further declared that the feared desacralisation of the world, because of secularisation and the rise of atheism among the masses, was actually deeply Christian because, like Christ's defeat of the demons, it demystified the false gods and demons and their hold on human consciousness.[57] The role of the Church in the world was not to consecrate it, because the Incarnation had declared that 'la distinction entre profane et sacré est dissoute'.[58] Therefore, it is in the construction of the world, not its consecration, that the Church and its laity are properly engaged. Despite their confusing interchangeability in *Lumen gentium*, Chenu distinguished between sacralisation of the world and the sanctification of humans. For him, consecration involved separation, an ontological change, whereas sanctification meant the recapitulation in Christ of all created things to participate in the divine life: 'Consécration du monde, c'est sanctification

---

53. '«Consecratio mundi»', in *Nouvelle Revue Théologique* 86 (1964): 608–18; which was expanded upon in 'Les Laïcs et la «consecratio mundi»' Guilherme Baraúna OFM and M-J Congar OP, editors, *L'Église de Vatican II* (*Unam Sanctam* 51c, tome III) (Paris: Cerf, 1966), 1035–1053. A further version appeared in 1966 as 'Les Laïcs et la "consecration" du monde' in *Peuple de Dieu dans le monde* (Paris: Cerf, 1966), 69–96.
54. Much later Chenu described this in terms of the Church's liturgy before Vatican II: 'La liturgie était un phénomène aristocratique réservé aux moines.' *Un théologien en liberté*, 92.
55. Pius XII: 'La *consecratio mundi* est, pour l'essentiel, l'oeuvre des laïcs eux-mêmes', in *Osservatore Romano*, 23 March 1962 cited in '«Consecratio mundi»', 608, n 2.
56. '«Consecratio mundi»', 611.
57. '«Consecratio mundi»', 612–613.
58. '«Consecratio mundi»', 616.

des hommes.'⁵⁹ He also resisted the theocratic tendency in the term making the laity's task in the world that of a 'une société lévitique, «cléricale».'⁶⁰ In the 1966 versions, he also commented that the use of '*consecratio mundi*' deliberately avoided dealing with the controversial problems raised by the baptismal extension of the threefold charism of Christ, as priest, prophet, and king, to the laity. While he does not name this problem as the concept of the 'priesthood of all believers' proclaimed by the Protestant Reformers, it could be implied.⁶¹ Chenu identified that '*consecratio mundi*' bore significance well beyond its intended use and would seem to counter the Church's involvement in the world as developed in *Gaudium et spes*.⁶² The shift to lay and Church 'présence' in the world, which his writings had so advocated before Vatican II, were at risk of being smothered by a '*contemptus mundi*'.⁶³ He noted thankfully that the term did not appear in the Pastoral Constitution, perhaps a result of his and others' efforts to challenge the use of '*consecratio mundi*'.⁶⁴ Chenu's objection to '*consecratio mundi*' represents most fully the anthropological priority in his ecclesiology as through it he emphasised the inherent value of the humanity of the laity and how the mission of the Church is best effected through the witness of this humanity, rather than in an increase of sacralised ministers imported into the world with some vague sacramentalising capacity for announcing its salvation. Chenu instead insisted that it was the humanity of the laity that revealed most profoundly the mystery of the Incarnation to fellow humans and the immersion of these Christians in the 'profane' world reproduced most faithfully the condition of Christ on earth. This constituted a theological re-positioning not only of the role of the laity in the Church's mission, but of mission itself and of the Church's affirmation of the humanity it exists to serve.

---

59. '«Consecratio mundi»', 618; 'Les Laïcs et la «consecratio mundi»', 1051.
60. '«Consecratio mundi»', 610.
61. 'Les Laïcs et la «consecratio mundi»', 1050.
62. 'Les Laïcs et la «consecratio mundi»', 74–5.
63. 'Les Laïcs et la «consecratio mundi»', 81.
64. 'Les Laïcs et la «consecratio mundi»', 1052. This is reflected in Gérard Philips comment: 'Différentes raisons expliquent cette réserve [re 'consecrent'] . . . La sanctification mise en vedette ne prive d'aucune manière le monde sa valeur propre'. *L'Église et son mystère au II Concile du Vatican. Histoire, texte et commentaire de la constitution Lumen Gentium* (tome II) (Tournai: Desclée, 1967-8), 33.

Conclusion

Chenu was not alone in insisting on a less theocratic understanding of the Church's relationship to the world, but it was his persistent promotion of the role of the laity, mission as constitutive of the Church, and the faith being realised in history, that led to the wide dissemination and adoption of these themes in the major Conciliar documents. In this sense, he had extended Möhler's teaching of 'continuing Incarnation' in the Church to include all humanity and the world as the site of 'continuing Incarnation'. This more Incarnational and Christological understanding of the community of the church had been his ecclesiological project since the 1930s. Its anthropological significance rested on a Thomist respect for the autonomy of created things and the recognition that the socialisation of humans through technological and industrial civilisation was not a block to their sanctification in Christ. Such a prophetic reading of the otherwise negatively received secularisation situated his ecclesiology in a daring dialogue with modernity, but Chenu continued to perceive theological possibilities in the modern world and to discover there a refreshment of the Gospel mission of the Church. Chenu's contribution to Vatican II ecclesiology remains largely underestimated, yet this may be understood as reflecting the prophetic quality of his anthropological turn and the long-term resolution of such innovation in ecclesial understanding. Chenu would revel in the developments of lay ministry, both within the Church and its mission in the world since Vatican II, more thoroughly than any of the other theological forerunners of the Council. There is no reported regret from Chenu to match that of Lubac and Daniélou's disaffection with the post-Conciliar direction of the Church up to the pontificate of John Paul II. Even the more moderate concerns attributed to Congar indicate hesitation about the Council's outcomes that Chenu would not have equally shared.[65] Rather, Chenu called for an even greater reform of the Church that would constitute a deeper commitment to the potential of its human membership, recognising more fully the human character of the Church, while engaging with the humanity of the world in an activation of its mission that found even in secularisation

---

65. See Gabriel Flynn's conclusion in *Yves Congar's Vision of the Church in an Age of Disbelief* (Aldershot: Ashgate, 2004).

the seeds of the Gospel that characterise the risk of the Incarnation in each age.⁶⁶

In this sense, his prophetic and theological efforts bore the fruit in Vatican II that he himself had long proclaimed: 'Théologiens et prophètes cohabitent dans une Église en bonne santé.'⁶⁷ It is the historical perspective on this often bumpy cohabitation that outlined for Chenu a theology of history in which the 'ruptures' of doctrinal development played a crucial role. This theology of history is explored in the next chapter.

---

66. 'Le Christianisme, lui, de manière sensationelle, trouve et réalise son identité dans la modernité.' Chenu, 'Modernité', La Lettre nos 346–347 (1987), 5–7, 5.
67. Chenu, 'Un peuple prophétique', in *Esprit* 364/10 (1967): 602–11, 608.

Chapter 5
Chenu's Theology of History

> 'Une histoire parfaite de la théologie aboutirait,
> s'il en existait une, à une théologie de l'histoire.'
> Chenu, *La théologie au douzième siècle*
> (Paris: Librairie Philosophique J.Vrin, 1957), 14.

Late in Chenu's career, Congar observed that among the works he regretted Chenu had not completed, due to silencing and incessant pastoral activity, was 'un ouvrage formellement consacré à l'histoire, sa nature, son objet, sa méthode. La matière d'une telle étude existe éparse dans son oeuvre.'[1] For Chenu, history and his theological projects were interdependent, grounded in an historical methodology, predicated on the historical character of Christianity. From as early as *Une école de théologie: le Saulchoir*, Congar noted, Chenu sought 'l'idée d'une histoire intégrale', a history which reconstituted 'tout le tissu humain'.[2] For Congar and Chenu, the study of history was intrinsically theological, exposing a dialectical relationship between Revelation and general history, and between past meaning and present accessibility of doctrine. The sources-study approach that both learned from the *Le Saulchoir* school of theology favoured contextual interpretation over the rationalist form analysis of 'modern scholasticism' that reigned under Garrigou-Lagrange at the *Angelicum*. This was a turn to historical criticality as intrinsic to the understanding

---

1. Congar, 'Le Père M.-D. Chenu', 783.
2. *Une école de théologie*, 169 (100).

and representation of doctrine.[3] History not only made present the meaning of texts; it was key to the renewal of theology. Applying Lagrange's historical-critical exegesis to Thomist studies was more than an appropriation of a method; it introduced a way of defining theology as historical, material, and human. For Chenu, historical criticality located theology in the reality of human enterprise rather than in the abstraction of eternal and universal truths. Metaphysics had been succeeded by history in theology. History continues to reveal divine truth and that understanding of this truth is located by humans in history: 'je sentais que la Parole de Dieu est dans l'histoire, et qu'entrer dans l'histoire est un moyen d'atteindre la Parole de Dieu.'[4] In this chapter, the theology of history that Chenu operated through will be explored across his writings with specific attention to his historical works and the Christian anthropological consciousness that they represent.

Total history for a total theology

Chenu's starting point, that history is constitutive of theology, required a more 'total' historical approach than the positivist history of the nineteenth century.[5] Chenu began employing Lagrange's historical exegesis to read Aquinas' *Summa Theologiae* as the construction of a particular historical conjunction, whose context disclosed further its meaning. This use of historical method emphasised the difference between the truths of Revelation and their historically conditioned

---

3. This is evident as early as 1923 when Chenu considered the debate about the effects of time on faith as the background to Thomas' treatise on faith: 'l'élément «temps» (passé, présent, futur) vis-à-vis d'un objet de foi est-il obstacle à l'immutabilité de la foi, y introduisant des variations essentielles?' 'Contribution à l'histoire du traité de la foi.', 36.
4. *Un théologien en liberté*, 37. cf also *Introduction à l'étude de Saint Thomas d'Aquin*, 261: 'l'histoire évidemment, ici plus qu'ailleurs, sera maîtresse, car elle sera, au sens fort du mot, révélatrice'.
5. Chenu observed that: 'Michelet parlait de la résurrection qu'accomplit l'histoire. Mais la résurrection d'une pensée passée exclut la perspective du présent. . . . Mais revivre, ce n'est pas vivre, et une survie dans ces conditions serait précaire, artificielle et de pure érudition. Ainsi nous voyons au XIXe siècle des travaux marqués d'historicisme. L'érudition, disait Valéry, est une défaite. On connaît l'antinomie marquée par Nietzsche entre l'histoire et l'instinct de création du présent.' Chenu, 'L'étude historique de saint Thomas', *Revue Philosophique de Louvain*, 49 (1951), 735–743 (736).

human reception. Similarly, Chenu's method distinguished between dogma based on Revelation and Aquinas' more innovative theological enterprise. Chenu recognised in the twelfth century a *'conjonction'* of different expressions of critical consciousness, concurrent with the socio-economic revolution of mercantilism, from which a theological awakening (*un reveil*) had emerged. From these he mapped the '*mentalité*' of an age.

> Le tâche de l'historien . . . progresse au-delà des sources et des contextes pour découvrir dans son irréductible originalité l'esprit qui les exploite et, par ses intuitions maîtresses, crée en quelque sorte de nouvelles intelligibilités. Cette création personnelle cependant n'est pas livrée à ses contingences psychologiques, et, ultime matière de l'historien, une logique interne commande le développement des intuitions en constructions systématiques selon des principes synthétiques choisis.[6]

Chenu's application of historical critical method released from Aquinas' texts a picture of the total '*mentalité*' that produced him, and from which he re-produced a new critical theological method. He did not limit his recovery of the theological past to the works of Aquinas but included other medieval sources, the missing writers and thinkers through whom he ascertained the overall climate or milieu in which Aquinas had appeared. He unearthed the shift that occurred between the theologies of his predecessors Anselm and Abelard, and Aquinas' synthesis of doctrine and the 'new' philosophy. He also highlighted the influence of neo-platonism on Aquinas, especially represented in the *exitus-reditus* structure he postulated for the *Summa*.[7] Chenu's contextual reading identifed other 'intuitions maîtresses' from minor mystics of the twelfth and thirteenth centuries, which underpinned Aquinas' thought. From this insight, Chenu determined that any theological reading of Aquinas is conditioned by the difference between its historical situation and that of Aquinas, and this is decisive for any interpretation.

---

6. *Une école*, 163.
7. As noted earlier, this reading of Thomas' plan of the *Summa* has been disputed among others by Rudi Te Velde, Rudi, *Aquinas on God: The 'Divine Science' of the Summa Theologiae* (Farnham: Ashgate, 2006), 10–15.

The use of historical method began with his thesis, an innovation warily noted by Garrigou-Lagrange, and radically extended Thomist *ressourcement* beyond the neo-scholastic free-standing textual analysis and proof-texting.[8] Chenu concluded that Aquinas' 'scientific' synthesis of revealed faith and human knowledge reproduced the expository method of the medieval *lectio* and the discourse of the *quaestiones disputae*.[9] This was not the fixed system rendered by later readings that responded to Cartesian and Kantian foundationalism.[10]

Chenu sought to incorporate but not homogenise the innovations and ruptures that failed to fit the established conclusions of the traditional history of dogma. So he departed from the genealogical analysis of the 'greats' by making an historical turn, locating medieval theological discourse within its intellectual, social, and economic contexts, but also finding contrasts with these contexts.

> Mais précisément ces maîtres en pensée ou en institution ne sont intelligibles que dans les ensembles contemporains, disons, puisqu'il s'agit de théologie, dans la communauté d'Église qui les porta. L'historien ne peut se résoudre à juxtaposer les vicissitudes des psychologies individuelles; il a l'ambition de saisir les corps sociaux eux-mêmes, les conditions de leur fonctionnement, mental ou institutionel.[11]

Chenu anticipated the *Annales* approach of a 'total' history, emphasising the wider social and material documentation, the interrelation of theological and socio-economic themes, and the identification of the tensions that constitute the broader coherence of movements. In his study of 1927, *La théologie comme science au XIIIe siècle*, Chenu contextualised Aquinas, his precursors, and contemporaries in their own time, and not against the philosophical debates of the sixteenth to eighteenth centuries where neo-scholasticism or 'modern-scholasticism' had exclusively couched them. In this work, Chenu inaugurated

---

8. 'Le théologien devra donc, dans l'usage qu'il fait des documents, respecter à la fois leur autorité et leur origine, ce qu'il ne peut faire qu'en les intégrant dans une pensée historique et non pas seulement en les prenant comme point de départ.' 'Histoire du salut', 26.
9. Chenu, *Introduction à l'étude de Saint Thomas d'Aquin*, 257.
10. Chenu, *Une école*, 165 (95): 'la philosophie de saint Thomas n'est pas ce qu'on appelle un «système». Ce n'est pas comme à un système que nous y adhérons.'
11. Chenu later described his method in: 'Avant-propos', *La théologie au douzième siècle* (Paris: Librairie Philosophique J.Vrin, 1957), 12.

his own theological version of the '*longue durée*' perspective upon the conceptual development of the 'science' of theology before Aquinas, then through his two revisions, generated extensive contemporary discourse, which advanced the further retrieval by other twentieth century theologians of the history of the interpretation of '*sacra doctrina*' through the centuries.

Chenu's early recognition of the *Annales* movement reflected a concurrence in method and subject matter.[12] Its focus on the complexity and durability of structures, rather than 'the great men' or 'great events' on human activities beyond politics, and on incorporating into historical study sociology, psychology, geography, economics, and semantics, parallelled the comprehensiveness of Chenu's interest in filling-out the centuries-long development and shifts that produced the medieval synthesis of cosmos, self, and God:

> mes recherches historiques se conjuguaient, par une coïncidence significative, avec l'historiographie nouvelle, dégagée de l'histoire des grands hommes, penchée sur la vie quotidienne, les sensibilités élémentaires, les mentalités, l'anonymat des masses, l'oralité des récits, bref de la foi *vécue*, et pas seulement de la foi *enseignée*.[13]

Chenu's historical theory was closer to the early *Annales* historians like the medievalists Bloch and Febvre, than the later movement following Braudel.[14] He shared their interest in the sociology of history, with its Marxist political implications, but Chenu wrote more a his-

---

12. The *Annales* school took its name from Marc Bloch and Lucien Febvre's journal *Annales d'histoire economique et sociale* begun in 1929 (which in 1946 became *Annales: Economies, sociétés, civilisations*). It is also known as 'l'histoire totale' and 'l'historiographie nouvelle'.
13. Chenu, 'Post-scriptum 1985', *Une école*, 176.
14. Fernand Braudel researched the longitudinal histories of *La Méditerranée et le Monde Méditerranéen à l'Epoque de Philippe II* (1949), and *Civilisation Matérielle, Economie et Capitalisme, XVe-XVIIIe* (1979). Jacques Le Goff notes that Chenu added the history of intellectual development to Marc Bloch's treatment of the twelfth and thirteenth centuries: 'Le Père Chenu et la société médiévale', *Revue des sciences philosophiques et theologiques*, 81 (1997), 371–380 (373). Although Chenu extensively used the concept of '*conjoncture*' and employed '*la longue durée*' perspective, his use anticipated Braudel's articulation of their theory. (for example in 'Position de la théologie' (1935), 135; *Dimension nouvelle de la Chrétienté* (1937), 22; 'L'unité de la foi' (1937), 18—where '*conjonction*' is used along with equivalent words).

tory of ideas and beliefs, understood as *'mentalités'*, albeit represented materially in the doctrinal disputes.[15] The collection of articles in *La théologie au douzième siècle* (1957) traced the gradual distinguishing of nature and history from allegorical conceptions of creation through the themes of symbolism and analogy and grammar, against the background of evangelical revivals and the transfer of the centres of learning from the monasteries like Clairvaux to the Cathedral schools of Chartres and Salisbury. In his introduction, Chenu declared an *Annales* preference for elaborating these social, economic, and conceptual turns in collective consciousness instead of focusing on the individual agency of 'l'un des maîtres de ce temps' or on their dogmatic equivalent 'l'une ou l'autre des doctrines majeures explorées dans les controverses':

> dégager les méthodes, et sous les méthodes enseignées, les mentalités implicites, qui, au delà des systèmes et des controverses, déterminent l'évolution de ce siècle, unanimement considéré comme la charnière du moyen âge occidental, dans ses institutions comme dans sa religion.[16]

Chenu resisted the interpretation of this *réveil* as the progressive displacement of a mythological consciousness by a proto-scientific one. Instead, his research revealed residual and revolutionary elements coexisting in the complex of appropriations of competing allegorical and natural science perspectives.

> Mais l'historien n'a pas seulement à observer les enchaînements de causalité, entre les idées ou entre les faits; il discerne aussi l'implication de certaines continuités, mentales ou institutionelles, qui donnent un soutien à des aspirations spirituelles.[17]

---

15. See especially the bibliographical article *Les études de philosophie médiévale*. (Paris: Hermann et Companie, 1939), which le Goff commends as decisive for his own research in 'Le Père Chenu et la société médiévale'.
16. 'Avant-propos', 11; also, 'L'histoire, croyons-nous, doit atteindre les sous-sols des textes, des controverses, des systèmes, des génies eux-mêmes, s'il est vrai que la génie est celui don't les paroles ont plus de sens qu'il ne pouvait leur en donner lui-même.'
17. Chenu, 'Cur Homo? Le sous-sol d'une controverse' (1953) in *La théologie au douzième siècle*, 52–61 (59–60).

The synthesis of this humanist *'mentalité'* was presented not as sequential development but rather as being comprised of erratic waves of historical consciousness, with different stages of realisation about the autonomy and causality of nature. Chenu cited the anomalous coexistence in John of Salisbury of a vehement defence of Thomas à Beckett's theocratic polity, alongside his construction of a political theory of a secularised society.[18]

In the key first chapter 'La nature et l'homme: la Renaissance du XIIe siècle', Chenu focused on the theological reception and implications of the discovery of 'nature' as a universe, a reality in itself rather than a mere backdrop to the drama of salvation, and of how humanity came to be conceived as constituted within this nature while apparently acting upon it like some force from without.[19] In *Annales* mode, he cited as material articulations of 'la prise de conscience' examples of lyrical literary and eroticised sculptural representations of a reality no longer only sacramentalised.[20] The new awareness was further demonstrated in a secularised political psychology evidenced in the demands for the restriction of clerical rights and the popularity of anti-clericalism, and through the forensic appropriation of causality shown by the introduction of rational proof in courts of justice. But to allay any impression given by this diversity of representations that the new consciousness was universally and uniformly acquired, Chenu noted the collision between old and new mentalities: 'l'idéalisme naturaliste de Chartres', which exalted the power and wisdom of a God who ordered the universe at his own pleasure and the 'new thinking' that conceived nature as an observable ordered whole independent of miraculous explanations and attributing all causality to continuous direct intervention by the First Cause. Chenu described the new thinking as emanating from 'le sens concret d'une histoire où les

---

18. 'La nature et l'homme: la Renaissance du XIIe siècle', 50–51.
19. 'C'est la prise de conscience qui s'effectua alors, dans les hommes du XIIe siècle, qu'ils avaient affaire à une réalité extérieure, présente, intelligible, efficace, comme à une partenaire . . . dont les forces et les lois appelaient composition ou conflit, au moment même où par un choc parallèle, ils se rendaient compte qu'eux-mêmes étaient pris dans ce jeu de la nature, qu'ils étaient eux aussi une pièce de cet univers qu'ils s'apprêtaient à dominer.' 'La nature et l'homme: la Renaissance du XIIe siècle', 21–22.
20. These included *La Romain de la Rose* and bas-relief sculptures of human occupations on the arches of Chartres cathedral.

libertés, divine et humaine, jouent au-delà des determinismes de la nature.'[21]

While Chenu's compilation from literary and cultural sources could appear a limited operation to '*abbatre les cloisins*',[22] he was revolutionising theology by weighting its thought with its concrete relationship to time and space, and by locating the 'mentalités' that produced such thought. This is literally illustrated in his *St Thomas d'Aquin et la théologie*, not a biography but a history of Thomas' intellectual and spiritual representativeness of the '*mentalité*' of his era, materially embellished with contemporary and later images from manuscripts and sculptures.[23] Significantly, none of Chenu's writings were biographical. From his later examination of the breakthrough in medieval consciousness comes his articulation of the interrelation of context and the flowering of human intellectual endeavour.

> Ni Abélard, ni Héloïse, ni saint Bernard, ni saint Thomas d'Aquin, ne furent des inspirés, soudain tombés du ciel et livrés à leur charisme: ils étaient saisis dans les conditionnements socio-culturels de toute part enveloppant et engendrant. Mais, loin de réduire leur inspiration, leur génie, leur charisme, ces conditionnements furent le terrain de leur genèse et de leur fécondité.[24]

All theology he proposed comes with a history because it is the product of history. For Chenu, history is revelatory. Revelation is manifested in history, and in turn, the interpretation and proclamation of this Revelation is formed within a particular history. So, doctrine and theology are always historically and materially located, but while the *Annales* approach enriched Chenu's methodology and content,

---

21. 'La nature et l'homme', 24–25.
22. The *Annales*' technique of extending research areas beyond the confines of separate disciplines.
23. Under the sub-heading 'Conjoncture' at the beginning of *St Thomas d'Aquin et la théologie* Chenu distinguished his method from hagiography: 'Ce n'est pas réduire la valeur hagiographique de cette aventure, ni en éliminer les expressions naïves, que d'en découvrir le sous-sol sociologique dans la conjoncture contemporaine; c'est en déceler la profondeur significative dans la Chrétienté en évolution, bien au-delà de l'épisode personnel d'une vocation contrariée.' 6.
24. Chenu, *L'éveil de la conscience dans la civilisation médiévale* (Montreal/Paris: Institut d'Études Médiévales/Librairie J.Vrin, 1969), 80.

his objectives differed. Chenu's historical studies aimed to recover the historical dimension of theology, which in turn, presumed a *theology of history*.

The later *Annales* historian Le Goff recognised the difference between Chenu's project and *Annales* historiography at work in Chenu's insistence that the advent of scholastic dialectic in the twelfth century did not banish symbolic interpretation from theological discourse to the margins of popular faith.[25] Chenu was fighting the Enlightenment prejudice that failed to appreciate the continuing historical importance of symbolic expressions of faith. Le Goff judges Chenu's criteria that symbolic thinking carries 'plus d'efficacité chrétienne que les procédés dialectiques'[26] as reflecting a '*parti pris*' that is not historically demonstrable.[27] Le Goff rightly detected that Chenu's approach involved vested judgements about the continuity of faith within the radical changes in the intellectual history of the twelfth century. This was a theological appeal to the stability of the content of faith over the succession of conceptual forms. Chenu here departed from the *Annales* objectification of data, and anticipated the more subjective and symbolically sensitive historiography of Michel de Certeau.

> Nous avons délibérément tenté, au bénéfice de cette intelligence intérieure, une interprétation des faits et textes, non certes par un transfert idéologique au service d'une thèse ou d'un système, mais par une recherche passionnée des liaisons internes, des apparentements à demi-conscients, des déterminismes institutionnels ou spirituels. Les objets eux-

---

25. Elsewhere Le Goff commends Chenu's important historical contributions, especially to the concept of time transformed by the new mercantile culture in 'Conscience de l'histoire et théologie' in *La théologie au douzième siècle*, 62–89, cf Le Goff, 'Au Moyen Age: Temps d'Église et temps du marchand' in *Pour un autre Moyen Age: Temps, travail et culture en Occident* (Paris: Gallimard, 1977), section I, chapter 2. But he also notes: 'Le P. Chenu ne parle d'ailleurs pas beaucoup de la culture populaire. . . . c'est une vision globale de la société qu'il propose.' 'Le Père Chenu et la société médiévale', 377.
26. Chenu, 'Avant-propos', *La théologie au douzième siècle*, 14; Chenu sustained this argument through 'La mentalité symbolique' (Chapter VII) and 'La théologie symbolique'(Chapter VIII) in *La théologie au douzième siècle* (Paris: Librairie Philosophique J.Vrin, 1957), 289–308 (308).
27. Jacques Le Goff, *Medieval Civilisation*, translated by Julian Barnes (Oxford: Blackwell, 1996), 344.

mêmes d'ailleurs, quelle que soit l'originalité des esprits qui les ont traitées, ont leur déterminisme'.[28]

Chenu's history has a strong sense of the *'longue durée'*, detecting the persistence of the sacramentalised apprehension of reality well beyond its Renaissance demise. Despite the obituaries, the symbolic recurs. He recognised in this persistence a resistance, demonstrated in the material evidence of the sources for conflict, between these *'mentalités'* in subsequent eras of Western thought up to and including the neo-scholastic deracination of spiritual theology from speculative theology. Beyond a genealogical location of sources in their historical context, Chenu juxtaposed successive periods of theological thought and their context to demonstrate the interdependence of theology and history. The currents of twelfth century and successive theological and philosophical controversies recur throughout the centuries, persisting into twentieth century theological discourse. This indicates the grounds for Donneaud's condemnation that history was being put to the service of Chenu's theological agenda. Yet it is also the vitality of Chenu's theology because, rather like Walter Benjamin's angel, its historicity is comprehensively unlocked to a past while dynamically engaged in present and future, gathering up the theological residue.

While Chenu's theological project is not philosophically committed to the same ends as the later *Annales*, he did utilise their understanding that change in social structures is not a succession of results from a single causal event. Rather, change operates through different stages of realisation for different levels or planes of human activity. The *'longue durée'* of change affects structures in society not sequentially, nor simultaneously on different levels, but through the intersection and interpenetration of *'conjonctures'*. For Chenu, *'réveil'* is not a single event as such; it is more like a *'conjoncture'* or nexus within the *'longue durée'*.[29] The *Annales* doctrine was that structures are only eventually transformed and therefore elude the historical study of periods. There was much convergence between the *Annales* methods and his theological interests in Chenu's studies of the mutually stimulating effects of socio-economic change in the life of medieval towns and the emerging universities and of changes in conceptual under-

---

28. 'Avant-propos', 14.
29. This is the theme of Chenu's *L'éveil de la conscience dans la civilisation médiévale*.

standing.³⁰ This is particularly evident in the significance he bestows on the twelfth century awakening to '*novitas*' as an awakening to the desirability of change, not only to viewing change as catastrophic disorder. In theological terms, he detected an in-breaking of the Gospel through these imperatives for change emerging from the growth in human consciousness.

> Nous parlons ici de moyen âge occidental, pour autant qu'il apparaît comme une période homogène. Mais dans cette continuité, celle des consciences comme celle de l'histoire, il y eut des temps forts, des sursauts, des novations, dans les consciences précisément plus encore que dans les institutions, qui décidèrent d'une évolution alors inaugurée. Le XIIe siècle est sans conteste le pivot d'une de ces évolutions . . . le XIIe siècle est l'âge de l'éveil, avec ses ingénuités, sa novation, des séductions sommaires. Je m'y tiendrai ici, quitte à prologer le trait dans une référence prospective aux futurs maîtres de l'Université du XIIIe siècle, âge réflexe déjà d'une raison et d'une foi adultes, où précisément l'homme adulte sera défini par le retour sur soi (conscience) devenu l'axe et le critère de la moralité.³¹

Chenu welcomed an equivalent view of the changes wrought by twentieth century modernity as signalling another shift in 'humanisation', awaiting a corresponding theological openness to the 'royaume de Dieu toujours jeune dans une humanité toujours renouvelée.'³²

Chenu's historical turn coincided with the *Annales* method, because their understanding of history provided sufficient complex space or '*densité*' for the range of relations that make up what is human. This historical turn was his means for re-vivifying the 'sclerotic' theology of timeless universals by opening theology to the

---

30. Chenu acknowledged the influence of Bloch's medieval studies, especially in *Introduction à l'étude de Saint Thomas d'Aquin* and *La théologie au douzième siècle*, cf Marc Bloch, *La société féodale* (Paris: 1940); *Apologie pour l'histoire* (Paris: 1949). On the *Annales* school cf Peter Burke, *The French Historical Revolution: the Annales School 1929–89* (Cambridge: Polity Press, 1990); Georg G. Igges, *New Directions in European Historiography* (London: Methuen, 1984); Susan W. Friedman, *Marc Bloch, Sociology and Geography: encountering changing disciplines* (Cambridge: Cambridge University Press, 1996).
31. Chenu, *L'éveil de la conscience*, 12–13.
32. *Dimension nouvelle de la Chrétienté*, 7.

historical materiality and spirituality of the human quest for truth. Congar described how this historical turn pervaded Chenu's teaching: 'Il nous initiait à la perception du caractère concret, matériel, des réalités les plus sublimes que nous somme appelés à vivre dans le Temps.'[33]

'L'histoire de la théologie est intérieure à la théologie même.'

Chenu early perceived a coherence between theology and history beyond the static concept of the 'deposit of faith' and the fear prevalent in Catholic theology of relativism or evolutionism. In his programmatic introduction to *La théologie au douzième siècle*, Chenu declared that a 'perfect' understanding of the development of doctrine would amount to a theology of history. Preceding this statement was the basis of his claim: 'l'histoire de la théologie est intérieure à la théologie même.'[34] That history is *within* theology, not extrinsic to it, not related to it merely as a new methodology, nor some ideological or alien impost, is the starting point for Chenu's theology.

> C'est tout au long de son cours que l'histoire de la Chrétienté est source de connaissance théologique, portant en soi une intelligibilité toujours neuve de par la *présence* de la foi dans de nouvelles générations.[35]

Theology is historically located because of its origin in Revelation, as Chenu had long insisted.[36] 'La théologie est *réaliste*, parce qu'elle est l'intelligence de l'ordre du salut dans son histoire et sa réalisation concrète.'[37] Chenu underscored the historical nature of all human inquiry, even that of scholastic philosophy. Because the task of theology is to unfold the meaning of this Revelation for each new age, Chenu asked how any theology could then be exempt from historical elaboration and critique.

---

33. Congar, 'Le frère que j'ai connu', 243.
34. Chenu, 'Avant-propos', *La théologie au douzième siècle* (Paris: Librairie Philosophique J.Vrin, 1957), 14.
35. *Une école*, 99–100 (169).
36. 'Position de la théologie', 128.
37. 'Position de la théologie', 131.

> Si la Révélation s'insère ainsi dans le temps, au cours d'une histoire, histoire sainte, mais histoire, centrée sur le fait historique de l'Incarnation, si dès lors le donné révélé s'inscrit et se présente dans des faits et des textes historiques, nous voici directement et brutalement devant cette question: la théologie, comme la foi qui l'inspire, ne sont-elles pas alors justiciables d'une critique historique?[38]

Chenu was concerned to awaken theology to its historical character, but he was equally determined not to subsume Revelation to history nor equate history with theology:

> ni la nature ni l'histoire n'ont capacité de révéler le mystère de Dieu: sa Parole vient «d'en-haut», par l'initiative d'un amour gratuit, s'engageant dans une communion amoureuse. La grâce est grâce, et l'histoire profane n'est pas source de salut.[39]

While he would stipulate that history is not equivalent to Christian Revelation, he nevertheless insisted that 'sacred history' was not a super-addition to human history, but the meaning revealed by an historically critical theology, conscious of its own historicity through Creation and the Incarnation.

> Telle est donc l'économie de la Révélation, dans l'Ancienne et dans la Nouvelle Alliance: non pas une histoire dans laquelle se produirait une révélation, mais une histoire par elle-même révélante.[40]

History is not Revelation, but it reveals. For Chenu, the priority was on recognising the temporality of theology: not sacralising history but restoring the sense of the rupture and innovation that is proper to Revelation and to theological reflection on its doctrine. He emphasised the importance of '*conjonctures*' that rupture the apparent continuities in doctrinal history: 'On avance à travers les ruptures, les conflits, les haines. L'Histoire fait des détours, dans lequels se loge

---

38. *Une école*, 58 [134–5].
39. 'Histoire du salut et historicité de l'homme', 28.
40. 'Histoire du salut', 21–32 (26).

tout de même la grâce de Dieu.'[41] In this way, he departed from Braudel's version of the *Annales* method, which discounted attention to 'the event' as obstructing the continuities denied in traditional history.[42] Chenu's reason for focusing on '*ruptures*' was theological, in that it revealed the currents and other subtle changes that the ecclesial ideology of immutability would otherwise disguise. His target was that authoritarian tendency in neo-scholastic theology that 'détemporalisait la Parole de Dieu en une idéologie abstraite manipulée par un pouvoir magistériel.'[43] Chenu's theology of history understood the truth-value in historical critique as a counter to dogmatism in theology: 'Ce fut même là le ferment le plus actif du travail en cours, comme aussi l'immédiate occasion de la crise doctrinale.'[44] Instead of change being equated with disorder and alienation from the eternal order of creation, Chenu concluded that acute periods of change and historical convergence revealed the powerful rupture or return of the Gospel in the affairs of humans:

> le «retour à l'Évangile» est provoqué par la conscience d'une mutation violente d'une anthropologie vétuste et d'une société périmée: elles sont contestées au nom de l'Évangile.[45]

The themes of '*rupture*' and '*réveil*' represent for Chenu the in-breaking of the Gospel, the '*nouveauté*', which provokes individuals and social groupings to respond in human freedom to the challenges of the Gospel, especially when the institutional forms of Christianity have become moribund or smothered by 'les pesanteurs sociologiques.'[46]

---

41. Chenu, 'Civilisation technique et spiritualité nouvelle' (1948) in *La Parole de Dieu II*, 137–158 (156).
42. Chenu had more in common with the early *Annales* historians Bloch and Febvre, and later ones like Le Goff, who understood events and structures as interrelated elements of social reality.
43. 'La théologie en procès', Savoir, faire, espérer: les limites de la raison, (Bruxelles: Facultés Universitaires St Louis, 1976), 691–696 (693).
44. 'Mais cette réaction trop fruste couvrait en outre un conservatisme négatif attardé à défendre par routine des positions intenables, qu'il fallait abandonner bientôt précipitamment, après de vaines habiletés apologétiques ou des concordismes perpétuellement en retard.' *Une École*, 37 (116); 'L'histoire est une sauvegarde contre cet esprit dogmatique.' Chenu, 'L'étude historique de saint Thomas', *Revue Philosophique de Louvain*, 49 (1951), 735–743 (738).
45. 'La rénovation de la théologie morale', 291.
46. 'Histoire du salut', 23.

'C'est le retour de l'Évangile qui porte en lui la rupture avec les appesantissements collectifs autant qu'avec les désordres personnels.'[47] For Chenu, a theology of history identifies the significance of such changes and of what they reveal about the power of God's word in the world.

> Quand l'histoire avance peu à peu, régulièrement, il la suit; mais quand il y a un choc, que le mouvement se précipite, que des ruptures interviennent, alors le théologien est tout à fait en éveil—j'allais même dire que, d'avance, il est tout à fait heureux—parce que c'est une occasion unique pour observer la Parole de Dieu en travail dans l'histoire. Le monde dans ses mutations est un provocateur de la Parole de Dieu.[48]

In a longer study of Chenu's theology of history, the dialectic of 'rupture et présence' would provide a critical framework for examining his key historical-theological themes and the dynamic unity that underpins them. They recur throughout the themes in his theology: Creation (the world), Incarnation, the Holy Spirit in history, and eschatology; then there were the 'economic' and anthropological themes of human situation and corporeality, secondary causes, matter, and sacramentality, the city as the locus of history, 'the new', truth and freedom, prophecy, the Gospel and the poor, 'événement', and the 'signs of the times' in the economy of salvation. Here it is possible only to summarise their function for Chenu's Christian anthropology but they mark the progress and the restraint of humanisation in its struggle towards divinisation. Significantly, 'rupture et présence' are not opposed for Chenu: 'Rupture et présence: c'est le paradoxe de l'Évangile.'[49] Rather, they represent the interplay of freedom and truth within history, how the necessary urge for security and continuity in humans and the Church is historically tempered by Gospel-oriented outbreaks of reform and renewal, which Chenu notes may be 'authentiques ou déviées'.

> Mon métier d'historien m'a amené à observer avec complaisance ces expériences, authentiques ou déviées, et

---

47. *St Thomas d'Aquin et la théologie*, 15.
48. Chenu, *Un théologien en liberté*, 23.
49. *St Thomas d'Aquin et la théologie*, 11.

> donc m'a rendu ultra-sensible à la problématique présente, non pas tant dans ses articulations théoriques, si urgentes soient-elles, mais dans ses contextes communautaires.[50]

Chenu demonstrated the interplay of freedom and truth that is 'rupture et présence' in his historical and theology study: 'Vérité et liberté dans la foi du croyant'.[51] This article written for Esprit shortly after Mounier's untimely death was a demonstration of how 'ruptures' in doctrinal history had not prevented the truth of the Gospel prevailing. He cited the condemnation of Aquinas and his disciple Giles of Rome in 1277 by the intervention of the archbishop of Paris and the collusion of St Bonaventure, which threatened the freedom of theological inquiry. Chenu followed this with the example of the denunciation and imprisonment by Pope Paul IV (1555) of Cardinal Morone, who only after the Pope's death was freed and went on to become one of the authors of the Catechism of the council of Trent. His final case of 'ces conjonctures difficiles, souvent douloureuses'[52] was more modern: the censure of historical critical biblical exegesis by Pope Pius X in his 1910 encyclical *Pascendi* and the effect this had on the biblical scholar Marie-Joseph Lagrange OP. For Chenu, these events spoke for the resurgence of the truth despite or even enhanced by the checks upon persons and the continuity of their work. Clearly his own experience is in the background and his audience would have been aware of this and the many apparently lost opportunities for contemporary evangelisation of the laity. Yet for Chenu, this *'rupture'* and the prevailing *'présence'* of truth were the roll and tumble of human history, even or especially in the history of the Church.

> Ce sont là des tensions constantes de la pensée chrétienne, et leurs pressions ont parfois détérminé des ruptures dans l'équilibre d'une unique vérité.[53]

Ruptures allow 'l'évolution des cultures et des mentalités' and the intellectual and spiritual space to catch-up with those called to lead

---

50. 'La rénovation de la théologie morale', 288.
51. (1959) in *La Parole de Dieu I. La Foi dans intelligence* (Paris: Les Éditions du Cerf, 1964), 337–59. [First published in *Esprit*, avril (1959), 598–619.]
52. 'Vérité et liberté dans la foi du croyant', 340.
53. 'Vérité et liberté', 344.

ahead with the freedom of the truth.⁵⁴ This was what he detected in his study of Aquinas' theological development that '*rupture* et *présence*' are the recurring conditions of human life in the world.

> Rupture et presence: le paradoxe du Chrétien dans le monde, de sa presence divine à toute réalité humaine, la plus charnelle comme la plus spirituelle, ne joue pas en effet sur le seul plan de l'action, individuelle et collective; il s'étend, selon la logique totale de l'Incarnation et de l'Esprit, à la culture de l'intelligence.⁵⁵

Chenu's theology of history was wound round these dynamics and in his refusal to see setbacks as determining the value of historical movements for their pursuit of the Gospel. 'En Évangile, la rupture n'est que pour une présence.'⁵⁶ Rather, he ended 'Vérité et liberté' with a warning:

> Redisons avec saint Thomas que, à s'en tenir à l'*autorité* de la foi, sa *vérité* vivante en pâtirait, car le fidèle s'avancerait dans la certitude peut-être, mais dans la vacuité de l'esprit.'⁵⁷

For Chenu rupture tempered the dangers of certitude with the struggle necessary to seek the truth of the Gospel in the varied events of history.

From the development of doctrine to a theology of change

It was in this spirit of unabashed openness that Chenu's interest in the historical status of Christian theology developed, particularly due to the recently re-visited debates about the development of doctrine.⁵⁸ The problem of how to maintain the immutability of the revealed supernatural truth of dogma, while taking into account the human

---

54. 'Vérité et liberté', 340.
55. *St Thomas d'Aquin et la théologie*, 17.
56. *St Thomas d'Aquin et la théologie*, 17.
57. 'Vérité et liberté', 359.
58. Chenu quoted from Newman's 'très psychologique' approach (albeit Bremond's poor translation, 99, 33-4) to reinforce 'cette doctrine du caractère complexe et progressif comme énoncé humain.' *Une école*, 117, 140; 'La raison psychologique du développement du dogme d'après Saint Thomas' (1924), 57-58, n.3.

reception and understanding of that truth, retained its largely anti-protestant focus in Catholic theology until challenged by the late nineteenth century's historical criticism of scripture and the sources of tradition. Despite its limited initial influence, Newman's *Essay on the Development of Christian Doctrine* injected an historical and psychological perspective into the debate already advanced by Johann von Drey, Johann Adam Möhler, and Matthias Scheeben by recognising the historical contingency of doctrine without falling into a doctrinal relativism.[59] The suspicion accentuated by the 'Modernist crisis' led Francisco Marin-Sola and P. Schultes to offer carefully nuanced evolutionary explanations of development.[60] At issue was the concept of change that continued to inform the Roman dogmatism: that change and history threatened the eternal truth of Revelation because they evidenced disintegration from the unity of Being on the one hand, and the disorder of relativism, on the other. Chenu's integration of historical method in theology was deemed by his Roman critics to repeat the erroneous historicist reductionism of the modernist crisis. History was arraigned as necessarily ideological, the instrument of infiltration by Kantian subjectivism and Schleiermacher's experientialism,[61] the destructive force of 'the liberal philosophies of development' that refused the absolute authority of God, and the derived authority of monarchy and the Church.[62]

---

59. Yves Congar OP, *Tradition and Traditions* (New York: Macmillan, 1966), 186-197, 212-213; Schoof, *Breakthrough*, 167.
60. Francisco Marin-Sola OP, *L'Évolution homogène du Dogme catholique* (Fribourg: Imprimerie et Librairie de l'Oeuvre de Saint-Paul, 1924) [original Spanish edition: 1923], Section 7; P. Schultes, *Introductio in Historiam Dogmatum* (Paris: Lethielleux, 1922). Chenu later expressed indebtedness to Schultes' idea of evolution, despite regretting the absence of Newman's theology from Schultes' treatment. 'La raison psychologique du développement du dogme d'après Saint Thomas', 57–58, n. 3.
61. *Une école*, 36 [116].
62. Owen Chadwick identifies how the challenge to absolute authority represented by history was operating in the controversies over the development of doctrine. While he concludes that 'Newman was a prodigy. He was a prodigy because he came to believe in historical development without also believing in liberal philosophies of development. This is what made the *Essay* possible as a contribution to Roman doctrine.' 'This is why Newman—never in any sense Gallican in spite of his Anglican past ... can be said by Acton to have "blunted the edge of Ultramontanism"'. *From Bossuet to Newman: The Idea of Doctrinal Development*, Cambridge University Press, 1957, 194–5.

Consistent with the official theology's obsession with 'une conception rigide de l'immutabilité du dogme' was its defensiveness against the rapid political and social change descending on post-World War I Europe.[63] Many of the official theologians approved by Rome were also committed to the reactionary political agenda of Mauras' *Action française* and Mussolini's Fascism, which promised a return to the 'old order', that is civil restoration of Church privileges.[64] The pervasive attitude in these circles was that of nostalgia for a lost past, focused on a romantic vision of the 'order' of medieval Christendom, an ecclesial 'Pre-Raphaelite' revisionism.[65] Chenu recognised that critical historical research was the key to unlock this alliance from its appropriation of an idealised account of the medieval order. This allowed Chenu to demonstrate that mere appropriation of a past was as inadequate as any other proof-texting procedure. Ecclesiastical fear of historical relativism and change had been exacerbated by Catholic Modernism's 'confusion des méthodes et le jeu des préjugés philosophiques', which failed to demonstrate their independence from

---

63. Just as the restoration of neo-Thomism and neo-scholasticism represented an 'order'-providing reaction to the disorder and the vacuum in central authority that marked the nineteenth century after the 1848 revolution against the *Anciens Régimes* across Europe, and the unification of the Italian and German states.
64. Yvon Tranvouez, *Catholiques d'abord. Approches du mouvement catholique en France (XIXe-XXe siècle)* (Paris: Les Éditions Ouvrières, 1988), 181, 212; Komonchak, 'Theology and Culture at Mid-Century', 601-2, especially n. 67, where he cites two letters (12 and 19/12/46) from Maritain to Garrigou-Lagrange in which Maritain 'vigorously defends himself against Garrigou's use of the word "deviation" to describe Maritain's opposition to Franco', and a "mortal sin" to describe his support for de Gaulle over Pétain.
65. Beyond the more politically committed reactionaries, there was the intellectual reaction to modernity and its incipient totalitarianism represented by Nicholas Berdiaeff who had extensive influence on early twentieth century French Catholic thought. Berdiaeff judged modernity as a series of disasters with the collapse of European civilisation in World War I and the Bolshevik revolution resembling the fall of the Roman Empire under the barbarian invasions. He called for a new Middle Ages which would restore a social order above the ruins of liberalism and against communism. Nicholas Berdiaeff, *Une nouveau Moyen Âge* (Paris: Plon, 1927) cited in Tranvouez, *Catholiques d'abord*, 115-6. Tranvouez notes Jacques Maritain's rejection of this restorationist mentality despite his call in *L'Humanisme intégral* (Paris: 1936) for a profane Christianity, which would adapt the medieval principles to the new historical situation. Also the criticism by Étienne Borne in 'Pour refaire une Chrétienté', *La Vie intellectuelle*, 9 (1936) of the delusion of slavishly copying the Middle Ages, cited by Tranvouez, 124-5.

liberal and romantic ideological challenges to dogmatic authority.[66] Chenu's solution outlined in his 1937 manifesto *Une école de théologie: le Saulchoir* was to recover the scholastic period *par excellence* as it presented an obvious 'trojan horse' for an historical investigation of the development of doctrine, under the guise of conforming to neo-scholastic theology. Chenu noted that the disorder posed by the critical epistemological turn of late nineteenth century modernity had parallels in 'plusieurs reprises, selon les cycles de culture, dans la Chrétienté d'Occident', recognisable by the intensity of the 'réaction de défense' these engendered. The use of 'les cycles de culture' here is an ambiguous avoidance of the term 'history' while alluding to the historical passage of time. 'Cycle' was safely consistent with Thomas' more circular understanding of reality and recognisably liturgical. Chenu does not subscribe to a cyclic view of history, but proposed that 'grands cycles de culture' or (as he would later term them) '*conjonctures*' coalesce into non-consecutive but comprehensive shifts in the intellectual development of the Middle Ages, 'à l'intérieur de chacun dequels la croyance rencontre, comme en des lieux parallèles, les mêmes points critiques.'[67]

Rather than the caricature of the medieval era secured in static order by the theocracy of Christendom, Chenu listed the 'renaissances' that forced change during the early medieval period. Charlemagne's institutional reforms were accompanied by the intellectual upheaval that included the introduction of grammar as a critical tool for organising the interpretation of the sacred and other texts. The waves of theological renaissance in the twelfth and thirteenth cen-

---

66. *Une école*, 38 [117].
67. Chenu, 'Le sens et les leçons d'une crise religieuse', 359. Chenu often employed this term 'cycle', not to suggest repetition of historical events, but to explain the process whereby different eras (re-)awaken to the Gospel ('un reveil évangélique'). Elewhere he portrayed these moments as a '*rupture*' or a '*conjoncture*', the Annales concept of the cumulative effect (experienced as '*rupture*') of the co-incidence of different pressures for change, which otherwise would occur over different periods, as different levels and sectors become conscious and receptive of change. 'L'univers de l'historien se déroule dans le temps; il est quelque chose de successif, d'irréversible, selon des époques qui sont des étapes sur une route vers une destinée, dans une série d'événements purs, et non dans un retour éternel des générations et des corruptions, comme dirait Aristote.' 'Position de la théologie' (1935), 128.

turies were initiated when Abelard introducing dialectic reasoning into the articulation of theology, and brought to a climax in the acrimonious battles over the integration of Aristotle's thought, firstly in the faculty of arts then providing Saints Albert the Great and Thomas Aquinas with the new systematic structure for their theology. These changes in the history of theology demonstrated for Chenu the difference between safeguarding official teaching from relativism and perceiving a theology of history that would recognise the actual relativising of theology caused by contemporary neo-scholastic theology's rationalist analyses.

> Quant au dogme, sa valeur religieuse n'était soidisant sauvgardée que par un relativisme radical, où sa vérité dans l'histoire et dans l'esprit était en fait ruinée; tandis que d'autres ne ménageaient pas les vraies relativismes qui s'insèrent entre la révélation et les élaborations rationnelles qu'elle suscite.[68]

Chenu's many layered study of the 'conscience de l'histoire et théologie' in the twelfth century further contrasted the 'new' interpretations of time by Hugh of St Victor, Anselm of Havelberg, Otto of Freising, and John of Salisbury, distinguishing them from the traditional understandings attributed to the Bible, Augustine's *City of God*, and the ubiquitous 'seven ages of man'. These theologies of history, as he terms them, similarly arose from their proponents' need to explain the discrepancy between the questions raised by 'les événements du monde' and those asserted in sacred history.[69]

Chenu insisted that a study of Aquinas' theology in reference to the conflicts of his period, instead of its anachronistic deployment against Descartes, Kant, or Einstein, revealed that Aquinas assimilated differing contemporary and historical thought into 'cette «réduction» de cinq civilisations en l'unité d'une vie spirituelle'.[70] Chenu also raised the significant intellectual and cultural contributions of Eastern theology and Islam to medieval Christianity's self-

---

68. *Une école*, 38 [117].
69. 'Conscience de l'histoire et théologie', 84.
70. *Une école*, 105 (173).

understanding.⁷¹ Such alien formative influences on the epitome of so-called 'Catholicity' confounded the ideological revision of medieval Christianity as hermetic and changeless. Again, for Chenu, this history contained wider implications for contemporary Christianity besides its openness to movements and ideas beyond the restricted confines of the Church's understanding of mission. Christian faith had been formed in the past by exchanges and imports from various non-Christian sources and yet these critical correlations had enhanced rather than corrupted the truth of Revelation. The 'missing' factor of Islam in the history of Christian theology pointed not only to 'l'importance des sources arabes pour une étude technique des idées philosophiques au Moyen Âge' but to 'l'importance actuelle d'une religion comme l'Islam, à laquelle appartiennent plus de quatre cent millions d'hommes, qui a un passé tellement lié aux destins de l'Occident'.⁷² Again here, Chenu demonstrated from the presumed 'golden age' of Catholic theology the efficacy of theological engagement in the search for truth with the most hostile and exotic contemporary forces. From neo-scholasticism's claimed continuity with medieval Thomism then must proceed the implied affirmation of theological sources beyond the traditions of Christianity, and therefore the historical contingency of all theology. Instead of the ideological and nostalgic invocation of a selective past to resist the problem of change by ecclesial and political interests, Chenu concluded that change could no more be discounted from the medieval era than it could be ignored in the present.

> Chrétienté nouvelle, parce que le ferment qui fait lever la pâte est toujours neuf et frais; nouvelle, parce que la vraie conservation est une création continue.'⁷³

---

71. 'Philosophie Arabe', Section VI of 'Les études de philosophie médiévale', Philosophie: Chronique annuelle de l'Institut Internationale de Collaboration Philosophique, 813.III (1939), 1-87 (33-41). Le Goff acknowledges this influence, Jacques Le Goff, 'Le Père Chenu et la société médiévale' Revue des sciences philosophiques et theologiques, 81 (1997), 371-80 (375).
72. Chenu writing about Père Anawati, who was 'très attentif au mouvement des idées, à l'animation des cultures, aux possibilitees enrichissantes des échanges culturels', and the Dominican foundation of the Cairo Institute in 1938 cited in Brosse, 86.
73. *Dimension nouvelle de la Chrétienté*, 7.

'Je me présente comme historien de l'Évangile dans le Peuple de Dieu'[74]

Chenu recognised that history provided theology with a methodology that was not accidental to it but that inhered the reality of theology itself, as much as grammar, dialectic, and other philosophical methods adopted by theology. 'Aujourd'hui, après la grammaire, après la dialectique, après la science, c'était l'histoire qui se proposait comme instrument rationnel à la théologie.'[75] No longer could historical development in theology be dismissed as relativist without thereby endangering the veracity of historical Revelation, because the Gospel is history at work in the people of God.

> Il y avait là non seulement méconnaissance d'un ordre légitime de recherches, sur le plan de l'histoire, mais erreur théologique, s'il est vrai que c'est la loi même de l'économie de la révélation que Dieu se manifeste par et dans l'histoire, que l'éternel s'incarne dans le temps où seulement l'esprit de l'homme le peut atteindre.[76]

Here Chenu summarised his theology of history, typically centred on Revelation, the Incarnation, and continuing human participation in the development of theology. History is the locus and means chosen by God to disclose the economy of revelation. What is eternal, therefore timeless, chooses to be incarnated in time and enters history. Only through Revelation in history can humanity reach towards the eternal and incarnated mystery of God. For Chenu, the question of the development of doctrine required answers that upheld the historical and human mode of God's Revelation, what he termed the 'realism' of the human encounter with God in faith. In this way, Chenu's theology is historical and 'economic', in the Trinitarian sense, concerned with God's action in the world and history, while also formally 'théo-logique' in his concern to articulate God revealed through this world.

Chenu mapped a theology of history that is neither evolutionary nor a progressive convergence towards realisation of a divine Abso-

---

74. Chenu, 'La rénovation de la théologie morale. La loi nouvelle', *Supplément de la Vie Spirituelle*, 22.90 (1969): 287–297 (288).
75. *Une école*, 39 [118].
76. *Une école*, 37 [116].

lute, yet it includes an evolving understanding of Revelation and a progressive humanisation in history.[77] While Chenu acknowledged an Hegelian legacy through Möhler and Gardeil, this is checked by his Thomism, which maintains a strict ontological difference between the divinisation of humanity and God, the source of that divinisation. Chenu understood the economy of salvation to have an eschatological dynamic to it; God's plan is already being realised in history and contemporary affairs. The dynamic of the in-breaking of the Kingdom of God not only confounds a view of history that depicts humanity as passive before an unfolding progression in time, but it re-instates ordinary human affairs as revelatory of the divine will and its ends, just as the Incarnation made revelatory Christ's humanity and the ordinary human affairs Jesus inhabited. Chenu drew his understanding of history from Paul's and Irenaeus' doctrine of recapitulation of all things in Christ, that the Incarnation continues to renew all of creation, including humanity, until it reaches its fullest eschatological resolution in history.

> Cette vision d'une histoire par laquelle continuellement l'homme se fait, et dans laquelle, continuellement aussi, le Verbe se manifeste, a de quoi rénover la révélation biblique de la Création, et alimenter une «théologie de l'événement», sous la récapitulation de toute réalité dans le Christ.[78]

Yet history functions within the human condition of sin, hence ruptures bear the ambiguity of being moments of Gospel opportunity or measures of human limitation due to human tendencies to sin and destruction. Chenu's theology insisted that these moments cannot be prejudged to be inherently sinful without limiting the continuous realisation of Creation and Incarnation in history. Rather, as 'la double cause de la «novation» permanente', the newness in Creation and the Incarnation defines the Christian's response to the world and human affairs. Faithfulness to the double dimension of the divine mystery, according to Chenu, is 'la *présence* au monde' enacted in reading the 'signes des temps' to discern in human and world affairs salvation active in history.

---

77. *Une école*, 65 [140].
78. 'La rénovation de la théologie morale', 293.

> C'est précisément cette distention dans le temps (et dans l'espace) qui introduit dans la fidélité à une identique économie les surfaces psychologiques, sociales, politiques de l'histoire de l'humanité. Les impacts évangéliques seront discernés là où les événements sont les «signes des temps».[79]

Fundamental to Chenu's conversion of these events into 'signes' was the Thomist respect for the autonomy of natural causes and human freedom, which is enhanced by the convergence between human aspirations for good and the Gospel vision of the future.

> sa conception de l'homme-dans-le-monde fournit les bases d'une sociologie où l'efficacité et l'intelligibilité des cause secondes, loin de concurrencer l'éternelle providence de Dieu, la réalisent dans le temps et dans la vérité terrestre de l'histoire, la sainte et profane.[80]

So it is no coincidence then, in his view, that just as in general human affairs a new historical consciousness emerged, so Christianity came to understand itself less in timeless, continuous, and institutional terms, than as the herald of the Revelation of God's hopes for humanity now and into the future.

> ce n'est pas par hasard que le chrétien devient plus attentif à l'originalité de l'économie du salut, au moment où l'homme prend une très vive conscience de l'historicité de sa nature. Convergence normale, s'il est vrai que la foi, incarnée dans le sujet humain, se moule dans ses structures et dans ses évolutions.[81]

Chenu identified the watershed evangelical awakening of the twelfth century with subsequent breakthroughs in the history of western thought, intending resonance with the eighteenth century 'Enlightenment', while suggesting a check on its claims to be the exclusively critical breakthrough. He cited the 'monde «moderne» du Quattrocento' and the 'nouveaux types d'intelligibilité', which he lists as

---

79. 'La rénovation de la théologie morale', 292.
80. Chenu, 'Situation humaine: corporalité et temporalité' (1958), in *La Parole de Dieu II: L'Évangile dans le Temps* (Paris: Éditions du Cerf, 1964), 427.
81. 'Histoire du salut', 29.

'Léonard da Vinci, Copernic, Galilée,—Descartes surtout', and finally the historical critical turn of the late nineteenth and twentieth centuries.[82] For Chenu, the parallel was in the dramatic turns these '*conjonctures*' marked, the challenges they made to the preaching of the Gospel, and the subsequent reforms or shifts they demanded of the Church. Primarily these were shifts from a sacralised world-view to one which engaged the Church to bridge the sacred and the secular, for him an opposition rendered redundant by the Revelation of Creation and the Incarnation.

Conclusion

More than a new theological method or a correlative source for theology, history is itself revelatory for theology. As early as *Une école de théologie: le Saulchoir*, Chenu developed the theological link between history and 'l'économie de la révélation' as the *locus* and means by which the Gospel is revealed. For Chenu, this is a theology of history in the strictest sense: God, the object of theology, enters history as Creator and incarnate Saviour, so the reality of God consists of a reference to time and history and all the disruptions and setbacks that punctuate human existence in the world. Modern industrialisation posed for the Church another rupture of significant proportions that evidenced for Chenu an opportunity for a new evangelisation through a revision of theological understanding of the human activity of work. 'La théologie du travail' was Chenu's most extensive theological subject after the Church and in the next chapter provides evidence for the specifically anthropological starting-point of all his theology.

---

82. *Une école*, 88 [159]

Chapter 6
Chenu's Socio-political Christian Anthropology

> 'Double et unique transformation qui bouleversait les rapports de l'homme et de la nature. Le passage de l'outil à la machine a non seulement ouvert une nouvelle phase de l'économie, mais inauguré un nouvel âge de l'humanité'.
> Chenu, *Pour une théologie du travail* (Paris: Seuil, 1955), 13–14.

Of all Chenu's writing, that on work and the theological significance of the working classes presents his most developed theological anthropology. While work was the focus through which Chenu examined the challenges posed by the alienation of industrialised labour and Marxism to the contemporary Church, this chapter will argue that his theology of work is more a theology of the new understanding of humanity that emerged from the struggles of organised labour in the twentieth century. This assertion goes someway towards explaining the very abstract quality of his theology on work and the paucity of experiential reflection, which is atypical of his theology. It also heightens the focus on humanity, instead of the over-sacralised emphasis on the Incarnation in some readings of his theology.

This is evident in Chenu's programme in the eponymous chapter of the collection of essays in *Pour une théologie du travail*. There he proposed that a fuller Christian response to work could draw on four anthropological sources for constructing such a theology: 'l'homme et l'univers', 'l'homme lui-même', 'l'économie totale du salut', and 'l'Incarnation'.[1] These offer a thematic framework for determining how Chenu addressed a Christian anthropology through his theolo-

---

1. Chenu, *Pour une théologie du travail* (Paris: Seuil, 1955), 28–30.

gising on work. In this chapter, these subjects will be employed as themes that Chenu identified about the new humanity of industrial work: the condition of humanity, humanity and the universe, and humanity in the whole economy of salvation. Chenu's understanding of the Incarnation underpins each of these themes. This chapter will also demonstrate how some critics of Chenu have underestimated this anthropological stress as the principal object of his writing in their judgement of his theology on work.

A theology of work?

Chenu first wrote about 'Le monde du travail, lieu privilégié de l'Incarnation' in 'Dimension nouvelle de la Chrétienté' in 1937, 'Classes et Corps mystique du Christ' in 1939, then in the pamphlet *Spiritualité du travail* in 1941.[2] The pastoral and political context for these works was France's rapid post-World War II industrialisation and the surge in atheism across the wider population partly influenced by popularisation of Marxist and existentialist unbelief. Chenu addressed his theology of work for an audience consisting of worker-priests and their fellow Christian-activist workers, a specialist group of workers committed to theological reflection on their lives and work.[3]

Pour une théologie du travail (1955) collected three articles originally delivered at the annual *Semaines sociales* for worker-priests: the earliest was 'L'«homo œconomicus» et le chrétien' of 1945; then 'Le devenir social' (1947); and a reworked version of the 1952 'Pour

---

2. 'Dimension nouvelle de la Chrétienté', in *Vie Intellectuelle*, LIII (1937): 325-351. 'Classes et Corps mystique du Christ' (Bordeaux: Semaines sociales de France, session 31, 1939), [republished in *La Parole de Dieu. II. Évangile dans le temps*, 477-494.]; *Spiritualité du travail* (Paris: Éditions de temps présent, 1941). Other early publications on work include: a section in 'La foi en Chrétienté' (1944) [republished in *La Parole de Dieu. II*, 109-132], 'Révolution économique et révolution spirituelle', in *Revue de l'Économie contemporaine* (juin 1944): 30-32, 'La notion de profit et les principes chrétiens' (Toulouse: Semaines sociales de France, session 32, 1945), [republished in *La Parole de Dieu. II*, 495-514], 'Civilisation technique et spiritualité nouvelle', in *Masses Ouvrières* (mai, 1948): 14-37, [republished in *La Parole de Dieu. II*, 137-158], and 'Corps de l'Église et structures sociales', *Jeunesse de l'Église* (1948), 145-153, [republished in *La Parole de Dieu. II*, 159-170]
3. Robert Wattebled, *Stratégies Catholiques en monde ouvrier dans la France d'après-guerre* (Paris: Éditions Ouvrières, 1990), 22-25, 128-130, 178-181.

une théologie du travail'.[4] 'Pour une théologie du travail' provides an introduction to the argument of the other earlier pieces. All three articles appear to be in some dialogue with the topics and historical examples in Marx's *The German Ideology*.[5]

Chenu was early exposed to the problems faced by industrialised labour, initially in collaboration with Fr Joseph Cardijn's young workers' movement, *Jeunesse Ouvrière Chrétienne* (JOC), at the Belgian site of Le Saulchoir in 1924. The Dominicans offered sympathetic assistance in the formation of JOCist leaders and with Abbé Guerin introduced the movement to France in 1926. Significantly, also in 1934 Chenu encouraged two of his young student friars to do their pastoral experience working as miners in Charleroi, Belgium.[6] For Chenu and the worker-priests, this urgently needed evangelisation was not understood solely as a struggle for the workers' souls against the evils of communism, but rather as the contemporary manifestation of the Gospel witness to all peoples, regardless of class. The crucial issue for Chenu was the place of history in theology, all history. This was a pertinent example of historical reality unfolding in contemporary events, demanding the attention of theology: 'une attention directe à son contenu objectif, pour discerner la valeur originale que ce contenu, économique et humain, pouvait contracter, à le considérer dans sa relation possible avec le gouvernement de Dieu sur le monde.'[7]

---

4. 'L'«homo œconomicus» et le chrétien. Réflexions d'un théologien à propos du marxisme', in *Économie et humanisme* (mai-juin 1945): 225–236. [republished in *Pour une théologie du travail*, 43–65.]; 'La conception du devenir social' (Lyon: Semaines sociales de France, session 34, Paris, 1947). [republished in *Pour une théologie du travail*, 69–108.]; 'Pour une théologie du travail', in *Esprit* (janvier 1952): 1–12. [republished in *Pour une théologie du travail*, 9–39.] The 1955 version also added an appendix of nine pages, 'Un texte de saint Maxime († 668) sur le rapport de l'homme et de la nature' added by Chenu at the time of publishing. RJ Keller OP, 'Toward a Contemporary Roman Catholic Theology of Work' (unpublished doctoral thesis, Graduate Theological Union, University of San Francisco, 1993), 44.
5. Karl Marx and Friedrich Engels, *The German Ideology*, Part 1 (London: Lawrence and Wishart, 1977). There is no direct evidence from Chenu to identify this source, nor which edition or French translation he used.
6. Chenu in *Un théologien en liberté*, 144; *cf* also Leprieur, *Quand Rome condamne: Dominicains et prêtres-ouvriers* (Paris: Plon et Cerf, 1989), 23.
7. 'Pour une théologie du travail', 12.

Definition of work

Chenu chose the theme of work to present his theology of humanity because it is the daily reality commonly experienced by all humans, more participated in than politics and contemplation or worship. Typically, his definition of work was consigned to a footnote while he devoted paragraphs to charting the human *situation* of work, in creation, the world, history, social evolution, and at the nexus ('jonction') of matter and spirit:

> Le mot *travail* est toujours pris ici, comme dans la langue et dans la mentalité contemporaines, dans son sens complet, au-delà de sa matérialité, avec tout l'engagement corporel, psychologique, social, qui comporte la fabrication à tous ses niveaux. [8]

Clearly, Aquinas' encompassing concept of labour was behind this definition.[9] Chenu was also influenced by Marx's emphasis on the universality of the phenomenon of human work, which rejected the Christian denigration of work as a punishment for fallen humanity.[10] Work was also not to be understood in terms of a romantic dignifying of pre-industrial peasant or artisan labour, nor as an educating discipline, nor as an asceticism that mimics post-lapsarian suffering.[11] Chenu questioned the social division of labour that assigned to the world of ideas greater value than that of manual labour. While a moral duty specific to one's station in life applied to all work, for Chenu this insufficiently defined the theological magnitude of work.[12]

---

8. 'Pour une théologie du travail' in *Pour une théologie du travail*, 13, n 1.
9. 'Sciendum tamen quod sub opere manuali intelliguntur omnia humana officia ex quibus homines licite victum lucrantur, sive manibus, sive pedibus, sive lingua fiant' ['But it should be noted that by manual labour are understood all the human activities by which men lawfully earn their livelihood, whether by the use of their hands, feet or tongue.'] Aquinas, *Summa theologiae* IIa IIae. q. 187, a.3, responsio.
10. Chenu also rejected the concept of work as an expiation for sin in *La 'doctrine sociale' de l'Église comme idéologie*, 23.
11. 'Pour une théologie du travail', 15. Chenu's longer assessment of the individualism implicit in the peasant-worker model and its ideological origins in 'le droit «inaliénable et sacré» de la propriété' of the French Revolution appeared in *La 'doctrine sociale' de l'Église comme idéologie*, 40–41.
12. 'Pour une théologie du travail', 12.

The influence of Marx can also be seen in Chenu's observation that while humans have always worked, the awareness needed to discern the ends and historical purpose of work only occurred with the emergence of the collective consciousness initiated by industrialisation. Through industrialisation, all life has been affected to a degree unparalleled in the pre-industrial world; modern work has completely changed the relations between humanity and nature.[13] Unlike twentieth century Marxist-Leninism, Chenu did not atttribute the absolute meaning of humanity to work.[14] Humanity is made for more than work. Its consubstantiality of matter and spirit, body and soul, physicality and mindfulness impels it beyond itself and work, so that its further destiny in God is revealed. Chenu conceded to the Marxist view that the advance in knowledge brought by work's rational and virtuous manipulation of nature had redefined a new humanity.[15] Chenu accepted the Marxist assertion that the social division of labour is an ideological superstructure, which falsely claimed priority for consciousness, the spiritual, over all work, because work involved a demeaning engagement with matter:

> le travail qui les fait accoucher, est un acte majeur de l'homme adulte, et il ne faut, ni à droit, ni à gauche, le contreposer à la contemplation. Le sage chrétien, à l'encontre de l'aristocratique sage grec, comme du spiritualiste cartésian, trouve son unité dans ces deux fonctions conjugées.[16]

Chenu goes beyond Marx in insisting that work overcomes the classically conceived resistance of matter through its spiritual transformation of matter, challenging the long-held discontinuity between matter and spirit. The vocation of all humanity, then, is its ontological and existential consubstantial union of matter and spirit, in turn transforming matter and history through its material-spiritual invention.

---

13. 'Pour une théologie du travail', 13.
14. 'Marx—in spite of his successors and his enemies—never tried to reduce the human person to a *Homo œconomicus*.' Otto Maduro, 'Labour and Religion according to Karl Marx', in G Baum, editor, 'Work and Religion', in *Concilium* 131 (1980), 14.
15. 'Pour une théologie du travail', 18.
16. 'Pour une théologie du travail', 19.

> L'homme est précisément l'être qui, indissolublement et consubstantiellement matière et esprit, est apte par-là même à porter dans l'histoire le mystère de l'esprit.[17]

Through work is disclosed the ultimate spiritual destiny of humanity in history.

At times, Chenu's theology of work fails to acknowledge the destructive results of this industrialisation. His optimism about the new humanity emerging through this work does tend to damp the alienation and repetitious determinism affecting workers. He dismissed discussing the negative effects of the assembly-line on humans, as these were already studied psychologically.[18] This is not an abdication of theology to peripheral observation only, as proscribed by the ideologues of the Enlightenment.[19] Rather, Chenu is adamant about the autonomy of human knowledge, that it cannot be checked by 'le cléricalisme intellectuel'.[20] So what could appear to be disengagement with the lot of the workers is a call for the appropriate use of theology, not in a clericalist wariness of the social sciences.

Yet, while Chenu was not proposing an ideal assessment of industrialisation nor a rose-coloured picture of the actual experience of mechanised industry, he fails to discuss the conditions of industrialised work. This is because he addressed people who actually worked in the factories and on the docks: he did not reprise their experience. Instead, he sought to theologise from their experience, while acknowledging the dehumanising conditions, refusing to abandon this industrialised world to existing outside of the theological domain. He discerned in the experiences that they had shared in the JOCist reflection process, the presence of an awakened humanity which offered an understanding beyond the too apparent exploitation

---

17. 'Pour une théologie du travail', 24.
18. 'Pour une théologie du travail', 31.
19. Chenu asserted: 'L'autonomie des objets et des méthodes est la loi essentielle du savoir humain', 'L'homo oeconomicus', 43; also 'Le devenir social', 71. John Hughes misses the context of such critical comments by Chenu and reads him as separating theology from critical involvement with human knowledge, like economics. This converts Chenu's position into the very isolation of faith from life that he thoroughly resisted. *The End of Work* (Oxford: Blackwell, 2007), 16.
20. 'L'homo oeconomicus', 43-4.

and alienation of industrialisation.[21] Therefore, Chenu's writings on work were a middle stage of a process of theologising, concluded by the workers' discernment of their praxis in the future.[22] The absence of material on work itself, while unsatisfactory for a reader seeking such content from a 'genitive theology' of work, points both to the responsive style of Chenu's theology, in the process of theologising on work, and the anthropological focus of this theology. Further, this demonstrates how his theological method employed contemporary human experience without falling into what Congar criticised as the tendency to fuse theology and life in the style of *Lebenstheologie*.[23] For Chenu, the true subject of his theology of work is the relationship of this 'new' humanity to God: a Christian anthropology.

Chenu's theology and Marxism

Chenu drew on Marxist thought as the contemporary interlocutor of his theology of work, while he critically engaged Marxism. He accepted what he called the metaphysical Marxist analysis of work: in the relations of production, the alienation of work under capitalism, its communal power, and the historic possibilities in proletarian consciousness. While he rejected the ideology of work as the total conception of humanity, class struggle and communist totalitarianism as tragically erroneous, he welcomed the recognition of the historical mission of work in the rise of the proletariat and the democratising of freedom and justice. Chenu judged that while contemplation may be the highest expression of the life of the spirit in us, it is pretentious to assert this in the face of the reality that it is work where spiritual and material unity is most experienced by most people.[24]

---

21. The *JOC*ist reflection process employed the actions of 'see', describing the person's lived reality in terms of events; 'judge', evaluating the participants and dynamics of this experience in the 'light of the Gospel'; and 'act', discerning an appropriate response. I would locate Chenu's theology of work in the 'judge' stage.
22. The *JOC*ist method for Chenu was equivalent to how he understood the medieval theological process of *disputatio* provided the genre for his interpretation of Aquinas' method in the *Summa theologiae*. Chenu, *Introduction à l'étude de Saint Thomas d'Aquin*, 82, 73–81.
23. Fergus Kerr OP, 'Yves Congar and Thomism' in Gabriel Flynn, editor, *Yves Congar Theologian of the Church* (Louvain: Peeters, 2005), 67–97, 71–72.
24. 'L'«homo œconomicus» et le chrétien' in *Pour une théologie du travail*, 56.

> Produire, fabriquer, c'est l'activité typique de l'homme, celle qu'il peut mener à son terme, parce qu'elle est à la mesure de son esprit, d'un esprit incarné dans la matière et trouvant sa perfection dans le traitement des objets matériels, tandis que contempler est oeuvre surhumaine, démésurée pour notre âme corporelle.[25]

He was emphatic that theology cannot merely select from Marxist economics without negotiating the atheism of Marxism that permeates every level of this humanism. This judgement no doubt was partly shaped by the antagonism to communism in Catholicism and international politics at that time.

Today, the typical poverty and social disadvantage of the industrialisation of the mid-twentieth century has moved to the emergent capitalist developing economies. In the information technology revolutions of the late twentieth and twenty-first centuries, the developed post-industrial economies engender different social injustices, like under-employment and unemployment. Chenu's optimism about the 'new civilisation of work' could present as rather dated, yet this does not appear to have diminished interest in his theological-anthropological analysis of work, as evidenced in recent writing, and its implications for the Christian community. As later theologians have shown, there is value in a more dynamic reading of the Marxist critique of religion, with its challenge to convert faith from its ideological collusion with capitalism.[26] But Chenu also emphasised that while theology has no economic expertise of itself, because of the significance of economics to human experience, it needs to be addressed by theology.[27]

Pour une théologie du travail—a thematic Framework

Chenu defined theology as reflection on human reality as it shares in and relates to the economy of salvation.[28] In 'Pour une théologie

---

25. *Pour une théologie du travail*, 57.
26. Nicholas Lash, *A Matter of Hope: A Theologian's Reflections on the Thought of Marx* (London: Darton, Longman and Todd, 1981); Otto Maduro, 'Labour and Religion according to Karl Marx', 19–20; Philip West, 'Towards a Christian Theology of Work: A Critical Appropriation of the Thought of Jurgen Habermas', unpublished PhD thesis, University of Cambridge, 1986.
27. West, 'Towards a Christian Theology of Work', 45.
28. 'Pour une théologie du travail', 11.

du travail', Chenu chose as his starting point a survey of work in its human and material reality, tracing the ontology of work in Creation and the human condition.[29] Then he considered work in history, observing that before an adequate theology for modern work could be developed, a theology that acknowledged scientific autonomy was necessary. Biblical and pre-modern theological sources were therefore inadequate being bridled to pre-modern economic contexts.[30] So work is presented as a valid subject for theology. Workers are understood as agents in sacred history because of their material agency in world history, as explored in 'L'homo œconomicus et le chrétien'. The movement of human society into collective consciousness is charted as thick with signs of the reign of God in the eschatological social anthropology of 'Le devenir social'.[31] Like the social ruptures of the twelfth and thirteenth centuries responded to by earlier Dominicans, Chenu called for similar recognition by the church of the workers in the twentieth century: 'Plus ils sont fidèles au ferment évangélique, plus, dans cette pureté, ils peuvent s'incerner dans ce monde nouveau'.[32] Hence while Chenu's topic was a theology of work, through it he reveals the comprehensive density of his Christian anthropology.

Human condition

In the article 'Pour une théologie du travail', Chenu announced that humanity had assumed a new understanding of its condition through its reason and the discoveries this produced. Humanity was creating 'un monde nouveau, un monde humain.'[33] Through this theme it can be considered how Chenu conceived the theological meaning of this understanding in Christian anthropological terms.

Chenu concurred with the Marxist view that labour is not only a means of human survival but is also the locus for understanding the meaning of contemporary humanity and its purpose. Marx's rejection of Hegelian idealism paralleled for Chenu his own theological rejec-

---

29. 'plus l'homme travaille, plus Dieu est Créateur.' Chenu, 'Théologie du travail' in *La Parole de Dieu II: L'Évangile dans le temps*, 543–570, 558.
30. 'Pour une théologie du travail', 13–14; Chenu, 'Travail' in *Encyclopédie de la foi*, volume VI (Paris: Cerf, 1967), 371.
31. 'Pour une théologie du travail', 35–37.
32. 'Le devenir social' in *Pour une théologie du travail*, 83.
33. 'Pour une théologie du travail' in *Pour une théologie du travail*, 17.

tion of the idealism on which Catholic social doctrine was based.[34] He particularly welcomed the Marxist derivation of the meaning of work from actual human experience. Marxist humanism provided a total conception of humanity, including beliefs and values, elaborated by participation in work and its economy with a vision of the future. Yet these were inseparable from a truly spiritual understanding for Chenu: 'C'est à une révolution spirituelle que nous assistons, au sein même d'une révolution économique.'[35] Marx's promotion of the unique role of the proletariat in human history provided Chenu with the example of an anthropology grounded in realism, which could be employed theologically to address humanity's alienation from the value of its labour. Chenu believed that theology needed to emulate how Marx had accorded philosophical and historical significance to work and the humanity it advanced, in order to be faithful to the Incarnational affirmation of humanity.

Chenu did not dispute with Marxism as did Jacques Maritain in *Humanisme intégral*, exhorting the restoration of a Christian political presence in society.[36] Chenu frequently cited Maritain and Emmanuel Mounier, the founder of *Esprit*, especially for their recognition of the new condition and consciousness of humanity as workers and their historic role.[37] Chenu's project was not restorationist; instead, he consciously reproduced Albert the Great's and Aquinas' contemporary engagement with Aristotelian thought, by employing Marx-

---

34. This is more fully developed in his critique of Catholic social doctrine in Chenu, La *'doctrine sociale' de l'Église comme idéologie* (Paris: Cerf, 1979).
35. 'L'homo œconomicus et le chrétien' in *Pour une théologie du travail*, 55. Here he echos Emmanuel Mounier's gloss on Peguy's aphorism about the necessity for the economic revolution to be moral as well. R William Rauch, *Politics and Belief in Contemporary France: Emmanuel Mounier and Christian Democracy, 1932-1950* (The Hague: Martinus Nijhoff, 1972), 82-3.
36. Jacques Maritain, *Humanisme integral* (Paris: Aubier, 1936). Chenu later commented that 'Maritain n'a pas appliqué expressément cette formule [*Distinguer pour unir*] en réunion des deux opérations dans le registre politique', despite Chenu's debt to his *Humanisme intégral*. Duquesne, 77-8.
37. 'L'homo œconomicus et le chrétien', 54. An example of the difference in approach of Maritain and Chenu is Maritain's application of Aquinas' thought to the twentieth century to reclaim the Christian past of Europe, while Chenu understood that the Gospel requires more real engagement with the movements of each era rather than the restoration of Christendom, especially a 'spiritual Christendom'. Chenu developed this further in La *"doctrine sociale" de l'Église comme idéologie*.

ist insights, historical examples and methods in his theology. In the article 'L'homo œconomicus et le chrétien', Chenu found in Marx's realism and historical materialism a profound human understanding that was 'mystique et prophétique autant que doctrinal', rather as Aquinas had drawn on the realism of Aristotle's metaphysics.[38]

Chenu's anthropology also proceeded from Aquinas' principle of the ontological unity of matter and spirit, body and soul in humanity.[39] This key theme of 'consubstantiality' paralleled the consubstantiality of the human and divine natures in Christ and the coexistence of the individual and others in society, in a way that such collectivism does not cancel out the uniqueness of the person.[40] It is in work that humanity brings together the material and spiritual in order to preserve human life, but also transforms and directs life towards the fullness of being, the union of humanity and God in Christ, the fullness of humanity.[41] Chenu insisted that like 'carnal love', work is the vehicle of God's love in the world, consubstantially uniting matter and spirit and restoring the unity of grace and nature in human history.[42] In terms he borrowed from Mounier, humanity becomes itself through work, as '*homo artifex*': '*la nature de l'homme c'est l'artifice*', through the human urge to discover, to reason, and human virtue, a new world is created, a more human world.[43] This quality is why the reduction of a human's work merely to the function of a commodity

---

38. 'L'homo œconomicus et le chrétien', 59.
39. 'Le devenir social' in *Pour une théologie du travail*, 104–5.
40. 'Pour une théologie du travail', 36; also Chenu, 'La révolution communitaire et l'apostolat', *Masses ouvrières* (mars 1944), 23-24. [republished in *La Parole de Dieu. II. Évangile dans le temps*, 363-378].
41. 'Pour une théologie du travail', 36, and 'Le devenir social', 105. Also in the notes 'Un texte de saint Maxime († 668) sur le rapport de l'homme et de la nature' citing Balthasar's gloss on Maximus the Confessor, 117: 'La base de cette vision du rôle de l'homme, dans son rapport avec la nature, est évidemment la conception selon laquelle matière et esprit le constituent dans une union consubstantielle.'
42. 'Pour une théologie du travail', 25. Chenu's equation of 'carnal love' (ie not only as procreative love) and collective work here with propagating God's love is all the more remarkable on both counts given the traditional functionalist view of sexual ethics prevalent when Chenu was writing this piece.
43. 'Pour une théologie du travail', 17, citing Emmanuel Mounier, 'Pour un temps d'apocalypse' in *La petite peur du XXe siècle* (Paris: Éditions du Seuil, 1948), 29. On the use of "artifice" here see Chenu's observation on the medieval meaning of 'artificialis' as 'abstract' (in the creative sense not disparaging) in *Introduction à l'étude de Saint Thomas d'Aquin*, 136.

for use is falsely objectifying and thereby alienating of their humanity. Similarly, for Chenu, the pious objectification of the worker into a recipient of 'charity for the poor' is equally objectionable.[44] This theological appropriation of work as constitutive of human nature demonstrates how much Chenu's anthropology was developing beyond traditional theological loci.

Chenu claimed that work has not changed human nature, but the human condition has been changed by the change in work. It is through socialised work and its often dehumanising alienation that humanity is driven to claim itself, discovering its self-realisation in both the possibilities and the restrictions on its freedom occasioned by this new form of work. Chenu described this as a change of accidents in the metaphysical makeup of humanity.[45] It is noteworthy here that Chenu recognised again the possibilities, not merely the 'échecs', that the new conditions of work provided in human history. Yet he was alert to the dangers for humanity of alienating work:

> C'est que dans la mesure même où l'homme s'aliénait dans le travail, il perdait Dieu en même temps que lui-même. Le travail ne pouvait plus avoir un sens religieux, parce qu'il n'avait plus de sens humain.

No wonder he concluded that work has been deified by some in their attempts to satisfy their need for the sacred in their lives.[46] At the same time, Chenu was critical of how Christians resisted these revelations about their common humanity. 'Misère d'une certaine piété qui n'a pas compris ce que c'est pour Dieu que de se faire homme.'[47] He lamented how the social responsibility so integral to the Gospel appeared insufficient to equip Christians to respond to human misery except through charity. While it was an esteem for the poor and the dignity of the dispossessed that promoted the Gospel hunger and thirst for justice, contemporary Christianity had failed to be drawn into such brotherly communion.[48] Chenu argued that these characteristics should be magnificent resources for appreciating the trag-

---

44. 'Pour une théologie du travail', 15.
45. 'Pour une théologie du travail', 31.
46. 'Pour une théologie du travail', 27–28.
47. 'L'homo œconomicus et le chrétien', 60.
48. 'L'homo œconomicus et le chrétien', 60.

edy of the masses under industrialisation. His question, 'Comment le chrétien assiste-t-il à cette émouvante découverte de l'homme?',[49] indicated the theological-anthropological significance of such denial. For Chenu, this was not a moral failure on the part of Christians but a lack of humanity, a refusal to become more human and create a new future from the invitation revealed through modern industrialised work. His more damning contrast was to note Marx's extensive response to these new conditions, which included a metaphysics of work, a sociology of community, and a dialectic of history. 'Il construisit même, son messianisme à lui seul en fait foi, une religion, une "théologie". Mais ce fut dans l'athéisme.'[50] Marx's atheism filled the vacuum with a regard for humanity that Christianity failed to see.

In this massed work, humans began to transcend their own individual and familial interests for a collective identity that also called them into the service of each other. It created a new social energy that extended human interests beyond working for survival.

> Au lieu de la juxtaposition opaque, de la présence brute, 'objective' des individus les uns aux autres, c'est une présence spirituelle, dans un instinct fraternel développant une température sociale jusqu'alors insensible.[51]

If human societies are to survive into the future, he proposed, they cannot be merely collections of individuals but will be communities of persons in terms of their reciprocity to others, who find in this spiritual and economic collaboration their destiny.[52] It is from the dynamic tension between person and society that Chenu found the profound reality inscribed in the very nature of humanity: the expression of this social evolution, what it means to enter into the course of history.[53] Greater involvement in community has been the significant outcome of the emancipation of people across the centuries.[54] Also with the emergence of the collective consciousness of the proletariat, Chenu saw the movement of humanity toward its created destiny as

---

49. 'L'homo œconomicus et le chrétien', 59
50. 'L'homo œconomicus et le chrétien', 61.
51. 'Pour une théologie du travail', 22.
52. 'Le devenir social', 100.
53. 'Le devenir social', 74.
54. 'Le devenir social', 73.

involved with the salvation of the world: 'Les masses prolétariennes sont destinées à faire passer dans l'être cette volonté et cette espérance: elles rachèteront le monde.'[55]

Chenu concluded that the task of theology was to address the problem of humanity through these new resources proclaimed initially by a non-Christian prophetic movement in personal and communal, metaphysical, and historical dimensions. Humanity through work had come to a new understanding not only of itself but also of its relation to the whole of creation.

Humanity and the universe

The 'humanisme du travail' revolutionised relations between humanity and nature. Work is the key factor in humanisation, the pivot of socialisation, and decisive for humanity's impact on creation: 'L'homme et l'univers: le travail est leur jonction.'[56] Chenu described how the shift to mechanised production initiated a qualitative transformation of work that modified humanity's relationships as a whole and gave the encounter between humanity and nature a new significance.[57] Chenu emphasised how this refuted the prejudice against technology: work is neither a profane nor defiant Promethean effort to dominate nature. Human reason discerns the causalities and purpose in things in the universe using the same rationalisation of time and resources that marked industrialisation. This rational output affirms that humans are made in the image of God, while, through the unique power of the dual nature of these functions, humans also operate in autonomous, epistemologically sophisticated and interior freedom that does not eliminate their reflection of God.[58] The utilisation of our reason in the technical organisation of work propels humanity into a collective self-understanding, which is a shift equivalent to the human developmental shift into adulthood. It is a movement beyond what Chenu termed the infantile Enlightenment world-view of Newton and Descartes.[59] The result of their desacralising the world and deeming it inanimate was that they could allow

---

55. *Pour une théologie du travail*, 58–9.
56. *Pour une théologie du travail*, 28.
57. 'Pour une théologie du travail', 16.
58. 'Pour une théologie du travail', 18.
59. 'Pour une théologie du travail', 19

the world only the life they were able to see, just as a child's totally self-referenced perception of reality discovers and fixes on one thing to the exclusion of all else.[60] Chenu concurred, then, with Marx that the transformation of work brought about by industrialisation inaugurated a new age for humanity in the universe.[61]

Work, in the theological understanding of Genesis, is a dynamic relationship whereby humanity is a collaborator and participant in the continuation of creation. In contrast to a deist view of God's separateness from creation, Chenu asserted that God did not create a finished universe, static and indifferent to the lives it produced. Humanity is called to participate in the divine creativity.[62] This identification of 'l'homme collaborateur de la création et démiurge de son évolution' was not an idealisation of human work. Chenu understood that work imposes a responsibility that is theological in its implication: going beyond the moral duty of creaturehood, work is humanity's relationship to the Creator through the human transformation of matter. Through the socialised work effected by industrialisation, humanity realises this role and the freedom it confirms economically as an agent and cause. Yet it is only through these same economics of industrialisation that humanity had its relationship to matter clarified, and becomes conscious of its historic and cosmic significance. 'La machine est l'instrument de cette entreprise créatice.'[63] Chenu concluded that humanity is not reducible merely to an analysis of concepts and statistics; rather, it is inscribed already in history. 'La science de l'homme . . . s'inscrit dans le mouvement historique qui réalise l'homme et construit la communauté.'[64] Humanity constructs community through struggle with the conflicting forces of chaos. 'Le monde a été donné à l'homme pour qu'il en achève la création, là même où il en tire de quoi satisfaire ses besoins.'[65]

---

60. Chenu here refered to another theme of Mounier's that he had cited earlier: 'l'homme européen a achevé vers l'aurore des temps modernes une sorte de vie utérine'. E Mounier, 'Pour un temps d'apocalypse', 30.
61. 'Pour une théologie du travail', 20.
62. 'Travail' in *Encyclopédie de la foi*, volume VI (Paris: Cerf, 1967), 371; *Pour une théologie du travail*, 28.
63. *Pour une théologie du travail*, 29.
64. 'L'homo œconomicus et le chrétien', 58.
65. 'L'homo œconomicus et le chrétien', 57.

Chenu was concerned to link the creation and redemption which had been too often separated in theology, in terms of the relationship of nature and grace.[66]

> Est expurgée, ou presque, cette néfaste disjonction entre la Création qui fonderait la *nature* et la Rédemption qui conférerait la *grâce*. Ce dualisme, qui a infecté la structure même de la théologie, est désormais évacué, sans détriment d'ailleurs pour les opportunes distinctions que comporte l'analyse de deux ordres, lors même qu'on les articule dans une histoire unique.[67]

Chenu added that this humanisation through work is the final end of humanity, the restoration and realisation in grace of the Creator's intention for all humanity and creation. 'C'était à la fois réhabiliter le travail sous toutes ses formes, et restaurer le primat de la Création dans la vision théologique de l'histoire'.[68] It is because God's grace finds its point of insertion into all life through the human life of Christ, that human work, 'la spiritualisation de la nature', continues to reveal the creative and saving acts of God.[69] Chenu recalled Irenaeus' under-

---

66. Chenu did concede that strictly speaking 'man is the "co-creator" is theologically inaccurate' with the reservation: 'He is charged with the task of assembling and recapitualting in himself the whole series of being . . . Man in his freedom, with intelligence and love, is the demiurge of that return.' Chenu, 'The Need for a Theology of the World', in R Hutchins and M Adler, editors, *Great Ideas Today* (Chicago: Encyclopaedia Britannica, 1967), 54–69, 61. *Cf* also Stanley Hauerwas, 'Work as Co-Creation: A Critique of a Remarkably Bad Idea' in John W Houck and Oliver F Williams, editors, *Co-Creation and Capitalism: John Paul II's Laborem Exercens* (Lanham: University Press of America, 1983), 42–58. JPG-Chenu concurs that: 'man is the "co-creator" of the universe, although, strictly speaking, this is theologically inaccurate.' but distinguishes humanity as both active and passive in the new creation, within the neo-platonic "exitus-reditus" paradigm: 'He is charged with the task of assembling and recapitualting in himslef the whole series of being. . . . Man in his freedom, with intelligence and love, is the demiurge of that return.'
Marie-Dominique Chenu, 'The Need for a Theology of the World', in Great Ideas Today, edited by R. Hutchins and M. Adler, [supplement to Great Books of the Western World] (editor) (Chicago: Encyclopaedia Britannica, 1967), 54–69, 61
67. Chenu, 'Trente ans après', in *Lumière et vie*, 4 (1975): 72–77, 73–74.
68. 'Trente ans après', 74.
69. 'Pour une théologie du travail', 28.

standing to support this.⁷⁰ Human work especially reflects the creative and redemptive activity of God since humanity is *homo artifex*, not merely *homo œconomicus*. Chenu located this revelation in the traditional anthropological terms of the relationship of nature and grace:

> Mais le dialectique de la nature et de la grâce peut jouer vis-à-vis de l'*homo oeconomicus* comme vis-à-vis de l'*homo naturalia*, car la grâce aujourd'hui précisément travaille à trouver toute sa dimension terrestre, dans une économie où la matière *dans* l'homme, est elle aussi sauvée.⁷¹

This called for the elaboration of a theology alert to the development of humanity as salvific across civilisations and history.⁷²

Humanity in the whole economy of salvation

Chenu's Christian anthropology identified an eschatological understanding of modern humanity, its destiny, and salvation. 'Le cosmos y entre, par l'homme, par le fait transformateur de l'homme précisément. Les cieux nouveaux et la terre nouvelle.'⁷³ This transformation does not naively ignore the reversals of sin and death while anticipating God's future. 'La perspective eschatologique accomplit, malgré la rupture de la mort, et n'évacue pas la perspective terrestre.'⁷⁴ The role of 'la perspective eschatologique' limits an erroneous optimism about the future. Chenu conceived this as founded in the ongoing reality of the Incarnation realised already in the positive outcomes of socialisation that emerge despite the negative outcomes of the initial stages of mass industrialisation.

> L'Incarnation continuée; le corps mystique du Christ; thème désormais classique d'une spiritualité' où le monde du travail trouve son équilibre et sa place chrétienne, et pas seulement par l'acquistion de mérites.⁷⁵

---

70. Irenaeus: 'Dieu a fait les choses dans le temps, pour que l'homme mûrissant en elles, donne son fruit d'immortalité.'
71. 'L'homo œconomicus et le chrétien', 65.
72. 'L'homo œconomicus et le chrétien', 65.
73. 'Pour une théologie du travail', 29.
74. 'Pour une théologie du travail', 29.
75. 'Pour une théologie du travail', 30.

Thus he rejected any bourgeois moralising about the value of human work as a counterfeit for the salvation already offered in the 'body of Christ' being realised in the world of work as much as any other part of creation. Yet he also recognised the risk of a naturalistic equating of the economy of salvation with human progress.[76]

This eschatological transformation was evidenced already for Chenu in the role of work in changing the structures of human organisation:

> sous la pression des déterminismes économiques et des progrès techniques, nous sommes, à tous les échelons de la vie sociale, comme acculés à un élargissement communautaire.[77]

He resisted what he termed a 'travailisme', which reduced the human to an isolated component of the industrial process.[78] Through work comes the human movement toward socialisation. Socialisation promoted through industrial work accelerates the full humanisation of persons and societies, through a concentration of people that extends each person's concern for the other beyond family and village commitments to a wider collective identity and purpose, which anticipates the wider communion of the reign of God.[79]

> Au lieu de la juxtaposition opaque, de la présence brute, "objective" des individus les uns aux autres, c'est une présence spirituelle, dans un instinct fraternel développant une température sociale jusqu'alors insensible.[80]

Crucial to this newly revealed collective nature of humanity were the working conditions of industrial production economies, not the pre-industrial skilled labour of individuals or trade-based small collectives. 'La civilisation du travail' emerges from the concentration of

---

76. 'Travail' in *Encyclopédie de la foi*, 371.
77. 'Le devenir social', 107–8.
78. 'Pour une théologie du travail', 21 and 'L'homo œconomicus et le chrétien', 63. 'Travailisme' for Chenu (94) was Taylor's US mass production 'scientific' work management, as in 'time and motion' studies. cf Frederick Winslow Taylor, *The Principles of Scientific Management* (New York: Norton, 1911).
79. 'Pour une théologie du travail', 25.
80. 'Pour une théologie du travail', 22.

populations and the raising of workers' consciousness.⁸¹ This affected all life, its spiritual as well as physical aspects. The relationship between humanity and nature was revolutionised and the economic structure of society was changed by the historic force of the proletariat. Chenu regretted 'le clericalisme intellectuel' that kept theology apart from this history entrenched in faith's timeless truths since the Enlightenment.⁸² This was a betrayal of the historicity of the Gospel, 'soit contre la théocratie l'autonomie du pouvoir politique'.⁸³

> Le monde moderne occidental est encore bâti à partir de principes et sur des fondements dont la sécularisation ne peut dissimuler l'origine religieuse. Le chrétien est donc tout disposé à observer, bien plus à favoriser, l'émergence de ces puissances nouvelles que l'homme portait depuis longtemps en lui et dont il prend conscience soudain à la faveur des révolutions dans la perspective d'une civilisation inédite.'

This concept of civilisation was not an abstract, universalised cultural identity, nor an elite culture for Chenu.⁸⁴ He recognised the initial violent disruption caused by industrialisation as an historical rupture leading to a re-integration of humanity with work and to liberation through its growing socialisation that would induce 'l'avènement réel de ces "communautés"'.⁸⁵

---

81. Chenu was citing J Lacroix: 'L'idée d'une civilisation du travail est autant philosophique que politique.' (36) from J Lacroix, 'La notion de travail', in *La Vie intellectuelle* (juin 1952): 11-12. [full reference cited in 'Théologie du travail' in *La Parole de Dieu. II*, 546, n 1.]
82. *Pour une théologie du travail*, 43-44.
83. 'Pour une théologie du travail', 50.
84. Chenu acknowledged Simone Weil's understanding of 'civilisation of work' in 'L'avenir professionnel de l'enfant' in the Bureau International Catholique de l'Enfance, *L'enfant et son avenir professionnel: Esquisse d'une théologie de la création et du travail* (Paris: Éditions Fleurus, 1959), 15, n 4. Later, he quoted her on theological dialogue with unbelievers: 'Il y a un propos très significatif de Simone Weil qui dit: «Ce n'est pas à la façon dont un homme me parle de Dieu que je vois si son âme a séjourné dans le feu de l'amour divin, mais c'est à la manière dont il me parle des choses terrestres.»' *Un théologien en liberté* (1975), 194. *Cf* 'Simone Weil and the civilisation of work', in Richard H Bell, editor, *Simone Weil's Philosophy of Culture: Readings Toward a Divine Humanity* (Cambridge: Cambridge University Press, 1993), 189-213, 192.
85. 'Pour une théologie du travail', 23.

Chenu was emphatic that a theology of work cannot be romantically nostalgic for an era when the artisan's work was buttressed by, and sustained the patriarchal family, small business, and private property.[86] The theological response must be in terms of the full realities of modern industrial work, with its destructive elements in view as much as any deeper liberative or eschatological meanings it may have. He also rejected the commonly negative theological depiction of industrialisation as reducing the labourer to moral abjection, and the demonising of mechanised technology as an embodiment of evil. Rather, he viewed it as a tool that allowed human autonomy. For Chenu, theology was faced with a more constructive challenge than this moralising hand-wringing or collusion with the dominant ideology.[87] It needed to demonstrate in doctrine, as in action, that faith was not divorced by industrialisation from humanity by challenging the economic analysis that reduced Christian faith to an ideology. The revelation of God became human in the Incarnation and all humanity's subsequent re-orientation towards God was needed to replace the bourgeois, anthropomorphised reduction of God that Marx had rightly rejected.[88]

Chenu's theological reflection on this 'civilisation du travail' envisaged a 'humanisme du travail' where human self-consciousness was advanced through work. This is in contrast to the totalitarianism of the mass movements of fascism and communism. This 'humanisme du travail' promised a transformation of all existing societies and economies, an eschatological destiny.

> Tout le tissu de l'histoire humaine, le développement des peuples, l'organisation du monde, et, en cela, la civilisation industrielle, sont le lieu de la Parole de Dieu, qui est Parole de Dieu à l'homme selon les catégories de l'homme et le rythme des civilisations. [89]

Chenu identified that mass industrialisation's ultimate revelation about humanity is that the poor and disadvantaged workers are the

---

86. 'Pour une théologie du travail', 15. Again here Chenu appears to be referencing *The German Ideology*'s treatment of the three aspects of social activity, 50.
87. 'Pour une théologie du travail', 15.
88. 'L'homo oeconomicus', 64.
89. Chenu, 'Trente ans après', in *Lumière et vie* (août-octobre, 1975): 72–77, 77.

recipients of the grace of Christ because they are most in need of it.[90] He equated industrial workers with the dispossessed poor in the Gospels who are the first to hear and respond to Christ. Emphasising the salvific character of their work, it is not their knowledge or virtue that saves 'les petites et les simples' but the consciousness that arises from their work. Chenu argued that collusion with the economic interests of capitalism was a distortion of the Gospel because it sectionalised the promise of salvation, instead of recognising the truth of the Incarnation seeking expression in the lives of the workers.

Criticism of Chenu's theology of work

Chenu's attempt to give priority to work as a locus for theology met with a mixed response since it was first published. The association with Marxism and the worker-priest initiatives led the order's leadership in Rome to proscribe *Pour une théologie du travail*. In more recent years, Chenu's work has continued to be reviewed in some theological circles, mostly in contrast to Pope John Paul II's encyclical on work, *Laborem Exercens*.[91] Chenu's theology is criticised for collapsing grace into nature and for pre-empting salvation through anticipating its occurrence through human affairs. Chenu rejected 'spiritualised Augustinianism' and 'Cartesian dualism' as failing to reflect the dynamic and power of the Incarnation and its continuing expression in the world. J-M Salamito accused Chenu of insufficiently distinguishing between creation and redemption, not subordinating the natural order to the supernatural order, putting humanisa-

---

90. 'Pour une théologie du travail', 30: 'Nous voici à l'heure où les petits et les simples sont disponibles, par leur état même de travailleurs, à la grâce du Christ.'
91. Charles Curran has commented that Pope John Paul II's *Sollicitudo Rei Socialis* refuted the critique of Chenu's later work *La 'doctrine sociale' de l'Église comme idéologie* (1979), whose thesis was that until Pope John XXIII's *Pacem in Terris* (1963) papal social teaching presented ideologically deduced principles with an ahistorical emphasis on continuity. Charles E Curran, *Catholic Social Teaching, 1891–Present: A Historical, Theological and Ethical Analysis* (Washington, Georgetown University Press, 2002), 63–65, 117. But John Paul II did favourably refer to Chenu among other French thinkers in *Letter to the Bishops Of France* (11 February 2005), 5 and also cited Chenu in the *Letter of His Holiness Pope John Paul II to Artists* (1999), 11.

tion above sanctification, and usurping God's place in creation.[92] He insisted that Chenu wrongly taught that there is a simple progression between creation and grace. This is a caricature of Chenu's dialectical understanding of nature and grace and ignores the detailed attention Chenu gives to grace in his theology. Chenu insisted on not reducing grace to some 'fixed capital' ecclesiastically reserved from sin and secularisation. Grace is diffused in time through the continuing Incarnation, invading all things and spreading through humanity collectively and individually, reconstituting and participating in the substance of matter in nature, which was created in the beginning by God and is recreated in Christ. Chenu compared Grace to the stock from which a grafted branch receives strength and structure. Rather than discounting Grace, Chenu called for a heightened sense of grace's power and presence and the salvific unity of God's actions in creation and redemption.[93] While Grace begins by supplementing our fragility, it becomes incorporated in us, but never at the risk of demeaning human freedom and autonomy. This is the tension that Chenu found in human work, while he acknowledged the painful conflict involved in bringing together Grace with nature in the limited working conditions of the present times. His theology of nature and Grace is not as fully developed as Lubac's, but its centrality to his understanding of work and humanity is inadequately understood by Salamito.

Jean-Yves Lacoste discussed work in terms of the conflict between technology and liturgy in the light of Heidegger's 'The Question concerning Technology'.[94] Lacoste's purpose is to locate liturgy in postmodern life, particularly in terms of its relationship to post-industrial work, work without the necessary production of goods. Services, information, and other post-industrial outcomes appear to eliminate the human transformation of matter in production. According to Lacoste, this challenges the relevance of theologies of work like Chenu's. Clearly, Chenu's theology did not anticipate this develop-

---

92. J-M Salamito, 'La Croix du Travail, le travail de la croix', in *Communio* IX/2 (1984): 4-15, 9-10.
93. 'L'homo oeconomicus', 46-51.
94. Lacoste, Jean-Yves, 'De la technique à la liturgie: un pas ou deux hors de la modernité', in *Communio* IX/2 (1984): 26-37; Martin Heidegger, 'The Question concerning Technology', in *Basic Writings*, David Farrell Krell translator (San Francisco: Harper, 1977), 287-317.

ment, but his concept of work was not limited to industrial labour.[95] In marking the shift in human work brought by mass industry, Chenu refused the classification of some works as superior to others, and accorded to the proletariat the full social and historical significance of their work along with its theological value. By contrast, Lacoste questions the Marxist utopianism where all work is *poesis*, and he instead divides work into two types: a production of goods or services that express the *person's* existence, and work where the human is only the tool for another's designs, anonymous and *personally* absent from their work, thereby alienated.[96] Chenu claimed value for all work as advancing the destiny of humanity through not only the transformation of matter into goods but also transforming humanity itself, socially and theologically, and cast the limitation represented in Lacoste's second category as a manifestation of the alienation, that is sin, which requires liberation. Work today is not only for earning our 'daily bread', also, 'il crée en quelque sorte de l'énergie sociale, immédiatement au service de l'entière humanité', even though the impoverished worker and the uninterested company director may fail to realise this effect. Chenu insisted that humanity is not rendered a tool by work because even work is not merely a tool for humanity, it is through work that humanity becomes more aware of itself, more humanised towards its ultimate destiny of union with its Creator.[97]

Lacoste judges Chenu's concept of the continuation of God's creation in human work as pretentious; instead he presents human work as being about 'de-creation' more than sharing in the creative action of God. He states that the 'proletarianism of human work' misuses power by alienating and dehumanising, and, in the context of technological 'overkill' and nuclear mass destruction, threatens total annihilation of the world. Lacoste accuses Chenu's theology of addressing only the perfection of what humanity makes rather than the perfection of humanity itself: a technological mode of operation completely replaces the relationship between the person and the world. Lacoste presents a pessimistic Heideggerian view of modern work, which fails to differentiate sufficiently the new humanity and socio-

---

95. Even theology, as opposed to 'intellectual clericalism', is work according to Chenu, and as work is its own critique. 'L'homo oeconomicus', 44.
96. Lacoste, 'De la technique à la liturgie', 28.
97. 'Pour une théologie du travail', 20.

economic relations raised by industrialisation.[98] Yet he recognises that work is also the fundamental mode of human fidelity, where vocation is proved.[99] Chenu was not merely optimistic in contrast to Lacoste's rejection of modernity; rather, he portrayed the same realities as instead pregnant with challenge. He saw in the new situation of more socialised work possibilities for humans to divest themselves of sectional and individualist interests through their awakening to the need for change in the face of these threats. Chenu was certainly not in idealistic denial:

> avec une irrépressible confiance, aux aspirations d'une humanité en marche, il me plaît de vous présenter cette vie en marche, il me plaît de vous présenter cette vie des sociétés humaines: la voici qui avance et progresse, au milieu des pires soubresauts et malgré d'humiliants échecs, et le chaos même qu'elle traverse souligne encore, à longue échéance, le déterminisme cosmique qui semble la promouvoir.[100]

Lacoste displays a partial reading of Chenu sieved through his sacralising conclusions that all work must be liturgical if humanity is to be unalienated, and that God's intervention with the human worker is the 'promesse d'une autre modalité, pour l'homme, de sa présence au monde'. This is more abstract and idealised than Chenu, whose subject was a humanity for whom work is central to identity and destiny. This is not a humanity located in some privileged economy above the means of production but theologically located in the contemporary world though which it proceeds to full unity with God. This critique of Chenu clearly refers only to the 'Travail' encyclopaedia article.[101] Lacoste's concerns are more with the relationship of technology and modernity than with the understanding of work derived by workers. Nor does he share Chenu's sense of the urgency for change in the understanding of work and in transformation of a 'civilisation of work'.

---

98. Heidegger missed the changed economic and social relations brought about by industrialisation, see Nicholas Boyle's critique of Heidegger's essay in *Who are we now? Christian Humanism and the Global Market from Hegel to Heaney* (Notre Dame: University of Notre Dame Press, 1998), 216–19.
99. Lacoste, 'De la technique à la liturgie', 31.
100. 'Le devenir social', 73.
101. 'Travail' in *Encyclopédie de la foi*, volume VI (Paris: Cerf, 1967).

Francis Schüssler-Fiorenza has criticised Chenu's theology of work for being a religious interpretation that overlooked 'the societal interests and concrete economics' affecting work and its relation to society, for its positive and objective valuing of work over and above its 'detrimental or constructive' effect on the worker, and for its romantic, abstract insistence on the vocational meaning of work, thus legitimating the dehumanisation of workers and ill-equipping them for the job-mobility and unemployment of post-industrialism. Schüssler-Fiorenza was writing during a revival of interest in theology of work and socialism that immediately preceded Pope John Paul II's encyclical *Laborem exercens* (1981). This later criticism depends on the advantage of hindsight, as the rise in unemployment and widespread computerisation of post-industrial production was unpredictable in the 1950s and Chenu deliberately based his theology on reading the current situation of the workers rather than establishing some eternal values about work. Schüssler-Fiorenza summarises his critique asking: 'whether a theology of work is adequate if it attempts to give meaning to work mainly by the theological application of religious beliefs to work' and whether this theology is only extending to work 'a meaning that was previously shared by the bourgeoisie or the intellectual strata of society but never by all members of society'.[102] These criticisms betray a cursory reading of *Pour une théologie du travail* with no reference to Chenu's wider corpus and a complete misreading of his focus on the human experience of work, which, critically, refused to provide 'an appropriate application of the religious tradition' *to* the subject of work. Schüssler-Fiorenza's tenacious hold on his own agenda, 'that a theology of work is inadequate unless it considers both the ambivalence of religious attitudes towards work and the ambiguity of work itself', dictates his reading of Chenu. Chenu examined both the ambivalence and ambiguity of work but did not end there, unlike the conclusions of traditional theology toward work. While Schüssler-Fiorenza claims not to be asserting 'that all Catholic theology has inadequately analysed work' he appears to be constructing a straw-man out of a particularly skewed reading of Chenu's *Pour une théologie du travail*.

---

102. Francis Schüssler-Fiorenza, 'Religious Beliefs and Praxis: Reflections on Catholic Theological Views of Work', in *Concilium*, 131 (1980): 92–102, 97–8.

In his historical survey in 'Le devenir social', Chenu cited the revolution in labour caused by the introduction of the horse-collar in the twelfth century. He compared this technical liberation, which freed up human labour for less arduous and more complex work, and its socio-political contribution to the abolition of serfdom, to the mechanisation of physical labour in the nineteenth and twentieth centuries. His intention was neither to romanticise this mechanisation, nor to ignore its improvement of human work and its socio-political revolution. Chenu was here in close dialogue with Marx's parallel historical survey of the rise of towns and the dismantling of serfdom leading to the rise of manufacturing in early modern Western Europe.[103] Schüssler-Fiorenza fails to acknowledge the significance of this contextual reference. Chenu considered it a non-worker's luxury, to sit on the side and bewail the evils of technology and fail to see from the workers' position how much labour-saving had occurred. He did not ignore the drudgery, fragmentation, and devaluation of labour that renders industrial work oppressive, but as an historian and a confidant of workers he is reminded as well of the positive outcomes of the evolution of work. Schüssler-Fiorenza's criticism is that Chenu's project fails because it attempted 'to give meaning to work precisely at a time when it appears to have become meaningless through industrialisation.'[104] Chenu would refute this as a failure to recognise the human significance of all work and its inherent transformation of humanity.

Where Chenu is vulnerable is Schüssler-Fiorenza's identification of his 'optimistic interpretation of technology and industrialism'. In a review thirty years after *Pour une théologie du travail* was published, Chenu acknowledged that the ecological threat posed by the glorification and mystification of human dominion over nature implied in works like his and Teilhard de Chardin's, and the consumerist fetishisation of the proletariat and Western society had put into question the optimism he promoted in the 1960s:

> Voici que, vingt ans après, la dure crise actuelle qui surprend les prévisions des technocrates, la sévère critique de la société de consommation, . . . a cédé mon diagnostic prométhéen, encore séduit par l'invention du feu.[105]

---

103. See Marx and Engels, *The German Ideology*, 68–79, 82–84.
104. Schüssler Fiorenza, 97–8.
105. 'Trente ans après', 75.

But he also insisted on reading this not morally as a failure of humanity, but theologically as:

> la fragilité de l'homme, à nouveau éprouvée, remet en bonne mémoire les vieux thèmes, j'allais dire les vieux mythes, y compris celui du péché originel, qui déjà tournaient en dérision les rationalisations de la *technê*.[106]

What was at stake for Chenu is not some religious claim about the abstract definition or idealisation of work, but whether the evils and limitations on freedom imposed by mass industrialisation overpower the Incarnation and Christ's victory over sin and death. Chenu was not imposing a religious ideology on the meaning of work, but sought where in the condition of the workers promise and possibility was offered. In other words, his optimism is a Christian hope seeking the eschatological signs in human reality that reveal God's creativity in all things. He made no apology for the distinctly Christian perspective of this, because he equally acknowledges the potency and vision of other eschatologies, especially those of Marxism and international capitalism.[107] Nevertheless, Chenu refused the secularist dismissal and marginalisation of faith from having something to share with the civilisation created by modern industrialisation.

Schüssler-Fiorenza also mistakes the purpose of Chenu's project: Chenu is neither providing remedies for 'the loss of the significance of work' nor appropriating 'the Christian tradition to give meaning to work within the human situation'.[108] Again, these judgements are more evidence of the position from which Schüssler-Fiorenza constructs his theology than Chenu's, particularly as his critique adopts the very abstraction from any particular location of the relationship between social analysis and praxis that he condemns. This resembles the contradictory fate of 'the fashionable insistence on "orthopraxis"' described by Lash: 'it is used as yet another device by means of which to avoid exposing theological affirmation to continual corrective

---

106. 'Trente ans après', 76.
107. Referring to Platonist and Cartesian philosophies of humanity, Chenu accepted the validity of all anthropologies precisiely because all of them are limited, even his preference, that of Thomas Aquinas: 'J'en accorde, certes, et la légitimit chrétienne, et la valeur humaine, non par éclectisme, mais par discrétion devant les limites de tout système, même en anthropologie.' 'Le devenir social', 104.
108. 'Le devenir social', 96, 98, 100.

purification from the particularity of human action and experience.'[109] Schüssler-Fiorenza's reading of Chenu assumes a moral focus which reduces work to only a site for sociological analysis and 'practical discourse' with an unrevealed other, certainly not the workers nor the Church whom Chenu was addressing. This moral emphasis collapses the dynamic tension Chenu identified between his *theological* reading of work and the ethics of work itself: he was not creating a meta-ethics with universal application but explored and recognised the theological implications of work and the internal coherence or 'densité' of its social, historical, and ethical orientation in humans, which is yet to be fully realised in the emancipation of the worker from the alienation of his labour.[110] Yet Schüssler-Fiorenza's concern with this theology's 'adequacy to our contemporary situation' does stand, and raises the issue whether any historically grounded theology is applicable in other historical situations. This is more than a question of relevance, nor is it solved in the appropriation of a method divorced of an historical context.

John Hughes' *The End of Work* offers a thorough and extensive treatment of the theological issues related to work from the historical context of post-industrialisation. While his treatment of Chenu is critical, it rightly examines Chenu's lack of criticality about his presuppositions from dialogue with Marxism and his 'cultural optimism'.[111] Chenu's confidence in the human transformation of matter does draw alarm about its ecological implications in a world where subjugation of creation has led to global destructiveness. To assert that 'La monde a été donné à l'homme pour qu'il en achève la création, la même où il en tire de quoi satisfaire ses besoins'[112] does not resonate adequately with today's ecological consciousness. While Chenu's anthropocentrism requires modification, it also proffers some insight into how subjugation of nature need not be the necessary outcome of an understanding of work as transformative. For Chenu, transforma-

---

109. Lash, *A Matter of Hope*, 30.
110. Such moral theological reduction was the response of Christians since the French Revolution about which Chenu was so critical: 'ils en restèrenet *à ce plan moral où les bonnes oeuvres recouvrent le souci ontologique des réalités. Ils n'eurent même plus la ressource d'un mauvais conscience.'* 'L'homo oeconomicus', 60.
111. *The End of Work* (Oxford: Blackwell, 2007), 15.
112. 'L'homo oeconomicus', 57.

tion of creation also transforms humanity, and this transformation would involve transforming human sinfulness and greed[113] to instead include more sensitivity to the scarcity of resources, awareness, and protection of the ecological interdependence of species and ecosystems, and human responsibility for our productivity and exploitation.

In his conclusion, Hughes suggests potential points of dialogue on the future of work that could engage with Chenu's theology. Rejecting utilitarian meaning alone for work, Hughes calls for 'a *vision* of true labour' which he qualifies may be 'manifest more in some forms than others'.[114] Chenu would seem to find such a 'vision' embedded in the recognition of the unity of matter and spirit in humans, which is then exercised as transformative through work. All work is therefore the means of emphasising the spiritual destiny available for all matter through the natural nexus of matter and spirit in the human.[115] Hughes and Chenu differ on the types of work that can be said to bear analogous qualities to divine creativity. While Hughes rejects Arendt's 'hierachical division of labour', there is a similar tendency in classifying artistry as being more analogous than other work to God's creation.[116] He examines this concept further and concludes, in a way that Chenu would agree: 'This is precisely what we mean by the transformation or redemption of work, and as our work participates more fully in divine labour so to some extent the oppositions we have noted begine to be overcome, even if never finally.'[117] Chenu understood work as in itself a participation in divine labour, but that the redemptive nature of participation was not fully realisable in the initial stages of industrialisation. For Chenu, work is always eschatologically incomplete, not redemptive in itself. Like Hughes, he does not rescind from the responsibility of socio-political engagement even though the eschatological resolution means that no temporal economic or political system can 'solve the problem'. Human activity

---

113. Chenu discussed the implications of greed and the dominance of economics in 45–46.
114. Hughes, *The End of Work*, 224
115. Chenu: 'ce travail ne va déhumniser que parce que, de soi, conduit selon sa loi, il serait capable d'humaniser.' and 'c'est en produisant une oeuvre, en sa subordonnant à elle en se soumettant à ses lois dans la matière, que l'homme au travail trouve sa perfection d'homme.' 'Pour une théologie du travail', 31–32.
116. Hughes, *The End of Work*, 226, n 18; 225.
117. Hughes, *The End of Work*, 228.

cannot afford the privilege of a 'counter-cultural' parallelism with contemporary society and its ills. For Chenu, work, like the cross, demonstrates the limitless possibility in the Incarnation's transformation of the otherwise un-divine in human life. Hughes rightly poses the problem of destructive work, for example, arms production, and the varieties of continuing exploitation of workers, through job mobility, casual employment, and other de-humanising through atomisation of work. Chenu's theology of work does not provide answers for these post-industrial developments.

Overall, Chenu's theology of work is limited by its contemporary situatedness. His advocacy of socialisation as a signal of greater humanisation can suggest an uncritical acceptance of socialist politics. Yet I would understand these as the necessary outcomes of a theology so focused on dialogue with its temporal situation and its then interlocutors, socialists and Marxists. A situated theology always bears the limitations of its situation, and Chenu was adamant that his theology was not repeating the ahistorical approach of 'modern scholasticism'. This chapter has also claimed that the topic of work was secondary to his interest in discerning theologically the impact on humanity of this new civilisation of work. It is in the transformation of our understanding of humanity by industrial work that I believe Chenu indicates the ways by which such theology can open to the problems and challenges facing humanity in more recent technological times. The key is Chenu's Thomist refusal to see any human situation as beyond the activity of grace, to regard all creation and human activity as sufficiently orientable and responsive to divine invitation to be transformed, even given its inherent sinfulness and resistance. While this is denigrated as an optimism, for Chenu it was rather a true sign of hope and the eschatological possibility already being realised in contemporary experience.

Chenu's Christian anthropology and work

Chenu's theology of work marks a shift in his Christian anthropological perspective beyond the Church's pastoral concern for an enfranchising of the industrialised working classes, and beyond his recognition of the contribution that these classes and their lay-Catholic collaborators offered for the reform of the Church's theological self-understanding, particularly in terms of the growing role of the active laity. His attempts at theologising on work made a more profound connection with the humanity being transformed in work. In this, Chenu moved to consider humanity theologically, more explicitly as the subject of theology rather than as an object of Church practice. In this he drew from the drudgery and dehumanisation of contemporary work an understanding of the human not merely transcending this reality in a liturgical appropriation of the value of work, but rather insisted on the ontological nature of work for humans, an ontology that too often has only been cast in terms of a repressive ontology of violence. Chenu insisted on the analogy of work with the creative act of God, initiating and transforming matter, not out of a pre-lapsarian battle between chaos and order, but the divine infusion of spirit into matter, specifically in the creation of the nexus of matter and spirit in the human. So objections to his claiming for humans a co-creator role miss the point when they focus only on the ontological difference between humans to God. Chenu instead presented the human as part of God's creative and transformative activity. Not merely an instrument of God, but, even in the simplest, least satisfying work, continuing the transformation of matter. Too often such critics fail to see that intellectual and society-building activities, not only productivity, continue God's creation in Chenu's theology. Similarly, the greed, destruction, enslavement, and oppressive conditions that mark industrialised work as sinful are acknowledged but not the final focus of Chenu's understanding. Instead he identified that humans also share in the continuing work of the Incarnation and salvation from sin and death. So the matter (the whole creation in Thomist understanding) at the heart of work, the unity of matter and spirit in the human being, and the ultimate restoration of creation won by Christ assuming human nature are for Chenu in continuity, open to God's grace and transformation. While I have asserted that work was less his focus than the new understanding of humanity produced by industrialisation, it would be negligent of Chenu's process of theologising not to register that work provided the context for naming the theological enterprise that he understood as human. It is not the quality of the work that is determinative of its revelatory character. Chenu would dispute with Lacoste and Hughes about valuing some work as liturgical over other work that is deemed without divine value. For Chenu, even unconscious, repetitive, apparently soul-destroying work has within it the capacity for socialisation and humanisation that is ultimately redemptive. Chenu envisages not so much a value-adding to such work, but its dehumanising increasingly forcing a rejection of such practices and the subsequent implementation through organised labour of more just conditions and more meaningful engagement of the worker. In some ways, the widespread replacement of production-line tasks by automative technologies since the end of the twentieth century has demonstrated such a transformation of work through the further innovations of human ingenuity. Rather than lamenting the loss of these monotonous jobs, a theology in Chenu's terms would welcome this further advance from the human degradation of such work, just as he welcomed the medieval invention of the yoke for animal husbandry as eliminating the use of serfs. Yet we are left with the question whether this is still a much too idealised depiction of work, when globalisation has only shifted the locations of the worst conditions of industrialisation to unregulated populations in the two-thirds world?

Conclusion

Pour une théologie du travail demonstrates the way in which Chenu privileged contemporary thought and human experience as he strove to situate theology in human history on the basis of the Incarnation. His theology of work was concerned with what work meant for people in the mid-twentieth century: its nature, its material and human sources, its unique value, and its economic and human content considered in its possible relation to God's reign in the world.[118]

Work is where human destiny is oriented and realised, but Chenu insisted it is only a secondary end, not the means of perfection of humanity as in the definitive accomplishment of the proletarian dictatorship, 'the last revolution'.[119] For Chenu, the separation of dogma from morality is untenable, so, just as religious alienation clearly accompanies economic alienation, economic freedom is inconceivable without religious freedom.[120] Chenu recognised the critical significance of the steep rise of atheism among the working classes—'l'athéisme positif'—as distinct from the empiricist or nega-

---

118. 'Pour une théologie du travail', 10–12.
119. 'Pour une théologie du travail', 35.
120. 'L'homo oeconomicus', 58–59, 63–64.

tive atheism of the philosophically educated.¹²¹ As humanity becomes alienated in its work, work loses its human meaning then the human loses itself, because of the centrality of work to its identity. When work has no human significance it cannot have a religious one; its reflexivity is arrested. There is a danger in the Marxist exaltation of work of deifying it, of finding in work a satisfaction of the need for the sacred that refuses to die even with the apparent loss of belief in God, but Chenu chastised theologians for not responding adequately to this need for realisation of the sacred in the experience of industrialisation: 'Il ne faut certes point diviniser le travail; mais ceux qui succombent à cette idolâtrie, destructrice des personnes et négatrice de Dieu à la fois, ne font que satisfaire au besoin du sacré.'¹²² Ultimately it is the differences in starting point and ends that distinguish Chenu from Marxist thought, despite his very fruitful engagement with it. Whereas Marx sees matter as the nexus between humanity and nature, Chenu found humanity where spirit and matter unite. Chenu asserted that this consciousness of humanity, based in and continually corrected by the social reality, determined humanity's becoming into the future through the force of spirit and freedom on the transformation of matter.¹²³ In the last chapter, Chenu's articulation of a theology of humanity is focused on its ontology, the unity of matter and spirit in the human initiated in the creative transformation of matter by God.

---

121. J Maritain, *La signification de l'athéisme contemporain* (Paris: Desclée, de Brouwer, 1949).
122. 'Pour une théologie du travail', 27–8.
123. 'Le devenir social', 93.

Chapter 7
The Human Truth of Matter: Towards a Christian Anthropology

> 'C'est, il semble bien, le message de nos générations, inspiré par des évolutions convergentes, que de déterminer enfin, dans sa dimension historique, *la vérité humaine de la matière*, dont les filons passent par la vie collective de l'humanité, comme par la vie physiologique des âmes.'
>
> 'Réflexions chrétiennes sur la vérité de la matière' (1948) in *La Parole de Dieu II. L'Évangile dans le temps* (Paris: Cerf, 1964), 447–451, 449.

Chenu did not complete any systematic treatment of Christian anthropology, despite the anthropological grounds of much of his writing. Most of Chenu's theology responded to contemporary questions: it was not a systematic exposition of doctrines. In this he resembled other contemporaries like Rahner.[1] Yet Congar's lament at Chenu's failure to complete a treatise on Christian anthropology suggests that such a project was not so far from Chenu's intention.[2] Where Chenu's anthropological thinking did emerge throughout his writings, it proceeded from Aquinas' anthropological understanding, but moved in a more historical and eschatological recasting of the human enterprise in response to the new challenges posed by the technological civilisation of the mid-twentieth century. Various articles on the theology of matter present his most articulated discourse with anthropological

---

1. As earlier referred: Karen Kilby, 'The *Vorgriff auf esse*: A study in the relation of philosophy to theology in the thought of Karl Rahner' (unpublished PhD thesis, Yale University, 1994), 202–209.
2. Congar, 'Le Père M-D Chenu' in R van der Gucht and H Vorgrimler, editors, *Bilan de la théologie du XXe siècle*, volume II (Paris: Casterman, 1970), 783.

themes more specifically than his theology of work, and this chapter will employ these writings in order to attempt to shape what might have been his Christian anthropology.

Previous studies of his theology have emphasised its Incarnational foundation, such as the comprehensive treatment by Potworowski.[3] While Potworowski's analysis is very thorough and convincing, his unease with Chenu's definition of the Incarnation (especially 'la loi de l'Incarnation' in Potworowski's last chapter on 'Incarnation and Christology') suggests there may be a more basic starting point for Chenu. I believe that Chenu's concern with the human, as matter and creature, provided the starting-point for his theology. While Chenu was very Incarnational in his theology, he started with the humanity assumed by Christ, as well as his divine nature in the Incarnation.

> Dieu ne peut être atteint qu'à travers le Christ-homme, et que c'est par l'homme, et donc par une anthropologie, que j'atteins une théologie.[4]

Throughout his major works, 'l'homme' was the subject, represented as an historical reality, in human reason and contemplation accompanying faith, in social and ecclesial communities, and engaged in work as a transformer of matter. Potworowski also observes that Chenu was more theological than Christological, more theocentric than Christocentric.[5] Here again, Chenu's Thomism is evident in this cosmological and anthropological approach. While Chenu repeatedly insisted that the true object of theology is God, not the doctrinal formulations of 'the deposit of faith', it was this that reinforced his focus on the relationship of humanity with God, as part of God's creation and as the object of the Incarnation.

> L'objet de la théologie, en effet, ce n'est pas proprement et premièrement cette économie où de fait l'homme reçoit par le Christ foi et grace; c'est Dieu en sa réalité même; toutes ses productions, au cours de l'histoire, toutes les oeuvres de

---

3. Christophe F Potworowski, *Contemplation and Incarnation. The Theology of Marie-Dominique Chenu* (Montreal and Kingston: McGill-Queens University Press, 2001).
4. *Un théologien en liberté: Jacques Duquesne interroge le Père Chenu*, 195.
5. Potworowski, *Contemplation and Incarnation*, 210.

création et de recréation... sont traitées et jugées formellement *sub ratione Dei.*⁶

It is through this focus on God that Chenu properly distinguished his anthropological focus. His emphasis was not an over-divinised representation of the Incarnation, but was informed by what is understood by Christ being fully human and, therefore, what is the corresponding fullness of humanity that all humans are redeemed by Christ to become. Chenu repeatedly rejected any tendency to Docetism. For him, the Incarnation showed:

> une nouvelle lumière sur l'homme aujourd'hui vient soutenir une redécouverte de l'Incarnation comme humanisation historique de Dieu, le centre de gravité christologique du christianisme place aussi l'homme sous une lumière nouvelle. Anthropologie et christologie, christologie et anthropologie, deviennent ensemble l'une par l'autre, le lieu géométrique de la théologie dans l'intelligence plénière du mystère.⁷

The humanising of God in history changes theological understanding of what it means to be human now. Christology and anthropology are related while not symmetrical. More than about developing an Incarnational Christology, Chenu's theological project sought to understand humanity as a continuing of the Incarnation, as humanity becomes more humanised through the advances of contemporary technological society.

Chenu is often accused of being too optimistic about humanity and too little concerned with its sinfulness. While there is not an examination of sinfulness in his theology, he did acknowledge the reality of sin: 'L'homme a péché. Il vit dans le péché.'⁸ Rather, he presumed that sin is the necessary condition of this humanity, clearly evidenced in the violence and destruction of the twentieth century, the social sin, which he identified early in his writings.

---

6. Chenu, *L'Introduction à l'étude de Saint Thomas d'Aquin*, 264.
7. Chenu, 'Histoire du salut et historicité de l'homme dans le renouveau de la théologie' in L. Shook and GM Bertrand, *La Théologie du renouveau*, volume 1 (Montréal, Paris: Éditions du Cerf, 1968), 21–32, 31.
8. Chenu, 'Chrétien, mon frère... pourquoi la guerre?' (1939) in *La Parole de Dieu II. L'Évangile dans le temps* (Paris: Cerf, 1964), 225–230, 229.

> c'est le régime même, où tout et tous sont en cause, qu'il fait juger. Non pas repêcher des individus dans la naufrage, mais sauver le bateau. *Car c'est le genre humain que le Chrétien prend en charge, et il constate plus que jamais la détresse des saluts personnels dans une économie désordonée.*[9]

In his later writing, he referred to sin as an ever-present ambiguity in human potential, which is taken up in the suffering of the Saviour, thereby human failure is redeemed in Christ's humanity.

> Là encore la réalité de l'histoire, de la toute douloureuse histoire des hommes, nous fait dépasser le moralisme d'un plate resignation: par le mystère de Dieu fait homme, entrent dans la recapitulation du Christ les échecs eux-mêmes, qui prennent sens et efficacité dans la passion et la mort du Messie Sauveur.[10]

He also distinguished between the over-emphasis on Original Sin by theologians influenced by Augustine and Pascal in contrast with Thomist theologians:

> Dans une anthropologie chrétienne commandée par la démesure du péché originel, le théologien augustinien ou pascalisant aura évidemment moins d'assurance sur les autonomies suffisantes et la promotion progressive de la solidarité humaine, qu'un disciple de saint Thomas.[11]

Perhaps here is some key to Chenu's negligence in dealing with sin: he clearly associated over-emphasis on sin with an Augustinian individualism. On this point I agree with Potworowski: 'Perhaps Chenu's mistrust of a theology focused on the individual and the individual's interiority, which he derisively calls '*spiritualisme*', can account for this.'[12] Chenu constantly shifted the theological agenda to the social

---

9. Chenu, 'La notion de profit et les principes chrétiens' (1945) in *La Parole de Dieu II. L'Évangile dans le temps* (Paris: Cerf, 1964), 495–514, 497.
10. Chenu, 'Une Constitution Pastorale de l'Église' ((1965) *Peuple de Dieu dans le monde* (Paris, Cerf. 1966), 11–33, 33.
11. 'Vérité et liberté dans la foi du croyant' (1959) in *La Parole de Dieu I. La Foi dans intelligence* (Paris: Cerf, 1964), 337–359, 353-4.
12. Potworowski, *Contemplation and Incarnation*, 214.

dimension of humanity, so when he considered it, his concern was more with social sin rather than individual sin.[13] His approach was a realised Christian hope.

Traditional Christian anthropology has had little to say about living humanity as opposed to the failure of human nature. While Chenu did not fully develop a theology of nature and grace,[14] he opened theological debate on ordinary human experience in work and other socialisation, the historicity of all human endeavour, and the particular role of women.[15] This was what Chenu sought to correct in his emphasis on the 'situation' of humanity, rather than its nature;[16] his project sought to expand existing Christian anthropological categories.

Following the mass collusion with ideologies that had reduced certain people to less than human status and the exposure of whole human populations to the mechanised destruction of World War II, Chenu recognised the need to restore the value of humanity, and the concomitant value of matter and the world. He was alert to the pastoral demands for a theology that addressed more directly the meaning of humanity in terms of these crises of the mid-twentieth century.[17]

---

13. See the treatment of social sinfulness of industrialised work and the dehumanisation it intensifies in 'Civilisation technique et spiritualité nouvelle' in *Théologie de la matière* (Paris: Cerf, 1967), 65-91, 83-85.
14. 'La théologie comme science ecclésiale', *Concilium*, 21 (1967), 85-93 (89-90) where Chenu commended Vatican II's Pastoral Constiution *Gaudium et Spes* for its rejection of the sterility of scholastic categories, like the nature-grace debate, in preference for concrete biblical language.
15. 'Ce sont les hommes, dit-on, qui font l'histoire; en tout cas, ce sont les hommes qui l'écrivent, et non les femmes. Aussi l'histoire de la civilisation serait-elle à récrire, en plusieurs chapitres, car elle n'a fait, jusqu'ici, que peu de place à la femme dans l'évolution de la vie sociale, culturelle, voire même familiale.'Chenu, 'Des femmes chrétiennes présentes à leur temps' *Témoignage Chrétien*, number 413 (Paris: juin 6, 1952), 1.
16. Chenu defined 'situation' as a theologically preferable descriptor for humanity to 'condition' because of its historical and relational references in 'Situation humaine: corporalité et temporalité' (1958) in *Théologie de la matière* (Paris: Éditions du Cerf, 1967), 31-63 (31-33).
17. Chenu reflected on this with prescience at the beginning of World War II in 'Chrétien, mon frère . . . *pourquoi la guerre?*', 228 and on the need for a more inclusive view of humanity after the War in 'Corps d'Eglise et structures sociales' (1948) in *La Parole de Dieu II. L'Évangile dans le temps* (Paris: Cerf, 1964), 159-169, particularly 162-3.

His approach was motivated by his positive appreciation of the same forces of socialisation creating new communal consciousness, despite their destructive harnessing by nationalism and racism.

> Il est bien vrai que nous sommes lies à la société, et, si nous y sommes trop souvent liés comme des prisonniers, il faut reconnaître que, à travers cette perversion, c'est la nature même qui nous lie, pour le statut et le progès de ma vie personnelle. C'est dans la communauté des autres hommes que l'homme trouve sa perfection.[18]

It is this constant orientation to find the good in what was generally held to be disastrous that also distinguished his later responses to secularisation, industrialisation, and de-colonisation.[19] His concern was rather with the causes of the depreciation of the human person. This he identified repeatedly as theological in origin, springing from the pervasive effects of the heretical (if common Christian) tendency to denigrate matter and the world, which he termed a Manichean rejection of Creation.[20] Such a rejection of all things material produced a negative theological view of humanity, which in turn risked distorting the Incarnation. For Chenu, this distortion resembled the heretical Monophysite and Docetist teachings that compromised the full humanity of Christ. They depreciated 'la verité humaine'. He acknowledged that such 'vulgarised' Augustinianism largely over-shadowed the more dynamic relationship in the matter of human and spirit propounded by Aquinas. To address this longstanding but more recently aggravated anti-human theology, Chenu tackled the popular 'Augustinian' understanding of human nature. His tools were Aquinas' teachings on the consubstantiality in the human of matter and spirit

---

18. Chenu, 'Destinée personnelle et morale communautaire' (1941) in *La Parole de Dieu II. L'Évangile dans le temps* (Paris: Cerf, 1964), 355–379, 359.
19. For example 'De même considérons-nous sans crainte l'accession des masses à l'existence historique, et le fait qu'elles jouent partout, même dans les régimes totalitaires, le rôle d'un facteur prédominant. Grandes forces humaines, que le chrétien refuse d'abandonner à la dépersonnalisation de l'instinct grégaire et à l'asservissement du trompeau.' Chenu, 'Liberté et engagement du chrétien' (1938) *La Parole de Dieu II. L'Évangile dans le temps* (Paris: Cerf. 1964), 331–354, 353.
20. Chenu identified the continuing menace of 'un manichéisme larvé' and the purity sought by the Cathars behind the problem of matter for Christians in 'Spiritualité de la matière' (1962) in *Théologie de la matière*, 15.

and the divine relationship to matter through the Creation and Incarnation. This questioned the relegation of matter to mere corruptibility.

From the end of World War II, Chenu addressed the theological problem of matter in a number of articles, many republished in 1967 as *Théologie de la matière. Civilisation technique et spiritualité chrétienne*.[21] The sub-title signalled that the purpose of this theology was to claim appreciatively the century's technological revolution and its impact on human society, as a benefit and not opposite to Christian spirituality. He argued repeatedly in this collection that material 'civilisation' was too often defined negatively in contrast to 'spiritualité'. This collection represents the closest Chenu came to compiling a theological anthropology from the positive human perspective that he discerned in the socialising effects of the technological developments of the industrial revolution, which was the project he previously treated in *Pour une théologie du travail* (1947, 1952, 1955).

The problem of matter

Chenu believed that a proper appreciation of matter and materiality is crucial to the understanding of humanity, the human body, social reality, and the world. The theological problem was how matter exists in relation to a Creator who is pure spirit, and what is the place of matter in the process of human divinisation.[22] The source of this problem was the conflicting attitudes to matter that the Judaeo-Christian theology of Creation and the Greek philosophical belief in the corruptibility and transience of matter represented, so a Christian 'spiritualisme' suspected matter of destroying what is spiritual. Further, in modern times, matter gained ideological notoriety through association with Marxist dialectical materialism. For Chenu, this presented a theological problem at the heart of any Christian understanding of what it means to be human because it denied the goodness of Creation. Following Aquinas' Aristotelian understanding of the unity of matter and spirit in the human,[23] he asserted that the role of matter

---

21. *Théologie de la matière. Civilisation technique et spiritualité chrétienne* (Paris: Cerf, 1967)
22. 'Spiritualité de la matière' (1962) in *Théologie de la matière*, 15.
23. Chenu noted that Aquinas' university lectures of 1268 on this are preserved in an edited form in the *Questiones disputatae* as 'De spiritualibus creaturis' and 'De anima'. *St Thomas d'Aquin et la théologie* (Paris: Éditions du Seuil, 1959), 101.

in humanity neither reduced the value of humanity nor its spiritual capacity because it is:

> la condition de l'homme, qui dans sa substance même et pour sa perfection, implique la matière. *La matière comporte donc, en lui et par lui, une verité humaine et une dignité spirituelle.*[24]

Chenu judged that this 'spiritualisme' is not only a result of the struggle of the spirit over the flesh but more profoundly of disbelief in the Incarnation because of a repugnance towards the whole of Creation, 'l'univers solidaire des corps et du cosmos'.[25] While allowing for Augustine's own ability to overcome such pessimism, Chenu observed that the Augustinianism that followed him had profound influence on negative Christian reactions to any scientific and technological advances that proceeded from human efforts or engagement with the material world:

> la vulgarization de cette philosophie «spiritualiste» pesa pendant plus d'un millénaire sur le comportement Chrétien, de plus en plus désaccordé avec une civilisation dont le dessein providential engageit avec la progrès de la science, la domination du monde de la matière.[26]

For Chenu, the problem of the denigration of matter was carried over in the aristocratic mentality that reduced work to the equivalent of slavery, because of the doubly negative engagement of sinful humanity with corrupted matter in servile work. Such moralising failed to affirm the autonomy of secondary causes and the co-operation of humanity with the Creator. The problem that a negative theology of matter created, according to Chenu, was a 'spiritualisme' that failed to find anything of value in what is created: 'Si Dieu crée, au sens fort et vrai du terme, la matière elle-même est voulue, est créée, est donc bonne.'[27] He insisted that in retrieving the theological value of matter, Christianity would also recover a deeper faithfulness to the doctrine of the Incarnation:

---

24. 'Présentation', 7.
25. 'Présentation', 7.
26. 'Présentation', 8.
27. 'Spiritualité de la matière', 455–6.

> En définitive, en retrouvant la vérité de la matière, la conscience de son corps, la condition sociale de sa nature, la sensibilité à l'histoire, l'homme aujourd'hui approfondit sa foi, sa «fidélité» à l'Incarnation.[28]

This understanding of matter provided a heuristic nexus for his Christian anthropology.[29] Because of their materiality appreciation of the worth of the human body, the social reality of humanity and its location in history and in the world meet. This was in contrast to 'une manière d'impérialisme spirituel',[30] which dislocated these elements from divine value since it deemed matter corrupted and apparently beyond the reach of grace.

Chenu's anthropology was conceived on this nexus of matter: uniting humanity, work, and the world. Only through retrieving the value of matter, as Aquinas had done, could the modern loss of spirituality be reversed through claiming *'l'efficacité de la matière tant dans la métaphysique de l'univers que dans la psychologie de l'homme et l'évolution de la société.'*[31] So a theology of matter was for Chenu the key to a theology of the human person that would sufficiently take into account the reality of what it means to be human in relation to the world and in response to the technological threats and challenges of the modern industrial age.

> Si l'on situe sur l'espace vital de l'homme l'essor extraordinaire de la technique, c'est évidemment dans le secteur où l'homme rencontre la matière, est comme immerge dans la matière, à cette jonction subtile où le dépassement de l'esprit est garanti par son incarnation même. C'est pourquoi *la civilisation*

---

28. 'Présentation', 10-11.
29. Chenu did not use the term 'nexus', but employed the synonyms 'la conjoncture' 'la jonction' and 'le pivot' to refer to humanity's relationship to the cosmos in 'Pour une anthropologie sacramentelle', *La Maison-Dieu*, 119 (1974): 85-100 (95). He also used 'un noeud' or 'les entrelacs'. See 'Civilisation technique et spiritualité nouvelle' (1948), 'Condition nouvelle faite à l'homme dans la civilisation technique (1960) in *Théologie de la matière* (Paris: Cerf, 1967), 66, 72, 73 n 6, 85 ('un noeud'), 86 ('les entrelacs'), 87 ('un noeud'), 98, 100 ('un noeud'). Also 'Une Constitution pastorale de l'Église' (1964) in *Peuple de Dieu dans le monde* (Paris: Cerf, 1966), 11-34, 22 ('le noeud')
30. *St Thomas d'Aquin et la théologie*, 120.
31. Chenu, 'Réflexions chrétiennes sur la vérité de la matière' (1948) in *La Parole de Dieu II. L'Évangile dans le temps* (Paris: Cerf, 1964), 447-51, 448-9.

> *technique met en question* non seulement l'équilibre moral des individus, mais *la conception même de l'être humain.*[32]

Chenu dared to claim that the compromised category of materialism was integral to his theology of humanity:

> Il y aura toujours des platoniciens dans l'Eglise, et des idéalistes; qu'ils sachent d'avance qu'ils seront dépaysés dans la civilisation nouvelle par son «materialisme».[33]

This is not merely to refute the over-spiritualising of previous theologies but to make a more profound claim (clearly with reference to the Marxist critique) that humanity's worth is brought to greater fullness through technological invention and production that enlarge human destiny as co-operative with the Creator.

> . . . contre le dualisme larvé qu'impliquent tous les «spiritualismes». *L'homme, esprit, est-il aussi et substantiellement matière?* Nous voici à la racine des refus, des réticences, de certaine pensée chrétienne face à la technique.[34]

No longer is humanity's realisation opposed to God but, through the human transformation of matter as co-creative with the Creator and through the materiality of the Incarnation, humanity unites with God through matter. This is the meaning of his slogan 'la loi de l'Incarnation': humanity is the continuing Incarnation, the continuation through matter, as matter and through the work of transforming matter. Idealisms that depreciate humanity as matter deny God's engagement with the world through the creation of humanity.

'The truth of matter'

For Chenu, '*la vérité humaine de la matière*' demanded a restatement of Christian anthropology in more positive terms. This 'vérité humaine' captured three crucial themes in his theology: the truthfulness of the human search for understanding, the divine truth of mat-

---

32. Chenu, 'Condition nouvelle faite à l'homme dans la civilisation technique' (1960) in *La Parole de Dieu II. L'Évangile dans le temps* (Paris: Cerf, 1964), 465–74, 499.
33. *La Parole de Dieu II*, 99.
34. *La Parole de Dieu II*, 99.

ter or creation, and the autonomy of secondary causes. Chenu found in Aquinas' assertion of the consubstantiality of matter and spirit, in the human as body and soul, the integration of matter that afforded its value or integrity in relation to the spirit. In 'Situation humaine: corporalité et temporalité', Chenu cited from Gilson's summary the premises of the unity of matter and spirit developed by Aquinas:

> La matière est donc, dans cette union hylémorphique, un bien et une source de biens, nullement la consequence d'une quelconque déchéance. Elle est meme plus qu'une simple condition de la conquête de l'esprit par lui-même.[35]

Humanity is individuated by matter, which is involved in both the substance and perfection of the human condition. Thomas refused to disqualify matter from a role in personhood.

> Entendez: l'homme, être spirituel libre, susceptible de dialogue et d'amour avec Dieu, est «individu» *par la matière que comporte sa nature.*[36]

In his shorter study of Aquinas, Chenu described the drama of Aquinas coming to this understanding of humanity in the face of trenchant opposition from St Bonaventure and the other theological masters of the University of Paris. Because Aquinas insisted that humanity is a unified being, not '«mixte»' where the soul might be seen as compensating for the body's inadequacies, Chenu observed:

> Contre tout dualisme, l'homme est constitué d'un seul être, où la matière et l'esprit sont les principes consubstantiels d'une totalité déterminée, sans solutions de continuité, par leur mutual inhérence: non pas deux choses, non pas une âme ayant un corps ou mouvant un corps, mais une âme-incarnée et un corps animé, de telle sorte que l'âme est déterminée, comme «forme» du corps, jusqu'au plus intime d'elle-même, à ce point que, sans corps, il lui serait impossible de prendre conscience de son être propre.[37]

---

35. 'Situation humaine: corporalité et temporalité' (1958) in *La Parole de Dieu II. L'Évangile dans le temps* (Paris: Cerf, 1964), 411–436, 429. Chenu referenced six formulae drawn from E Gilson's *Le thomisme* (Paris: Vrin, 1942), 258–275.
36. 'Spiritualité de la matière', 454.
37. Chenu, *St Thomas d'Aquin et la théologie* (Paris: Éditions du Seuil, 1959), 122.

In contrast to a spiritual priority, it is the soul whose being is more dependent on the body:

> C'est dans l'âme même qu'il faut chercher la raison d'être de son corps: inapte à subsister à l'état séparé, quoique sa nature spirituelle lui guarantisse survie une fois qu'elle existe, elle appelle, ontologiquement pour exister, psychologiquement pour agir, la conjonction substanielle à un corps.[38]

Chenu elsewhere distinguished that: 'La matérialisme est dans la «chair», non dans la matière, qui est encore une présence de Dieu.'[39]

The consubstantiality of body and spirit is not a static concept for Chenu. He sees this unity as an anticipation of the eschatological destiny of Creation towards which humanity is moving:

> l'homme est considéré, de par la consubstantialité de son âme et de son corps, comme *solidaire du cosmos*, dans son être, dans son action, dans sa conscience, dans son destin humain et religieux, alors il ne peut s'agir pour lui, dans la poursuite de sa plénitude, d'évacuer peu à peu cette relation *essentielle*, mais de lui donner sa valeur et son efficacité. Immanence au monde, qui ne ruine en rien la transcendence de son esprit.[40]

Then the provisional tension between matter and spirit, history and eschatology is resolved in the promised resurrection of the flesh:

> La résurrection de la chair, comme l'avènement d'une terre nouvelle, résoudront la provisoire opposition de l'histoire et de l'eschatologie, et, avec elle, celle de la matière et de l'esprit.[41]

For Chenu, the Incarnational truth of matter is revealed. This Christological re-creation, through which the intention of God's creation of matter is restored, identifies the truth of matter.

---

38. 'Situation humaine: corporalité et temporalité', 429.
39. 'La Fin de l'ère constantinienne' (1961) in *La Parole de Dieu II. L'Évangile dans le temps* (Paris: Cerf, 1964), 17–36, 28.
40. 'Condition nouvelle faite à l'homme dans la civilisation technique', 101.
41. 'Réflexions chrétiennes sur la vérité de la matière', 450.

Anthropological implications of this consubstantiality

According to Chenu, *De unitate formarum*, Aquinas' theology of matter and form, emerged from an intuition about humanity and its relationship to the world that led Aquinas to study Aristotelian anthropology. Chenu admitted to speculating about this, yet he judged it appropriate that the way the materiality of the Incarnation is restored in Christian theology should come through a theologian's openness to the contemporary challenges of philosophy.[42] As the form of the body, the soul is substantially united to the body, ontologically for existence and psychologically in order to act. This relationship between the soul and matter is a real unity, it is the total human being who is the subject of its actions, including the spirit: 'ce n'est pas l'âme seule qui pense, le corps seul qui sent, c'est l'homme qui pense, veut, aime, sent, agit, travaille'.[43] By this unity we are assured of the goodness of matter and, therefore, of the situation in which this consubstantiality exists:

> L'âme n'est nullement diminuée ni souillée à récapituler dans l'unité de sa propre perfection les opérations physiques, biologiques, psychologiques, techniques, économiques, auxquelles son corps se livre, apparement sous sa propre gouverne et selon l'autonomie relative de ses fonctions.[44]

Chenu concluded: '*l'unité de l'intelligence*, qui, *forme du composé humain*, résiste à tous les séparatismes. Il n'y a pas de faculté du divin.'[45]

Chenu drew out the significant consequences of the consubstantiality of matter and spirit for their psychological and phenomenological implications. This unity of forms means that the spirit is not the exclusive domain of human personhood, '*l'âme séparée du corps n'est pas une personne*'.[46] Rather, as matter individuates, the body is the site of personhood while the soul confers to the body organisation, life, and existence. As it is consubstantial with matter, the human soul lives and acts in time. It can never escape history, nor does humanity realise its perfection by fleeing the world: humanity becomes com-

---

42. 'Situation humaine', 429.
43. 'Situation humaine', 430.
44. 'Situation humaine', 430.
45. 'Situation humaine', 431.
46. 'Situation humaine', 432. [Chenu's emphasis]

plete in the completion of the world.⁴⁷ Human self-understanding is possible only in relationship to the real world it inhabits:

> La vérité humaine, la vérité divine sur l'homme, c'est que l'esprit pénètre profondement le domaine de corps, de son propre corps, mais aussi de tout ce corps du monde, en lui accompli.⁴⁸

Chenu declared that the physical temporality of the cosmos is related to human historicity, another indication of the historical foundation of his view of humanity:

> *Sans que soient effacées les discontinuitiés ontologiques, l'histoire de l'homme, l'histoire de l'esprit, embraye sur l'histoire de la nature.*⁴⁹

He expanded on this as applied to a cosmic sacramentality, which recapitulates creation in humanity:

> L'homme récapitule en lui le cosmos. Il est à la jonction de la matière et de l'esprit. Il est le pivot par lequel toute la matière est récapitulée en lui; il humanise la matière, et c'est par là qu'elle est divinisée. En humanisant le monde, l'homme en prend possession selon la voie de la creation, et c'est ainsi qu'elle est divinisée.⁵⁰

Finally, Chenu completed his profile of the human situation with the understanding that the full materiality of humanity is in its social reality:

> cette anthropologie—*les instants du temps et les libertés des individus ne deviennent une histoire que par et dans une sociabilité des hommes qui vivent dans ce temps.* L'histoire n'est pas une succession de biographies.⁵¹

---

47. 'Il s'accomplit lui-même en accomplissant le monde.' 'Situation humaine', 432.
48. 'Situation humaine', 432. Chenu alluded to Merleau-Ponty's concept: 'Être au monds à travers un corps.' Maurice Merleau-Ponty, *Phénoménologie de la Perception* (Paris: Gallimard, 1945), 357 cited in Chenu, 'L'homme-dans-le-monde' in Jean-Yves Jolif *et al*, editors, *Saint Thomas d'Aquin aujourd'hui* (Paris, Desclée de Brouwer, 1963), 171–175, 172, n 1.
49. 'Situation humaine', 434.
50. 'Pour une anthropologie sacramentelle', in *La Maison-Dieu*, 119 (1974): 85–100, 95.
51. 'Situation humaine', 434.

This is not a society of *laissez-faire* commodification where individual freedom and love are exchanged but not related in justice. Social progress is characterised by the intersubjectivity of love and the social objectivity of just relations. Humanity does not reach its destiny except with others.[52]

In 'Spiritualité de la matière' (1962), many of the same themes are covered along with the more detailed consolidation of the unity of humanity, in relation to Aquinas' argument on the virtues.[53] Chenu underscored the reality of the human subject credited with the goodness of its material and spiritual union by situating the virtues of temperance and fortitude with the passions of aggression and concupiscence that they guide. Following Aquinas' rejection of the distinction between the intellect, surrendered in contemplation of God, and reason, oriented toward knowledge and constructing the world, Chenu refused to separate the *ratio superior* and *ratio inferior*. He insisted that because the soul is one and fully embodied there cannot be such a dualist compromise of the tensions in human existence. The emotive passions are deemed as authentically part of the virtuous life because through this unity they participate in the dignity of reason and love: 'On «cultive» ses passions, selon leur propre engagement, selon les lois de leur nature, devenue alors digne sujet de vertu.'[54] So, negative anthropologies about human embodiment that presume the passions are outside of moral rule are erroneous, instead morality is integrated into embodied humanity.[55] He concluded this point by affirming the virtue of marital sex: 'Ainsi est-ce faire acte de vertu, pour des gens mariés, que d'user des joies inhérentes à leur état.'[56] This understanding of the goodness of sexuality was not commonly expressed by the Catholic moral teaching of that time and indicates the applicability of Chenu's anthropological understanding to the practical issues of human lives. As humanity is a unity, it is the lynchpin or 'jonction' of usually perceived opposing forces in the economy

---

52. 'le sujet n'est pas seulement la personne, mais le corps social'. 'Situation humaine', 434.
53. Chenu further elaborated on the virtues in 'Ratio superior et inferior. Un cas de philosophie chrétienne', in *Revue des sciences philosophiques et théologiques* XXIX (1940): 84-89 and Chenu, M-D, 'Les passions verteuses. L'anthropologie de saint Thomas', in *Revue Philosophique de Louvain*, 72 (1974): 11-18.
54. 'Spiritualité de la matière', 458.
55. 'Spiritualité de la matière', 458. See also St *Thomas d'Aquin et la théologie*, 141.
56. 'Spiritualité de la matière', 458.

of God. As already stated, the human person humanises matter and by it is divinised:

> je posséderai ma nature complète, et, en la possédant, je serai plus près de Dieu. Plus j'aurai ma matière, plus je serai près de l'esprit. Ainsi la matière entre en compte directement dans ma béatitude. L'âme séparée est mal assimilée à Dieu.[57]

In this realist conception of humanity, the body is the point of insertion in the world, at the same time as it takes part in the life of the spirit, and this is the basis of a truly anthropological spirituality:

> Ainsi réintegrée dans la *nature* humaine, et jusque dans la *personne* des hommes, la matière revêt une dignité que nous avons osé appeler une «spiritualité».[58]

In an early work from 1937, Chenu indicated the Christological significance of this humanisation by applying the dictum of Gregory of Nazianzus:

> Si le Christ s'est incarné, c'est pour assumer tout ce qu'il y a dans l'homme, car *tout* l'homme est racheté et divinisé en lui. Le Verbe a pris chair; il est homme jusqu'au bout, jusqu'à la tentation. Éviter ce faux idéalisme qui tendrait à ne voir dans le Christ que les apparences humaines (docétisme).[59]

This was to refute neo-scholasticism's inability to recognise the unity of spirit and matter and it established from within the neo-scholastic system a Thomist reference for the corporeal composition of human existence in material relationship to history and its collective materiality: 'Après la dignité du temps, la dignité de la matière, seconde implication ontologique de l'histoire.'[60] Chenu was continuing his subversion of the neo-scholastic hegemony through this re-claiming using Thomist warrants of the value of matter, in much the same way as he had re-sourced Thomas' *Summa* as historically conditioned. Even at this late stage after the Second Vatican Council's reforms were

---

57. 'Pour une anthropologie sacramentelle', 96.
58. 'Spiritualité de la matière', 459.
59. 'L'unité de la foi', 19.
60. 'Situation humaine', 428.

beginning to take effect in theological circles, he was still constrained by the need to work within a Thomist framework. Chenu was ever theologically committed to this Thomist understanding of humanity and while he anticipated the freedoms of the new ways of theologising, he remained a Thomist.

'La loi de l'incarnation'

Potworowski concludes that Chenu's ambiguity about the meaning of the Incarnation in his theology is due to a Thomist tendency to underplay the significance of the Incarnation. He attributes this to Chenu's theory of the plan of the *Summa*, which he understands (with others) misreads the place of Christology in the *Summa*'s structure. This interpretative transfer from the ongoing debate on the plan of the *Summa,* including Chenu's controversial contribution, at first appears compelling. Potworowski judges that:

> The relations between Christology and the various implementations of the law of incarnation lack systematic differentiation and thematization in the writings of Chenu.[61]

He finds in Chenu an underdeveloped Christology. Clearly this demonstrates the clash in traditions between the Thomist metaphysical approach, from which Chenu is drawing his Incarnational theology, and the more Christocentric approach of Catholic theology after Vatican II. Potworowski is correct in assessing Chenu as having a low Christology, but Chenu can also be understood as more Pauline and Johannine in his emphasis on the cosmic dynamic of the Incarnation.[62] While Chenu's theology may be judged as insufficiently Christological, I find this misses Chenu's preoccupation with the Incarnation in two ways. Firstly, it does not take sufficiently into account the non-systematic nature of Chenu's theology, nor does it appreciate his more cosmic-centred presentation of the Incarnation.

In the later period of his theology, Chenu indicated repeatedly that he was not concerned to create a system, like the neo-scholastic theology against which he was reacting, but a broader theologising on the 'economy' of the Incarnation:

---

61. Potworowski, *Contemplation and Incarnation*, 230.
62. 'Civilisation technique', 90.

> Le Christianisme est une économie—avec toute la densité du mot, classique chez les docteurs grecs—non un système, lors même que, en seconde instance, l'intelligence de cette économie, dans la foi, se développe, normalement et fructueusement, en un système disons mieux: en un savoir «scolastique».[63]

This theology had a particular audience. After his 1937 condemnation, this was not the theological circles of twentieth century Catholic theology, but the Catholic activists engaged with the industrial and commercial ministries of reclaiming the Gospel economy for the masses who had become disaffected from the Church. This did not reduce his theology to a perceived 'lower' rung of so-called 'pastoral theology'. That 'aristocratic' judgement missed the purpose of theology since Vatican II. Resisting the setting of theology against pastoral activity, Chenu argued against 'cette facheuse et vain disjonction entre doctrine et pastoration.'

> La théologie est par définition pastorale, réflexion organique sur l'Église en acte de salut, au point d'impact de son action dans le monde, à un moment donné de l'histoire.[64]

For Chenu, this audience was therefore about altogether different concerns than those of an academic constituency, while it was no less committed to clarity in theological procedure.

In an early address on Christian engagement with contemporary society from 1938, Chenu provided the articulation of 'loi de l'incarnation' of which Potworowski sought further definition. The context for this elaboration of his theology was a *Semaine Sociale* in the industrial hub of Rouen, where priests and Catholic activists reflected theologically on their mission of evangelising French workers who were estranged from the Church. Chenu argued that human freedom was the gift of God, not submission. From this he began describing the effervescence of the Incarnation within humanity:

---

63. 'Histoire du salut', 25.
64. Chenu, 'Une Constitution Pastorale de l'Église' (1966) in *Peuple de Dieu dans le monde* (Paris: Cerf, 1965), 11–33, 17. Chenu insisted that: 'Une théologie qui n'a pas d'expression pastorale est vaine.'

> C'est la loi de l'Incarnation, qui n'est pas seulement venue en chair du Verbe, mais mystère d'un Dieu chef de l'humanité. En ce sens, on a pu dire: Le christianisme n'est pas d'abord un mysticisme, mais un fait historique: le Fils de Dieu fait homme parmi les hommes.[65]

The 'loi d'incarnation', differentiated but in continuity with the 'loi de l'Incarnation', is then presented as the presence of the Spirit in humanity like Christ in the church understood as the body of Christ.

> Car voici précisément la loi de cette incarnation qu'inaugura et que réalise la présence de l'Esprit dans l'humanité: Si Dieu s'incarne pour diviniser l'homme, il faut qu'il prenne *tout* dans l'homme, du haut en bas de sa nature; ne serait pas racheté, ne serait pas libéré ce qui, dans l'homme, resterait en marge de son emprise, de son assomption. Tel est l'authentique régime de la vie divine inaugurée sur terre. Fausse reverence, le docétisme qui voudrait, pour ménager la transcendance de Dieu, limiter l'humanisation du Verbe.'[66]

Then he outlined the continuation of the Incarnation in this 'loi d'incarnation' as an ongoing presence of the Incarnation in humanity, not as an elimination of what is human but its fulfilment:

> Si telle est la loi de l'Incarnation dans le Christ, telle est aussi la loi d'incarnation de la vie divine, au cours des siècles, dans l'Église du Christ. C'est tout l'homme, selon toutes ses ressources et avec toutes ses oeuvres, qui est assumé par la grâce. La vie divine ne s'infuse pas en notre vie par une élimination de son contenu humain ou une réduction de sa structure native, mais par une élévation totalitaire au plan surnaturel.[67]

Chenu understood the extent of the Incarnation as continuing to embrace all of humanity well beyond the historical and specific Incarnation of the Word.

---

65. Chenu, 'Liberté et engagement du chrétien' (1938) in *La Parole de Dieu II. L'Évangile dans le temps* (Paris: Cerf. 1964), 331–354, 345.
66. 'Liberté et engagement du chrétien', 352.
67. 'Liberté et engagement du chrétien', 352.

What Potworowski seems to miss about 'la loi de l'Incarnation' is the capacity Chenu showed to find the salvific act of Christ being continued in humanity through its divinisation in Christ. Chenu held together two understandings of salvation: the mystery of the Incarnational efficacy of the event of Christ and the Eastern Orthodox belief in human divinisation as the purpose and end of human existence. The Thomist insistence on the human paralleling of divine consubstantiality gave him the ground for this symmetrical resolution of an otherwise asymmetrically impossible unity of the human and the divine in the realities of human existence in the world.

> En tout premier lieu et au plus profond, doivent être engagées, évidemment, les ressources constitutives de l'homme, celles qui conditionnent son être et son progrès,—et donc cette structure «sociale» de l'homme, en laquelle seulement il peut trouver sa perfection. Loi de nature qui devient loi de grâce.[68]

Here Chenu invoked the scholastic adage that grace builds on nature: not only grace affecting a single individual but the socialisation of humanity also incorporated into this Incarnational consubstantiality: 'Si l'Incarnation n'arrive pas à assumer cela ['cette vie sociétaire'], c'est une tranche d'humanité qui est rejetée au déchet.'[69] It is this socialisation of humanity into a broader entity than the Church that Chenu marked as bearing witness to the Incarnation in the twentieth century: 'solidaires humainement, solidaires divinement, puisque cette socialibilté, cette «socialisation» est matière et instrument d'incarnation.'[70]

Chenu argued that the Incarnation initiated the divinisation of humanity and world without overwhelming their autonomy. Potworowski's statement that 'Chenu's tendency is to affirm the autonomy of the secular in the light of the incarnation'[71] recognises the direction of Chenu's use of the Incarnation. Again the parallel with the Thomist understanding of the autonomy of secondary causes is operative in

---

68. 'Liberté et engagement du chrétien', 352.
69. 'Liberté et engagement du chrétien', 352.
70. 'Liberté et engagement du chrétien', 353.
71. Potworowski, *Contemplation and Incarnation*, 220.

this theologising.[72] Chenu understood this as not a confusion of the anthropological with the Christological but as evidence of Incarnational continuity, of the divine assumption of the human in Christ for all time. This is the economy of salvation after the Incarnation, prolonged for the time needed for effecting full human divinisation:

> l'économie chrétienne . . . s'incarne au jour le jour dans les plus terrestres solidarités.[73]

Therefore, the 'loi de l'Incarnation' is not so confused where it is replicated liberally throughout Chenu's writing. It indicated the unique place of the human in Creation, through its matter-spirit consubstantiality, and, as a continuation of the Incarnation of Christ, the eventual divinisation of the contemporary world.

Matter and theology of the world

Chenu perceived a nexus (*'une conjoncture'*)[74] between how matter is understood and the value placed on humanity, work, and the world. He sought to articulate the implications of this nexus.

> Il n'est pas possible de faire une théologie de l'homme sans une théologie de la nature, comme il est impossible de séparer une théologie du Verbe incarné d'une théologie du Verbe créateur.[75]

Again his concern was to explicate a Christian anthropology about the divine destiny for humanity on the link between Creation and Incarnation.[76] So Chenu declared that a theology of the world needed

---

72. 'Saint Thomas n'a rien d'un historien; mais sa conception de l'homme-dans-le-monde fournit les bases d'une sociologie où l'efficacité et l'intelligibilité des causes secondes, loin de concurrencer l'éternelle Providence de Dieu, la réalisent dans le temps et dans la vérité terrestre de l'histoire, la sainte et la profane.' 'Creation et histoire', in AA Maurer *et al*, *St Thomas Aquinas 1274–1974*, 398.
73. 'Classes et Corps mystique du Christ', 479.
74. Chenu referred to this concept as 'une conjoncture', and in other places 'un noeud'. I have added 'nexus' to capture the intersecting implications of the concept. *Cf* n 25.
75. 'Présentation' in *Théologie de la matière*, 13.
76. 'C'est que tout n'a pas été donne à la fois: la création continue, et l'homme est, dans le temps, le coopérateur du Dieu éternel.' 'Situation humaine: corporalité et temporalité', 426.

to be elaborated for there to be a true theological understanding of God come into the world. Again, he did not complete a theology of the world, but he proposed an outline for such a project, under the themes of: 1) humanity and the universe, with work providing the 'jonction' of spirit and matter alongside a critique of the Marxist concept of human nature; 2) humanity itself as the nexus of matter, work, and the world; 3) the total economy of salvation, eschatological and terrestrial, to avoid dualism; and 4) the Incarnation as the definitive theology of the world, as 'terre de grâce', where the creating Word becomes human so that humanity may become, in the world that is humanised by them, a power for divinisation.[77] These recall the themes he also proposed in 'Pour une théologie du travail'.[78] The world is the theological meeting point where the human, as unity of matter and spirit, through work transforms matter and brings about the rapid expansion of human consciousness and social responsibility.[79] For Chenu, then, the relationship of humanity to created matter, the world, is not accidental but integral to full humanisation:

> La relation de l'homme à la nature n'est donc pas un accident marginal et indifferent; elle est un lieu d'humanisation de l'homme, et donc de sa perfection.[80]

Because humanity shares materiality and is situated in Creation, in terms of the continuing Incarnation it resembles the Christological adage that the whole of Creation is recapitulated in Christ.

> L'homme récapitule en lui le cosmos. Il est à la jonction de la matière et de l'esprit. Il est le pivot par lequel toute la matière est récapitulée en lui; il humanise la matière, et c'est par là qu'elle est divinisée.[81]

---

77. 'Civilisation technique et spiritualité nouvelle', 89–91. In 1967 Chenu published 'The Need for a Theology of the World' in *Great Ideas Today* (1967): 54–69, which included an English version of 'Foi et religion', in *Études philosophiques* 21/3 (1966): 357–69 and the conclusion from 'Une Constitution pastorale de l'Église', 33: 'Verbe créateur, fait homme, pour que l'homme devienne, dans le monde qu'il humanise, une puissance de divinisation.'
78. See Chapter 6.
79. 'Civilisation technique', 90.
80. Chenu, 'Paradoxe de la pauvreté évangélique et construction du monde' (1963) in *Théologie de la matière* (Paris: Cerf, 1967), 113.
81. 'Pour une anthropologie sacramentelle', 95. Also 'Spiritualité de la matière', 23: '[L'homme] s'accomplit lui-même en accomplissant le monde.'

For this to be effective, the human and the Church must be understood as '*dans* le monde, et non pas juxtaposée à lui'.[82]

How Chenu defined the world is many layered: it is a physical category, 'espace, le temps, les intempéries, la végétation, les fleaux',[83] in a biblical sense it is equivalent to Creation and the universe, where humanity finds its end and 'La perfection de l'univers est entièrement immanente au monde';[84] most significantly, the world is where humanity is located and, by co-operating with the Creator, constructs the world in freedom and responsibility.

> En construisant le monde, grâce à l'extraordinaire essor de la science et des techniques, l'homme prend possession du *dominium terrae*, à ce point qu'il assume ainsi la responsabilité historique du cosmos, selon l'impératif biblique, éclairé désormais par l'humanisation du Verbe.[85]

Yet Chenu is not blindly optimistic about the ambiguity of the world:

> Certes ce monde est le lieu de drames et de violences qui déconcertent et mettent en cause ces resources et ces espérances. Leurs valeurs qu'il exalte sont ambigués.[86]

Yet it is the necessity of the world as the material reality that humanity is immersed in that makes human engagement with the world open to God's economy of salvation. The truth of matter for humanity in God's economy is not flight from the world to a spiritual state of super-terrestrial purity.[87] His theology of the world is best illustrated in Vatican II's *Pastoral Constitution on the Church in the Modern World* whose content and direction Chenu's work had anticipated since the late 1930s. This was the move away from the enclosed 'per-

---

82. *Un théologien en liberté*, 196.
83. 'Civilisation technique', 113.
84. 'Création et histoire', 395.
85. 'Une Constitution pastorale de l'Église', 29. See also 'L'Encyclique sur le developpement des peuples' *Economie et Humanisme*, 174/26 (1967): 1–4, 4.
86. Chenu, 'Un Concile à la dimension du monde' (1962) in in *La Parole de Dieu II. L'Évangile dans le temps* (Paris: Cerf, 1964), 633–7, 634. A further list of the problems of the worrld appeared in 'Une Constitution pastorale de l'Église', 15.
87. 'Sa perfection ne consiste pas à surmonter une existence-dans-le-monde, comme une conjoncture assez pesante, mais à réaliser dans ce monde le plein équilibre ontologique et moral de son être', 'Spiritualité de la matière', 23.

fect society' of the Church prevalent before Vatican II.[88] In *Gaudium et spes*, 'world' is not a defined concept as such. Defining the 'world' was problematic for the commission of Schema XIII (*Gaudium et Spes*), as its theologian and commentator Charles Moeller admitted, because this involved going beyond the ambiguous and negative senses given 'the world' in previous doctrinal use, without seeming 'to canonise the modern world.'[89] Chenu's use of world was both emblematic and metaphorical conveying the relationship between humanity and the universe as material: 'le cas suprême d'une structure générale de l'univers.'[90] When Chenu employed 'the world' it was primarily as the location of humanity: 'Plus Dieu est présent au monde, plus le monde est monde, dans sa mondanité.'[91]

World, for Chenu, stands for humanity active in and contributing to the construction of the world, a theme recurrent in his writing. This is the object of his theology of work as much as his theology of matter. Work is a metaphor for the world in Chenu's Christian anthropology: the world is the industrial reality of city factories which, rather than apparently reducing the concept of world, enhanced it by extending to it the human creativity of the transformation of matter. Matter operates similarly by extending the human enterprise from a dissociated experience from the spiritual to an embodied inspiring that refuses the separation of matter from spirituality. 'Ainsi réintegrée dans la *nature* humaine, et jusque dans la *personne* homme, la matière revêt une dignité que nous avons osé appeler une «spiritualité».'[92] So matter is the unifying characteristic of humanity, the world, and human work. Chenu retrieved the unity of matter and spirit and further

---

88. Its themes echo Chenu's anthropological and ecclesial interests: 'The Community of Mankind' (Chapter II), 'Man's Activity throughout the World' (Chapter III), and 'The Role Of The Church In The Modern World' (Chapter IV), and are previewed in the text of the Council Bishops' *Message au monde* that Chenu had initiated in 1962.
89. Moeller also makes mention of Chenu along with Congar, Montini, and Dom Helder Camara in relation to the genesis of an *ad extra* mentality at the Council. Charles Moeller, 'History of the Constitution', in Herbert Vorgrimler, editor, *Commentary on the Documents of Vatican II*, volume V (New York: Herder and Herder, 1969), 58–61.
90. 'L'Homme-dans-le-monde', 174.
91. Chenu, 'Modernité', in *La Lettre* nos 346/347 (sept-oct, 1987): 5–7, 6.
92. 'Spiritualité de la matière', 23.

restored their theological-anthropological meaning in a theology of the world.

Implications of Chenu's theology of matter on theological anthropology

Chenu saw the rediscovery of the human value of matter as the specific theological and sociological contribution of twentieth century modernity.[93] He further claimed for the twentieth century the vocation of pursuing a fuller understanding of the implications of the Incarnation:

> Il n'est pas présumptueux de penser que les époques de l'humanité possèdent chacune la vocation collective de découvrir et d'exulter l'un ou l'autre des valeurs humaines. Cette prise de conscience est sans doute, en ce XXe siècle, la cause occasionelle d'une intelligence plus profonde de la foi. Tradition vivante qui manifeste, siècle par siècle, les implications du mystère de l'Incarnation, continue dans l'Eglise, Corps du Christ.[94]

His theology of matter presented the Incarnation as a protest against the denial of matter and the world, and any pessimism about humanity. The implications for humanity are that the truth of the spiritual and material unity of humanity is re-claimed: human embodiment unites humans with the world, where humanity progressively discovers its own spiritual reality through human socialisation and the transformation of matter. While the pivot or nexus of this understanding is an appreciation of the truth of matter, its outcome is a redeemed theology of humanity. This is an embodied, fleshly, material humanity, not the disembodied *homo economicus* of capitalism or Marxism. This embodiment is 'thick' with real humanity: 'L'homme est le relais de l'expansion de l'amour créateur jusque dans l'épaisseur de la matière.'[95] Chenu's anthropology incorporated the burden of industrial workers in their sweat, women who had exclusively embodied the nega-

---

93. 'Réflexions chrétiennes sur la vérité de la matière' (1948) in *La Parole de Dieu II. L'Évangile dans le temps* (Paris: Cerf, 1964), 447–451, 448-9.
94. 'Présentation', 11.
95. Chenu, *St Thomas d'Aquin et la théologie* (Paris: Éditions du Seuil, 1959), 122.

tivity associated with matter, and even children, whose potential as students and workers does not overshadow their value as persons in themselves.[96] Chenu understood this corporeality as

> La vérité humaine, la vérité divine sur l'homme, c'est que l'esprit pénètre profondement le domaine de corps, de son propre corps, mais aussi de tout ce corps du monde, en lui accompli.[97]

For Chenu, an appreciation of the integral function of matter in God's Creation epitomised the fullest understanding of humanity and its purpose in Creation. Besides countering aristocratic notions of spirituality, Chenu was asserting the value of the concrete and of those connections with nature that have too often been depreciated as 'primitive' beliefs. Chenu's refusal to categorise matter as incompatible with the spiritual challenged the 'idea that the apophatic is the higher form of religious experience'.[98] Chenu's theology of the world also offers opening perspectives on Christian dialogue with other world inhabitants than those who ascribe to the 'great faiths'.

Chenu's theology of matter contributes a realist appreciation of humanity as matter and its agency in the transformation of matter and the co-operation with the construction of the world. Chenu assured through his theology that materialism not matter is the adversary of faith, but that even materialism could be converted to realising God's economy. Chenu sought to situate humanity within its reality, not sacralise it to achieve an extra spiritual value. 'Plus j'aurai ma matière, plus je serai près de l'esprit. Ainsi la matière entre en compte directement dans ma béatitude.'[99] The human value of matter is that it grounds human aspirations while it orients the human to

---

96. See 'Des femmes chrétiennes présentes à leur temps' (1952); Chenu's preface to Mathilde Landercy, *Figures de Femmes au sein du peuple de Dieu* (Paris; MédiasPaul, 1987), 7–9; Chenu, 'L'avenir professionel de l'enfant: perspectives théologiques' in *L'enfant et son avenir professionel: Esquisse d'une théologie de la création et du travail* (Paris: Éditions Fleurus, 1959), 11–47.
97. 'Réflexions chrétiennes sur la vérité de la matière' (1948), 449.
98. From Chenu's theological appreciation of matter, Frank Fletcher has extrapolated how the immanent religious beliefs of Australian Aborigines, in their materiality, can be valued by Christians. Frank Fletcher MSC, 'Towards a Dialogue with Traditional Aboriginal Religion', in *Pacifica* 9 (1996): 164–174, 172.
99. 'Pour une anthropologie sacramentelle', 96.

its source and object, the Creator God. Chenu's theology of matter realised the unity of the Creation and Incarnation and the truth they declare about the value of matter. The 'loi de l'Incarnation' is continued through the unity of matter and spirit in humanity and, through the continuing human construction of the world in history, the new economy of the Reign of God is initiated.

> *La résurrection de la chair, comme l'avènement d'une terre nouvelle, résoudront la provisoire opposition de l'histoire et de l'eschatologie, et, avec elle, celle de la matière et l'esprit.*[100]

The theology of matter situated Chenu's Christian anthropology at the centre of this unity overcoming the false divisions that alienated human life and the world from its divinely created orientation. Chenu's theology of humanity appropriately revolved on the two significant contributions of the twentieth century to human understanding: historical consciousness and the rehabilitation of materiality. Matter and history thereby constitute the framework for Chenu's Christian anthropology.

---

100. 'Réflexions chrétiennes sur la vérité de la matière', 451.

Conclusion

'Le monde leur tient lieu de cellule et l'océan de cloître.'
Chenu (1989)[1]

While Chenu never completed a Christian anthropology, this study has sought to extract the features of such a project through his published writings. To some degree, besides his theology being incomplete, this task returned an incomplete theological anthropology also. Besides some notable lack of coverage of the topics of sin and the sinner's relationship to God, Chenu's approach to the theology of humanity derived from a different perspective to that of traditional theological anthropology. Working from human experience in work, in the social context of Church and in the particularities of gender and development of the young, Chenu shaped a more grounded human subject as the object of his theology.[2] Early in his writing he identified his starting point in the dynamic of the 'theological humanism' of Aquinas, distinguishing this from a 'humanist theology' where the theology was confined by the humanist agenda.[3] Chenu's Christian anthropology was always focused on the God–human relationship

---

1. Chenu 'Le monde leur tient lieu de cellule et l'océan de cloître' (unpublished discourse on the occasion of the canonical visit of Damian Byrne OP, Dominican Master General, Couvent St Jacques, Paris: 12 March 1989). This was Chenu's last recorded theological reflection.
2. This is suggested in the class-transcending mutuality of a particular encounter between two women in 'Classes et Corps mystique du Christ' (1940), 494 and in his article about the public roles of women in 'Des femmes chrétiennes présentes à leur temps', Témoignage Chrétien, juin 6 (1952).
3. 'Position', 135.

and the implications of this for the destiny of humanity. This is evident in his applications of the understanding of nature and grace, particularly as it applies to humanity's relationship to God's creation and the co-creative role of humanity in the construction of the world. Humanity was identified as a locus of grace and consequently human endeavours, like the development of technology in industrialisation, hold out the possibility for furthering God's grace. There are two features of Chenu's Christian anthropology that emerged from this exploration of his writings: the divine truth of humanity is revealed in human history, that all human affairs remain open to the continuing Incarnation; and the comprehensive inclusion of all humanity, regardless of class, race, and gender, in the humanisation towards divinisation that is the Creator's destiny for humanity. While these may seem too obvious at this later stage of Christian theology, Chenu's coupling of these truths was a challenge to the abstract theological hegemony before Vatican II. Even now, such confidence about humanity is depicted as a dated optimism rather than the theologically embracing hope that it is. The problem represented by Chenu's ever-hopeful realism about humanity continues to affront and appear unsatisfactory from a contemporary perspective. Yet there is also something appropriately challenging in Chenu's overarching benevolence towards humanity and human potential.

The introduction presented his image of the bridge at Pont-St-Esprit, because this appeals as a metaphor for Chenu's work and life. His theology bridged the desiccated analytical 'modern scholasticism', which was such a rejection of the historical challenges of the nineteenth and early twentieth century and the human autonomy that they claimed. It stretched across the turmoil and destruction of the two world wars and the mass industrialisation of Europe, to reach expansive understanding of humanity and commitment to the world in the new ecclesial bridge of the Second Vatican Council's *Gaudium et spes*. Chenu not only spanned that century but was deeply immersed in its political and social struggles and some of the more innovative ecclesial responses to the needs that emerged from such upheavals. His advocacy of '*présence*' was at the cost of many '*ruptures*' in his theological ministry, yet he recognised such setbacks as opportune and vitally constitutive of the disruptive awakening to the new that the Incarnation continually calls for in the Church and in the world.

So it is not surprising that his last reflection would also be about the encounter with the world from even his friar's cell.

There are stylistic reasons why the evidence for compiling his theology of humanity is limited also. Chenu was not systematic in either his approach or product. Primarily, he is not particularly philosophical, but eclectic in his use of philosophical concepts and expressions. His aphoristic style recalls Pascal's *Pensées* but often lacked sufficient elucidation of his point despite the flourish of his passion. Clearly, Chenu intended this effect to communicate effectively with his audiences, who were not theologians. Chenu convinced people not by argument but through repetition and a grounded-ness that met and valued their experience. As well, Chenu's theology did not operate within the more familiar categories of Christian anthropology, yet his work cannot be reduced to merely a humanism. He frequently presented current ecclesial and world issues against the typology of the Incarnation and the Christological controversies of the early Church. Yet Christ was not the subject of his theology in the way that humanity was, this study has proposed. It was history and the world as the sites of the construction of humanity that shaped his theology; this was not an historical theology in the style of his student and colleague, Congar. While his earlier writings were historical studies of the theologies of the twelfth and thirteenth centuries, particularly the innovation of Aquinas, Chenu did not pursue a 'return to the sources' oriented *ressourcement* throughout the rest of his theological writing. He drew on Aquinas to legitimate his theological dialogue with modernity in the earlier period before World War II, but following the 1957 republishing of *La théologie comme science au XIIIe siècle*, Chenu did not substantially return to theological history. As his critics have observed, Chenu drew from history his theology rather than examined theology historically. In this sense, despite his protestations, there was some split between the 'deux Chenus': the medievalist and the contemporary twentieth century theologian.

Despite the limitations in capturing his 'missing' theology of humanity, this study has detected more than the prolegomena for such a theology. The preceding trawl through Chenu's theology indicated features of his Christian Anthropology that the study attempted to draw together and which have both relevance and value today, as much because of the continuing threat to humanity from its own negative portrayal of itself in the face of continually destructive forces that feed on the dualism that informs such negativity. Chenu's theological anthropology does emerge from his corpus as Christian in its sources and in the eschatological orientation of his vision of humanity. It also bears a Thomist confidence in God's creation of autonomy in secondary causes, through which humanity operates not as estranged sinner but with the possibility of being co-operator with the Creator in the construction of the world. Chenu's theology enriches understanding of the historical situatedness of humanity and how this necessitates belief in and communication of the Gospel in each new age. From this, his openness to God's grace working even through secularisation and the human ingenuity of further advances in technology rightly orients confidence in God's constant relationship with humanity. Most significantly, there is Chenu's own delight in humanity and its spiritual and material consubstantiality that leads to his optimistic outlook on human capacity to seek God in truth. These features of his Christian anthropology are manifested in the themes of the two pivotal collections of his writing, *La Parole de Dieu*: faith in understanding and the Gospel in time.

In Chapter 1, this thesis presented the historical grounds for all his theology but especially his understanding of the '*temporalité*' of humanity and the false idealism of a theology not informed by history. Chenu's own struggle with the Vatican and the theological authorities of his Dominican order outlined the pattern of '*présence*' and '*rupture*' in the history of the theology he studied and taught. An historically Incarnational faith bears the confidence that humanity is not defeated by the 'echecs' and 'ruptures' of human history, but that these can reveal to humanity its fullest potential in its vocation of the construction of the world. Chenu refused the timeless authority claimed by the theological approach of neo-scholasticism and so rejected the anti–Modernist dualism of history versus faith in a prelude to defining humanity in terms of faith and understanding.

In Chapter 2, his earlier theological writing was explored with its emphasis on retrieving Aquinas' methodology in its historical context. With particular emphasis on Aquinas incorporation of Aristotle's autonomy of human reason, Chenu argued for the breakthrough of Aquinas' portrayal of the unity of human understanding.[4] From

---

4. '*Cognita sunt in cognoscente secundum modum cognoscentis.*' ST IIa IIae, q. I, a. 2, *responsio*.

this, Chenu emphasised the necessary unity of faith and contemplation in the believer and, further, the unity of faith and reason in the theological enterprise. The integrity of revelation and the receptivity of reason to divine grace was asserted in humanity. From his earliest encounter with the Dominican life of contemplation and learning, he sought a theology 'où l'engagement dans le monde est facteur de vie contemplative, à l'encontre d'une scolastique intemporelle.'[5] The outcome of the Dominican character of his vocation led to a contemplation in the world that resisted the dualisms between faith and spirituality, faith and reason in humanity, and found a 'cohérence de la nature et de la grâce'.[6]

From this, Chenu explored the social nature of humanity expressed in the community of Church. In Chapter 3, his understanding of the Church as continuing the Incarnation through the community it encourages was introduced and was further developed in his theology of matter. Chenu's greatest contribution to ecclesiology was the realisation that the Church no longer alone could set the agenda for its theology. This was the understanding declared in *Nouvelle Dimension de Chrétienté*: a radical understanding of the impact of the laity in the life and any future theology of the Church. A new Christianity was emerging in tandem with the awakening of the laity, especially the politicised activists of the industrial movements, who challenged the separation of the Church from their world. Here, the ecclesially defined dualism of the sacred and the secular was rejected by Chenu as not Incarnational.

Vatican II appeared as a vindication of Chenu's position during the previous thirty years. In Chapter 4, the peripheral involvement by Chenu in the Council's deliberations was judged as insufficiently manifesting the significance of his contribution to its proceedings and documentation. From his initiation of *The Message of the Bishops to the World* at the outset of the Council to his vigorous disputing of the concept '*consecratio mundi*', Chenu's contribution maintained the church's engagement with the world that John XXIII had inaugurated. The full extent of Chenu's influence on the teaching of Vatican II remains to be assessed.

---

5. 'De la contemplation à l'engagement', in *La vie spirituelle* no 678, tome 142 (1988): 99–102, 101.
6. 'De la contemplation à l'engagement', 102.

His theology of history remained as unformulated as his Christian anthropology, yet it pervaded all his thought. In Chapter 5, Chenu's melding of historical method, particularly the history from below of the *Annales* school, with an understanding of the theological significance of history was traced. Chenu's identification of the recurrence of '*rupture*' in history as a bearer of change through the awakening to new conceptualisation and reforms was highlighted as distinctive in his theology of history. Chenu always situated human inquiry as the agent of such change.

In Chapter 6, how Chenu takes this historical and social reality of humanity further into the world, through the factories and the mass socialisation imposed by industrialisation, was presented. His exploration of the humanity realised in work as co-operating in creative continuity with God the Creator was explored against the competing Marxist understanding of humanity. Chenu refused the modern isolation of the subject in itself, and instead examined the human as matter and spirit, through the realistic contexts of worker and community member. Therefore, the oppositional divide between all human work and God's Creation is overcome. For Chenu, work is a metaphor for the city and the need for the re-location of Church mission to factories and other work-places, instead of the village centrality it had enjoyed. The industrialised city also signifies for Chenu the reality of the world that the Church must find its place in anew. Work provided the milieu for Chenu to develop his anthropological turn more explicitly and to outline the key features of his Christian anthropology through the areas of the human condition, humanity and the universe, and humanity in the whole economy of salvation.

Finally, in Chapter 7, the basis for Chenu's theology of humanity is located in Aquinas' understanding of the efficacy of matter. Here the ultimate and most pervasive dualism of Christianity is deposed. For Chenu, God, faith, and spirituality are not opposed to the world and matter. It is in humanity that this dualism is defeated, because the human cannot relinquish the material nature that links it to God as creature and through which the Incarnation links Christ with humanity. It is through his teaching on matter and its 'conjoncture', or nexus of the human and the world, that Chenu established the ground for his Christian anthropology. Matter, history, and the world are all linked through humanity to the Incarnation.

While this investigation of Chenu's writings has not produced a comprehensive or systematised treatment of his Christian anthropology, it has collected the crucial features of such a theological project and found hints of what Chenu might have developed had the ruptures in his long life not have inserted at the particular times they did. His theology, while dispersed over the three main themes of the reality of faith, work, and matter, suggests innovative insights that only now appear so familiar because of the widespread adoption of them in the correlative and inductive methodologies of theology since Vatican II.[7] Chenu presented a theology of humanity that called for confidence that God relates to humanity and the rest of creation in all ages and across all civilisations. As Frank Fletcher suggested, this even applies to the humanity lived by indigenous peoples whose materialism is often mistaken for an absence of the spiritual.[8] This derivation from Chenu's theology has implications for the new generations of post-secularised, materialist human populations. Not only are these the successors of the 'de-Christianised' moderns that Chenu initially addressed as the pastoral concern of the Church, they embody anew the continuous challenge of the Incarnation that Chenu identified then. Chenu's Christian anthropology offers even today an important bridge to the consumerist world of the unbelievers: an understanding of what it means to be fully human that reaches beyond the Church to those otherwise alienated by ecclesial tactics. To understand the world as taking the place of his cell and the ocean like the cloister captures the bridging of oppositions that characterises Chenu's Christian anthropology. Chenu's anthropological project presents as even more appropriate today, as much because the official distaste for theologies of grounded in terrestrial realities recalls the separatism of the pre-Vatican Church that Chenu sought to overcome with an openness to the truth and freedom of humanity.

---

7. 'Si l'histoire est ainsi consubstantielle au christianisme, tant dans l'intimité des vocations personnelles que dans la Communauté du Peuple de Dieu, il apparaît que, dans cette Constitution pastorale, le ressort de l'induction humano-divine qui en soutient l'élaboration doit être la condition humaine dans l'histoire, *in muno huius temporis*, et non la nature humaine abstraite, fût-ce sous prétexte de transcendance.' 'Une Constitution Pastorale de l'Église' (1965), 18–19.
8. Frank Fletcher MSC, 'Towards a Dialogue with Traditional Aboriginal Religion', in *Pacifica* 9 (1996): 164–174, 172.

Bibliography
Chenu—Books

Chenu OP, Marie-Dominique,

Dieu et l'homme d'aujourd'hui (Paris: Éditions du Seuil, 1958).
Dimension nouvelle de la Chrétienté (Paris: Éditions du Cerf, 1937).
Introduction à l'étude de Saint Thomas d'Aquin (Montréal/Paris: Institut d'études médiévales/J.Vrin, 1950).
L'enfant et son avenir professionnel. Esquisse d'une théologie de la création et du travail (Paris: Édition de Fleurus, 1959).
L'éveil de la conscience dans la civilisation médiévale (Montreal-Paris: Institut d'Études Médiévales-Librairie J.Vrin, 1969).
La 'doctrine sociale' de l'Église comme idéologie (Paris: Éditions du Cerf, 1979).
Les études de philosophie medieval (Paris: Hermann et Companie, 1939).
La Parole de Dieu I. La Foi dans intelligence (Paris: Éditions du Cerf, 1964).
La Parole de Dieu II. L'Évangile dans le temps (Paris: Éditions du Cerf, 1964).
La théologie au douzième siècle (Paris: Librairie Philosophique J.Vrin, 1957).
La théologie comme science au XIIIe siècle (Paris: Librairie Philosophique J.Vrin, 1957).
La théologie est-elle une science? (Paris: Athème Fayard, 1957).
Notes quotidiennes au Concile: Journal de Vatican II 1962–1963, edited by Alberto Melloni (Paris: Éditions du Cerf, 1995).
Peuple de Dieu dans le monde (Paris: Éditions du Cerf, 1966).
Pour une théologie du travail (Paris: Seuil, 1955).
Pour être heureux travaillons ensemble (Paris: Presses Universitaires de France, 1942).

Spiritualité du travail (Paris: Éditions de Temps Présent, 1941).

St Thomas d'Aquin et la théologie (Paris: Éditions du Seuil, 1959).

Théologie de la matière. Civilisation technique et spiritualité chrétienne (Paris: Éditions du Cerf, 1967).

Une école de théologie: Le Saulchoir (Kain-lez-Tournai/Etiolles: Le Saulchoir/Casterman, 1937).

Une école de théologie: Le Saulchoir edited by Giuseppe Alberigo (Paris: Éditions du Cerf, 1985). [1937 edition republished with additional essays].

Collections and Interviews of Chenu

Brosse, Olivier de la, editor, *Le Père Chenu: La Liberté Dans La Foi* (Paris: Les Éditions du Cerf, 1969).

M-D Chenu and Jacques Duquesne, *Un théologien en liberté: Jacques Duquesne interroge le Père Chenu* (Paris: Le Centurion, 1975).

Chenu's Doctoral Thesis

M-D Chenu OP, 'De Contemplationis Natura', unpublished STD thesis, Angelicum, Rome (1920).

Chenu Articles:

Chenu OP, Marie-Dominique,

'Albert le Grand et la révolution intellectuelle du XIIIe siècle', in *Blackfriars,* XIX (January 1938), 5–15.

'Anthropologie et liturgie' (1947), in *La Parole de Dieu I. La Foi dans intelligence* (Paris: Cerf, 1964), 309–21.

'Arts "mécaniques" et oeuvres serviles', in *Revue des sciences philosophiques et théologiques,* 29 (1940), 313–15.

'Au temps des ordres mendiants', in *Lumière et Vie,* 153/4 (1981), 143–49.

'Aux origines de la «science moderne»', in *Revue des sciences philosophiques et théologiques,* XXIX (1940), 206–17.

'Bilan du XIIe siècle', in *2000 ans de christianisme,* edited by Marie-Dominique Chenu, Michel Balard and Francis Rapp (Paris: Hachette, 1975), 160–63.

'Ce qui change et ce qui demeure', in *L'Église vers l'avenir*, edited by M Cornillon, M.-D. Chenu, Ch. Duquoc, P. Eyt *et al* (Paris: Cerf, 1969), 87–91.

'Chrétien, mon frère. Pourquoi la guerre?' (1939), *La Parole De Dieu II. L'Évangile dans le temps* (Paris: Cerf, 1964), 225–30.

'Chrétienté ou mission? A propos des «Mouvements de paix»' (1949), in *La Parole de Dieu II. L'Évangile dans le temps* (Paris: Cerf, 1964), 255–59.

'Civilisation technique et spiritualité nouvelle' (1948), in *La Parole de Dieu II. L'Évangile dans le temps* (Paris: Cerf, 1964), 137–58.

'Civilisation urbaine et théologie. L'école de Saint-Victor au XIIe siècle', in *Annales. Économies, sociétés, civilisations*, 29 (1974), 1253–63.

'Classes et Corps mystique du Christ' (1939), in *La Parole de Dieu II. L'Évangile dans le temps* (Paris: Cerf, 1964), 477–94.

'Communautés humaines et présence missionaire' (1957), in *La Parole de Dieu II. L'Évangile dans le temps* (Paris: Cerf, 1964), 261–64.

'Condition nouvelle faite à l'homme dans la civilisation technique' (1960), in *La Parole de Dieu II. L'Évangile dans le temps* (Paris: Cerf, 1964), 465–74.

'«Consecratio mundi»', in *Nouvelle Revue Théologique*, 86 (1964), 608–618.

'Contribution à l'histoire du traité de la foi. Commentaire historique de IIa IIae, q. I, a. 2' (1923), in *La Parole de Dieu I. La Foi dans intelligence* (Paris: Cerf, 1964), 31–50.

'Corps de L'Église et structures sociales' (1948), in *La Parole de Dieu II. L'Évangile dans le temps* (Paris: Cerf, 1964), 159–69.

'Création et histoire', in *St Thomas Aquinas 1274–1974 Commemorative Studies*, volume II, edited by AA Maurer *et al* (Toronto: Pontifical Institute of Medieval Studies, 1974), 391–99.

'De la contemplation à l'engagement', in *Vie Spirituelle*, 142/678 (1988), 99–102.

'Des femmes chrétiennes présentes à leur temps', in *Témoignage Chrétien* (juin 6 1952), 1.

'Destinée personnelle et morale communautaire' (1941), in *La Parole de Dieu II. L'Évangile dans le temps* (Paris: Cerf, 1964), 355–62.

'Déchristianisation ou non christianisation?' (1960), in *La Parole de Dieu II. L'évangile dans le temps* (Paris: Cerf, 1964), 247–53.

'Définition de l'unité de l'enseignement', in *Seminarium*, XXIII/2 (1971), 267–79.

'Expérience chrétienne', in *Spiritus*, 13 (1972), 131–41.

'Foi et religion', in *Etudes philosophiques*, 21/3 (1966), 357–69.

'Histoire du salut et historicité de l'homme dans le renouveau de la théologie', in *La théologie du renouveau,* volume I, edited by L Shook and GM Bertrand (Mont'éal/Paris: Cerf, 1968), 21–32.

'Journalisme et théologie' (1939), in *La Parole de Dieu II. L'Évangile dans le temps* (Paris: Cerf, 1964), 213–24.

'L'amour dans la foi' (1932), in *La Parole de Dieu I. La Foi dans intelligence* (Paris: Cerf, 1964), 105–111.

'L'économie du XXe siècle et la vertu de la promesse' (1960), in *La Parole de Dieu II. L'Évangile dans le temps* (Paris: Cerf, 1964), 617–29.

'L'Église aujourd'hui—Diagnostics: 4. La crise, dimension de notre foi au Christ', in *Lumière et Vie,* 93/XVIII (1969), 66–70.

'L'église des pauvres', in *La Maison-Dieu,* 81 (1965), 9–13.

'L'église et le monde des images', in *Peuple De Dieu Dans Le Monde* (Paris: Cerf, 1966), 145–56.

'L'encyclique sur le developpement des peuples', in *Economie et Humanisme,* 174/26 (1967), 1–4.

'L'équilibre de la scolastique médiévale' (1940), in *La Parole de Dieu I. La Foi dans intelligence* (Paris: Cerf, 1964), 229–39.

'L'étude historique de saint Thomas', in *Revue philosophique de Louvain,* 49 (1951), 735–43.

'L'Évangile dans l'économie. A propos de l'encyclique *Populorum Progressio*', in *Théologie de la matière. Civilisation technique et spiritualité chrétienne* (Paris: Cerf, 1967), 141–48.

'L'évangélisme de saint Thomas d'Aquin', in *Revue des sciences philosophiques et théologiques,* 58 (1974), 391–403.

'L'homme-dans-le-monde', in *Saint Thomas d'Aquin aujourd'hui,* edited by Jean-Yves Jolif *et al* (Paris: Desclée de Brouwer, 1963), 171–75.

'L'humanisation de la terre, dimension constitutive de l'Évangile', in *Lumière et vie,* 33 (1984), 87–90.

'L'itinéraire d'un théologien', in *L'Actualité religieuse dans le monde,* 19 (15 janvier 1985), 21–22.

'L'opinion publique dans l'Église', in *Censure et liberté d'expression* (Paris: Desclée de Brouwer, 1970), 124–34.

'L'unité de la foi. Réalisme et formalisme' (1937), in *La Parole de Dieu I. La Foi dans intelligence* (Paris: Cerf, 1964), 13–19.

'La 'doctrine sociale' de l'Église', in *Concilium,* 160 (1980), 119–25.

'La décadence de l'allégorisation. Un témoin: Garnier de Rochefort († v. 1200)', in *L'homme devant Dieu: Mélanges offerts au Père Henri de Lubac,* volume II (Paris: Aubier, Éditions Montaigne, 1964), 129-35.

'La fin de l'ère constantinienne' (1961), in *La Parole de Dieu II. L'Évangile dans le temps* (Paris: Cerf, 1964), 17-36.

'La fin des temps dans la spiritualité', in *Lumière et vie,* 11 (1953), 101-16.

'La foi en Chrétienté' (1944), in *La Parole de Dieu II. L'Évangile dans le temps* (Paris: Cerf, 1964), 109-32.

'La J.O.C. au Saulchoir' (1936), in *La Parole de Dieu II. L'Évangile dans le temps* (Paris: Cerf, 1964), 271-74.

'La littérature comme "lieu" de la théologie', in *Revue des sciences philosophiques et théologiques,* LIII (1969), 70-80.

'La nature et l'homme', in *Archives d'histoire doctrinale et littéraire du moyen age,* XIX (1952), 39-66.

'La psychologie de la foi dans la théologie du XIIIe siècle. Genèse de la doctrine de saint Thomas Somme théologique, IIa IIae, q. 2, a. 1.' (1932), in *La Parole de Dieu I. La Foi dans intelligence* (Paris: Cerf, 1964), 77-104.

'La raison psychologique du développement du dogme d'après Saint Thomas' (1924), *La Parole de Dieu I. La Foi dans intelligence* (Paris: Cerf, 1964), 51-58.

'La rénovation de la théologie morale. La loi nouvelle', in *Supplément de la Vie Spirituelle,* 22/90 (1969), 287-97.

'La Royauté Du Christ', in *Vie Spirituelle,* octobre (1959), 325-35.

'La théologie comme science au XIIIe siècle. Genèse de la doctrine de Saint Thomas', in *Archives d'histoire doctrinale et littéraire du Moyen Age,* 2 (1927), 31-71.

'La théologie comme science ecclésiale', in *Concilium,* 21 (1967), 85-93.

'La théologie en procès', in *Savoir, faire, espérer: les limites de la raison,* L'École des sciences philosophiques et religieuses (Brussels: Facultés Universitaires St Louis, 1976), 691-96.

'La ville. Notes de sociologie apostolique' (1953), in *La Parole de Dieu II. L'Évangile dans le temps* (Paris: Cerf, 1964), 515-36.

'Laics en Chrétienté' (1945), in *La Parole de Dieu II. L'Évangile dans le temps* (Paris: Cerf, 1964), 71-83.

'Le message au monde des Pères conciliaires (20 Octobre 1962)', in *L'Église dans le monde de ce temps—Réflexions et perspectives,* volume III, edited by Yves M-J Congar OP and M Peuchmard OP (*Unam Sanctam* 65c) (Paris: Cerf, 1967), 191-93.

'Le message du Concile au monde' (1962), in *La Parole de Dieu II. L'Évangile dans le temps* (Paris: Cerf, 1964), 639–45.

'Le monde leur tient lieu de cellule et l'océan de cloître' (Couvent St Jacques, Paris: unpublished discourse on the occasion of the canonical visit of Damian Byrne OP, Dominican Master General, 1989).

'Le plan de la Somme théologique de saint Thomas', in *Revue Thomiste*, 47 (1939), 93–107.

'Le sacerdoce des prêtres-ouvriers' (1954), in *La Parole de Dieu II. L'Évangile dans le temps* (Paris: Cerf, 1964), 275–81.

'Le salut est dans l'histoire', in *L'Église interrogée. 11 questions. 11 réponses*, edited by Claudio Zanchettin (Paris: Éditions du Centurion, 1975), 155–67.

'Le sens et les leçons d'une crise religieus', in *Vie intellectuelle*, XIII/3 (1931), 356–80.

'Le théologien et la vie', in *Informations catholiques internationales*, 233/1 février (1965), 28–30.

'Les catégories affectives dans la langue de l'école', in *Le Coeur, Études carmélitaines*, XXIX (1950), 123–28.

'Les communautés naturelles, pierres d'attente de cellules d'Église' (1964) in *Peuple de Dieu dans le monde* (Paris: Cerf, 1966), 129–43.

'Les études de philosophie médiévale', in *Philosophie: Chronique annuelle de l'Institut Internationale de Collaboration Philosophique*, 813/III (1939), 1–87.

'Les événements et le royaume de Dieu', in *Informations catholiques internationales*, 250 (15 octobre 1965), 18–19.

'Les laïcs et la «consecratio mundi»', in *L'Église de Vatican I. Études autour de la Constitution conciliaire sur l'ÉgliseI*, volume III, edited by Guilherme Baraúna OFM and Yves M-J Congar OP (*Unam Sanctam* 51c) (Paris: Cerf, 1966), 1035–53.

'Les lieux théologiques chez Melchior Cano', in *Le déplacement de la théologie: Recherches actuelles III*, edited by by Charles Kannengiesser (City: Éditions Beauchesne, 1977), 45–50.

'Les méthodes d'enseignement', in *2000 ans de christianisme*, edited by M.-D. Chenu, Michel Balard and Francis Rapp (Paris: Hachette, 1975), 122–26.

'Les passions verteuses. L'anthropologie de saint Thomas', in *Revue philosophique de Louvain*, 72 (1974), 11–18.

'Les sacrements dans l'économie chrétienne' (1952), in *La Parole de Dieu I. La Foi dans intelligence* (Paris: Cerf, 1964), 323–33.

'Les signes des temps', *L'église Dans Le Monde De Ce Temps—Constitution Pastorale 'Gaudium Et Spes'* volume II, edited by Yves M-J Congar OP and M Peuchmard OP (*Unam Sanctam* 65 b) (Paris: Cerf, 1967), 205–25.

'Les théologiens et le collège épiscopal. Autonomie et service', in *L'évêque dans l'Église du Christ*, edited by H Bouëseé, M-D Chenu, and A Mandouze (Paris: Desclée de Brouwer, 1963), 175–91.

'Lettre', *Concilium*, 115 (1976), 11–12.

'Liberté et engagement du chrétien' (1938), in *La Parole de Dieu II. L'Évangile dans le temps* (Paris: Cerf, 1964), 331–54.

'Matérialisme et spiritualisme' (1948), in *La Parole de Dieu II. L'Évangile dans le temps* (Paris: Cerf, 1964), 461–64.

'Maîtres et bacheliers de l'université de Paris v 1240—Description du manuscript Paris, Bibl. Nat. lat. 15652', in *Études d'histoire: Littéraire et doctrinale du XIIIe siècle* (Paris/Ottawa: Vrin/Institut d'Études Médiévales d'Ottawa, 1932), 11–39.

'Memoire et avenir de la foi', in *L'Actualité religieuse dans le monde* 49.15 (octobre 1982), 32–34.

'Milieu ouvrier et théologie savante', in *Lumière et Vie*, 27/140 (1978), 57–64.

'Modernité', in *La Lettre* nos. 346–347 (1987), 5–7.

Moines, clercs, laïcs. Au carrefour de la vie évangélique', in *La théologie au douzième siècle* (Paris: Librairie Philosophique Vrin, 1957), 225–251 (251).

'Nature ou histoire? Une controverse exégétique sur la création au XIIe siècle', in *Archives d'histoire doctrinale et littéraire du Moyen Age*, XX (1953), 25–30.

'Orthodoxie et hérésie. Le point de vue du théologien' (1963), in *La Parole de Dieu I: La Foi dans intelligence* (Paris: Cerf, 1964), 69–74.

'Orthodoxie-orthopraxie', in *Le service théologique dans l'église* (*Mélanges offerts au Père Yves Congar*), edited by G Phillips *et al* (Paris: Cerf, 1974), 51–63.

'Paradoxe de la pauvreté évangélique et construction du monde' (1963), in *La Parole de Dieu II. L'Évangile dans le temps* (Paris: Cerf, 1964), 389–404.

'Paroisses et œuvres. Les exigences de l'Action catholique', in *Revue Dominicaine (Ottawa)* mars (1934), 343–58.

'Position de la théologie' (1935), in *La Parole de Dieu I. La Foi dans intelligence* (Paris: Cerf, 1964), 115–38.

'Position théologique de la sociologie religieuse' (1950), in *La Parole de Dieu I. La Foi dans intelligence* (Paris: Cerf, 1964), 59–62.

'Pour un oecumenisme planetaire', in *L'Actualité religieuse dans le monde*, 38 (15 octobre 1986), 21–23.

'Pour une anthropologie sacramentelle', in *La Maison-Dieu*, 119 (1974), 85–100.

'Pourquoi et comment j'ai obéi', in *Il est une Foi*, 22–23 (oct–nov 1989): 22–23.

'Pourquoi l'insurrection?' (2 septembre 1944), in *La Parole de Dieu II. L'Évangile dans le temps* (Paris: Cerf, 1964), 231–2.

'Prophètes et théologiens dans l'Église. Parole de Dieu' (1963), in *La Parole de Dieu II. Évangile dans le temps* (Paris: Cerf, 1964), 201–12.

'Présentation', in *Théologie de la matière. Civilisation technique et spiritualité chrétienne* (Paris: Cerf, 1967), 7–13.

'Ratio superior et inferior. Un cas de philosophie chrétienne', in *Revue des sciences philosophiques et théologiques*, XXIX (1940), 84–89.

'Regard sur cinquante ans de vie religieuse' (1964), in *L'hommage Différé Au Père Chenu*, edited by Claude Geffré OP (Paris: Cerf, 1990), 259–68.

'Réflexions chrétiennes sur la vérité de la matière' (1948), in *La Parole de Dieu II. L'Évangile dans le temps* (Paris: Cerf, 1964), 447–51.

'Réformes de structure en Chrétienté' (1946), in *La Parole de Dieu II. L'Évangile dans le temps* (Paris: Cerf, 1964), 37–53.

'Réveil Évangélique et présence de l'Esprit aux XIIe-XIIIe siècles', in *Mélanges E. Schillebeeckx: L'expérience De L'esprit* (Paris: Édition Beauchesne, 1976), 167–71.

'Situation humaine: corporalité et temporalité' (1958), in *La Parole de Dieu II: L'Évangile dans le temps* (Paris: Cerf, 1964), 411–36.

'Sociologie de la connaissance et théologie de la foi' (1958), in *La Parole de Dieu I. La Foi dans intelligence* (Paris: Cerf, 1964), 63–68.

'«Spiritualisme» et sociologie' (1961), in *La Parole de Dieu II. L'Évangile dans le temps* (Paris: Cerf, 1964), 437–45.

'Spiritualité de la matière' (1962), in *La Parole de Dieu II. L'Évangile dans le temps* (Paris: Cerf, 1964), 453–59.

'Symposium IV: Les artes libéraux dans l'université du Xiiie siècle', in *Artes libéraux et philosophie au Moyen Âge* (Montréal/Paris: Institut d'Études Médiévales/Librairie philosophique J Vrin, 1969), 158–9, 74, 201.

'Théologie du travail' (1952), in *La Parole de Dieu II. L'Évangile dans le temps* (Paris: Cerf, 1964), 543–570.

'Travail' in Heinrich Fries (editor) *Encyclopédie de la foi*, volume IV (Paris: Cerf, 1967), 371–77.

'Un Concile «Pastoral»' (1963), in *La Parole de Dieu II. L'Évangile dans le temps* (Paris: Cerf, 1964), 655–72.

'Un Concile à la dimension du monde' (1962), in *La Parole de Dieu II. L'Évangile dans le temps* (Paris: Cerf, 1964), 633–37.

'Un peuple messianique. Constitution de l'Église, chap. 2, n. 9', in *Nouvelle Revue Théologique*, 89 (1967), 164–82.

'Un peuple prophétique', in *Esprit*, 364/10 (1967), 602–11.

'Un Pontificat entre dans l'histoire' (1963), in *La Parole de Dieu II. L'Évangile dans le temps* (Paris: Cerf, 1964), 189–98.

'Une confidence du Père Chenu', in *Vie spirituelle*, nov-déc (1993), 757–69.

'Une Constitution Pastorale de L'église' (1965), in *Peuple de Dieu dans le monde* (Paris: Cerf, 1966), 11–33.

'Une définition pythagoricienne de la vérité au Moyen Âge', in *Archives d'histoire doctrinale et littéraire du Moyen Age*, XXVIII (1961), 7–13.

'Une religion contemplative', in *Vie Spirituelle*, 43/1 (avril 1935), 84–89.

'Vie conciliaire de l'église et sociologie de la foi' (1962), in *La Parole de Dieu I. La Foi dans intelligence* (Paris: Cerf, 1964), 371–83.

'Vocations particulières et grâce baptismale', in *La Vocation religieuse et sacerdotale*, edited by M-D Chenu et al (Paris/Montréal: Cerf/Éditions Fidès, 1969), 7–21.

'Vérité et liberté dans la foi du croyant' (1959)), in *La Parole de Dieu I. La Foi dans intelligence* (Paris: Cerf, 1964), 337–59.

'Vérité évangélique et métaphysique Wolfienne à Vatican II', in *Revue des sciences philosophiques et théologiques*, 57 (1973), 632–40.

Forewords by Chenu

Chenu OP, Marie-Dominique,

'Préface', in Ambroise Gardeil OP, *Le donné révélé et la théologie*, 2nd edition (Juvisny: Cerf, 1932).

'Post-Scriptum', in *La Parole de Dieu II. Évangile dans le temps* (Paris: Cerf, 1964), 675–79.

'Préface: le théologien et son vocabulaire', in *Incarnation ou eschatologie? Contribution à l'histoire du vocabulaire religieux contemporain 1935-1955*, edited by Bernard Besret OSC (Paris: Cerf, 1964), 11–16.

'Préface', in *Somme théologique. La théologie: la Prologue et question 1*, translated by HD Gardeil OP (Paris: Cerf/Desclée, 1968), 5–9.

'Voorwoord', in José M Gonzalez Ruiz, Het *Christendom is geen humanisme: Schets van een theologie van de wereld* (Bilthoven (Madrid): H Nelissen (Ediciones Península), 1970), 5–7. [Translation of Spanish original: *El Cristianismo No Es Un Humanismo: Apuntes Para Una Teología Del Mundo* (Madrid: Ediciones Península, 1970).

'Préface', in *Les Dimensions Politiques De La Foi*, edited by René Coste (Paris: Éditions Ouvrières, 1972), 7–9.

'Introduction', in *Le Déplacement de la théologie: Actes du colloque methodologique de février 1976*, edited by M Bellet, J Audinet, M-D Chenu (Paris: Beauchesne/Institut Catholique de Paris, Recherches actuelles, 1977).

'Préface', in Gustavo Gutiérrez, *La Libération par la foi: Boire à son propre puits* (Paris: Cerf, 1985), 9–10.

'Introduction', in La Congregation pour la Doctrine de la Foi, *Liberté chrétienne et libération: instructions de la Congregation pour la Doctrine De La Foi* (Paris: Cerf, 1986), i–vii.

'Préface', inMathilde Landercy, *Figures de femmes au sein du peuple de Dieu* (Paris: Média St Paul & Éditions Paulines, 1987), 7–9.

'Présentation', in *Foi Au Christ Et Dialogues Du Chrétien*, edited by Michel de Goedt ODC (Bruges: Desclée de Brouwer, 1967).

'Présentation', in *La Parole de Dieu II. L'Évangile dans le temps* (Paris: Cerf, 1964), 7–11.

'Préface', in Claude Geffré OP, *Un nouvel age de la théologie* (Paris: Cerf, 1972), 3–5.

Chenu Publications in English

Books

Chenu, Marie-Dominique, OP

Faith and Theology, translated by Denis Hickey (New York: Macmillan, 1968). [Selection of articles from *La Parole de Dieu I. La Foi dans intelligence* and *La Parole de Dieu II. L'Évangile dans le temps* (Paris: Cerf, 1964)].

Is Theology a Science?, translated by AHN Green-Armytage (London: Burns & Oates, 1959).

Nature, Man, and Society in the Twelfth Century: Essays on New Theological Perspectives in the Latin West, translated by Jerome Taylor and Lester K Little (Chicago: University of Chicago Press, 1968). [Selection of chapters from *La théologie au douzième siècle* (Paris: Librairie Philosophique J Vrin, 1957)].

St Thomas Aquinas and His Theology, translated by Paul Philibert OP (Collegeville: Liturgical Press, 2002).

The Scope of the Summa of St Thomas, translated by Province of St Joseph Dominican Fathers (Washington: The Thomist Press, 1958).

The Theology of Work, translated by Lilian Soiron (Dublin: Gill and Son, 1963).

Towards Understanding Saint Thomas, translated by A-M Landry OP and D Hughes OP (Chicago: Henry Regnery, 1964). [*Introduction à l'étude de Saint Thomas d'Aquin* (Montréal/Paris: Institut d'études médiévales/Vrin, 1950)].

Articles

'A Council for All Peoples', in *Vatican II by Those Who Were There*, edited by Alberic Stacpoole OSB (London: Geoffrey Chapman, 1986), 19–23.

'Body and Body Politic in the Creation Spirituality of St Thomas Aquinas', in *Western Spirituality: Historical Roots and Ecumenical Routes*, edited by Matthew Fox (Notre Dame, Ind: Fides/Claretian, 1979), 193–214. [Previously published in *Listening*, 13 (1983), 214–31].

'Christian Liberty and Obligations', in *Blackfriars*, XX (1939), 263–76, 332–41.

'*Consecratio Mundi*', in *The Christian and the World: Readings in Theology*, edited by Alfons; Rahner Auer, Karl; Metz, Johannes B; Schlier, Heinrich; Durig, Walter; Scheffczyk, Leo; Chenu, MD (New York: PJ Kennedy & Sons, 1965), 161–77.

'Public Opinion in the Church', in *Rethnking the Church*, edited by M Cuminetti and FV Joannes (London: Gill & Macmillan, 1970), 113–128. [Published originally as *La Fine della Chiesa come società perfetta* (Milano, Arnoldo Mondadori Editore, 1968)].

'Ratio Superior et Inferior. A Note on the Interaction of Theology and Philosophy', in *Downside Review*, LXIV/198 (1946), 260–65.

'The Church's Conciliar Life and the Sociology of Faith', in *Cross Currents*, 12 (1962), 132–42.

'The Church's "Social Doctrine"', in *Concilium*, 140 (1980), 71–75.

'The History of Salvation and the Historicity of Man in the Renewal of Theology', in *Renewal of Religious Thought*, volume 1, edited by LK Shook (New York: Herder and Herder, 1968), 153–66.

'The Need for a Theology of the World', in *Great Ideas Today*, edited by R Hutchins and M Adler (Yearly supplement to Great Books of the Western World) (Chicago: Encyclopaedia Britannica, 1967), 54–69. [English translation of 'Foi et religion', in *Etudes philosophiques*, 21/3 (1966), 357–69 and another unidentified article].

'The New Trinitarian Basis of the Church', in *Concilium*, 146 (1981), 14–21.

'The Plan of St Thomas' *Summa Theologiae*', in *Cross Currents*, 2/2 (1952), 67-79.

'The Renewal of Moral Theology: The New Law', in *The Thomist*, XXXIV.1 (1970), 1-12.

'Theology as an Ecclesial Science', in *Concilium*, 21 (1967), 95-106.

'Truth and Freedom in the Faith of the Believer', in *Cross Currents*, 9 (1959), 267-81.

'Work' in K Rahner *et al* (editors), *Sacramentum Mundi*, volume 6 (London: Burns & Oates, 1970), 368-373.

'Vatican II and the Church of the Poor', in *Concilium*, 104 April (1977), 56-61.

Theses on Chenu

Dussart, J-M, 'L'évangile Dans La Réflexion Du Père Chenu. Sur La Méthode Théologique Des Années 1936 À 1939', unpublished PhD Faculté de Théologie. Université Catholique Louvain (1975).

Gallo, Luis-Antonio, *La concepción de la salvacion y sus presupuestos en M.-D. Chenu* (Rome: LAS, 1977).

Graczyk, M, 'La Doctrine De La «Consecratio Mundi» Chez Marie-Dominique Chenu', unpublished Doctorate. Strasbourg II, Faculty of Catholic Theology (1978).

Grbac, Josip, 'Lavoro E Vocazione Integrale Dell'uomo—Pre-Storia Della Constituzione Pastorale *Gaudium Et Spes* Nella Teologia Cattolica Dell'area Di Langua Francese', unpublished PhD, Gregorian University (1988).

Hanley OP, Terry, 'An Exposition of the Major Themes of the Theology of M.-D. Chenu for the Period 1920-1965', unpublished STL Faculté de théologie. Université de Louvain-la-neuve (1981).

Hoogen, Antonius Josephus Maria van den, *Pastorale Teologie. Ontwikkeling En Struktuur in De Teologie Van M.-D. Chenu* (Amblasserdam: Offsetdrukkerij Kanters BV [STD, University of Nijmegen, 1983).

Keller OP, Robert John, 'Toward a Contemporary Roman Catholic Theology of Work', unpublished PhD Graduate Theological Union, San Francisco (1993).

Kubicki, Dominik, 'La Logique De L'incarnation Selon M.-D. Chenu', unpublished PhD Université de Strasbourg 2 (1994).

Mazzarello, Maria Luisa, *Il Rapporto Chiesa-Mondo Nel Pensiero Del P. Marie-Dominique Chenu* (Città del vaticano: Tipografia Poliglotta Vaticana, 1979).

Potworowski, Christophe F, 'The Incarnation in the Theology of Marie-Dominique Chenu', unpublished PhD thesis, University of St Michael's College, Toronto School of Theology (1988).

Safi, Protais, 'La «Consecration Mundi» Et La Théologie Du Laïcat À La Veille De Vatican Ii', unpublished STD, Lateran University (1981).

Zanatta, Valentin, 'Por una Igreja encarnada na història—Linihas de Fundo do pensamento eclesiológico de M.-D. Chenu', unpublished PhD, Gregorian University (1989).

Secondary Sources on Chenu:

Alberigo, Giuseppe, 'Christianisme en tant qu'histoire et «théologie confessante»', M-D Chenu OP, *Une école de théologie: le Saulchoir* (Paris: Cerf, 1985), 11–34.

'The Announcement of the Council: From the Security of the Fortress to the Lure of the Quest', *History of Vatican II. Volume I*, edited by Giuseppe Alberigo and Joseph A Komonchak (Maryknoll/Leuven: Orbis/Peeters, 1995), 1–54.

'Un Concile à la dimension du monde: Marie-Dominique Chenu à Vatican II d'après son journal', *Marie-Dominique Chenu: Moyen-Âge et Modernité*, edited by Guy Bedouelle OP (Paris: L'Institut Catholique de Paris/Le Centre d'Études du Saulchoir, 1995), 155–72.

Arnal, Oscar, 'Theology of Commitment: Marie-Dominique Chenu', in *Cross Currents*, 11. Spring (1988), 64–75.

Aubert, Roger, *Le problème de l'acte de foi. Données traditionnelles et résultats des controverses récentes* (Louvain: Universitas Catholica Lovaniensis, 1945).

'La géographie ecclésiologique au XIXe siècle', *L'ecclésiologie au XIXe Siècle*, edited by Maurice Nédoncelle *et al* (Paris: Cerf, 1960), 11–55.

'La Théologie catholique durant la première moitié du XXe Siècle', *Bilan De La Théologie Du XXe Siècle,* edited by Robert van der Gucht and Herbert Vorgrimler. volume I (Paris: Casterman, 1970), 423–78.

'Le Théologie chrétienne: les grands courants', in *Bilan De La Théologie Du XXe Siècle* edited by Robert van der Gucht and Herbert Vorgrimler, volume II (Paris: Casterman, 1970).

'The Catholic Church from the Crisis of 1848 to the War of 1914: The Modernist Crisis and the Integrist Reaction', in *The Church in a Secularised Society. The Christian Centuries*, volume 5, translated by Janet Sondheimer (New York/London: Paulist/Darton, Longman and Todd, 1978), 186–203.

'The Half-Century Leading to Vatican II: The Life of the Church', 'Developments in Thought', in *The Church in a Secularised Society. The Christian Centuries*. volume 5, translated by Janet Sondheimer (New York/London: Paulist/Darton, Longman and Todd, 1978), 574–606, 607–23.

Barth, Maurice A, 'M-D Chenu', in *Tendenzen der Theologie im 20. Jahrhundert. Eine Geschichte in Porträts*, edited by HJ Schulz (Stuttgart: Kreuz-Verlag Stuttgart und Walter-Verlag Olten, 1966), 409–15.

Bataillon, L-J, 'Le Père Chenu et la théologie du Moyen Age', in *Revue des sciences philosophiques et theologiques*, 75 (1991), 449–56.

Bedouelle OP, Guy, editor, *Marie-Dominique Chenu: Moyen-Age et Modernité* (Paris: L'Institut Catholique de Paris/Le Centre d'Études du Saulchoir, 1995).

Bibliothèque Thomiste XXXVII, *Mélanges offerts à M-D Chenu, Maître en théologie* (Paris: Librairie Philosophique J Vrin, 1967).

Bonnefoy OFM, Jean-François, 'La Théologie comme Science et l'application de la Foi selon S Thomas d'aquin', *Ephemerides theologicae lovanienses*, XIV (1937), 421–46 and 600–31; XV (1938), 491–516.

Boureau, Alain, 'Le Père Chenu médiéviste: historicité, contexte et tradition', in *Revue des sciences philosophiques et theologiques*, 81 (1997), 407–14.

Brosse, Olivier de la, editor, *Le Père Chenu: La Liberté dans la Foi* (Paris: Cerf, 1969).

Cardijn, Joseph, 'Théologie du travail, théologie pour l'homme', in *L'hommage différé au Père Chenu* edited by Claude Geffré OP (Paris: Éditions du Cerf, 1990), 19–21.

Celada, Gregorio, 'Apotación de la historia a la comprensión de la Palabra', in *Ciencia Tomista*, 112/2 (1985), 315–39.

Chifflot OP, Th-G, *Approches d'une théologie de l'histoire* (Paris: Cerf, 1960).

'Par lui saint Thomas nous parle', *L'hommage différé au Père Chenu*, edited by Claude Geffré (Paris: Cerf, 1990), 207.

Colombo, G., 'Il «secondo Chenu» in Italia', in *Revue des sciences philosophiques et theologiques*, 75 (1991), 491–504.

Congar OP, Yves, *Journal d'un théologien 1946–1956* (Paris: Cerf, 2001).

Mon Journal du Concile (Paris: Cerf, 2002).

'Hommage au Père M.-D. Chenu', in *Revue des sciences philosophiques et théologiques*, 75/3 (1991), 361–2.

'Le frère que j'ai connu', in *L'hommage Différé au Père Chenu*, edited by Claude Geffré OP (Paris: Cerf, 1990), 239–45. (Published originally in English as 'The Brother I have known', in *The Thomist*, 49 (1985), 495–503).

'Le moment «économique» et le moment «ontologique» dans la *Sacra Doctrina* (Révélation, Théologie, Somme théologique)', *Mélanges offerts à M.-D. Chenu* (Paris: Librairie Philosophique Vrin, 1967), 135–87.

'Le Père M.-D. Chenu', in *Bilan De La Théologie du XXe siècle*, volume II, edited by Robert van der Gucht and Herbert Vorgrimler (Paris: Casterman, 1970), 772–90.

'The Role of the Church in the Modern World', in *Commentary on the Documents of Vatican II*, volume V, edited by H Vorgrimler (New York: Herder, 1969), 202–23.

Congar OP, Yves M-J, and M Peuchmaurd OP, *L'Église dans le monde de ce temps—Réflexions et perspectives*, volume II (*Unam Sanctam* 65 B) (Paris: Cerf, 1967).

Conticello, CG, '*De Contemplatione* (Angelicum 1920). La thèse inédite de doctorat du P M-D Chenu', in *Revue des sciences philosophiques et théologiques*, 75/3 (1991), 363–422.

Corbin SJ, Michel, *Le Chemin de la théologie chez Thomas d'Aquin* (Paris: Beauchesne, 1974).

Daniélou, Jean. 'Lettre 5 Mars 1942—Daniélou écrit à de Lubac', in *Bulletin des amis du Cardinal Daniélou*, 2 (1976), 64.

Domenach, J.-M., 'Célébration du Père Chenu', *L'hommage différé au Père Chenu*, edited by Claude Geffré OP (Paris: Cerf, 1990), 122–25.

Donneaud OP, Henry. 'Histoire d'une histoire: M.-D. Chenu et «La théologie comme science au XIIIe siècle»', in *Mémoire Dominicaine*, 4. printemps (1994), 139–75.

'La Constitution dialectique de la théologie et de son histoire selon M.-D. Chenu', in *Revue Thomiste*, XCVI/1 (1996), 41–66.

'M-D Chenu et l'exégèse de *Sacra Doctrina*', in *Revue des sciences philosophiques et théologiques*, 81 (1997), 415–37.

Doré, J. 'Un itinéraire-témoin. Marie-Dominique Chenu', in *Les Catholiques français et l'héritage de 1789. 1889–1989* (Paris: Beauchesne, 1989), 313–39.

'Bulletin de Théologie Fondamentale: I. Auteurs contemporains', in *Revue des sciences religieuses*, 73/4 (1985), 527–60.

'Liberté et engagement du chrétien selon M-D Chenu', in *Vie spirituelle*, I-II (1990), 89–103.

Durand, Jean-Dominique editor, *Cent ans de Catholicisme social à Lyon et en Rhône-Alpes: la postérité de Rerum Novarum* (Paris: Les Éditions Ouvrières, 1992).

Duval OP, André. 'Aux origines de l'«Institut historique d'études thomistes» du Saulchoir (1920 et ss). Notes et documents', in *Revue des sciences philosophiques et theologiques,* 75/3 (1991), 423–48.

'Présentation biographique de M-D Chenu par ses oeuvres essentielles', in *Marie-Dominique Chenu: Moyen-Âge et Modernité,* edited by Guy Bedouelle OP (Paris: L'Institut Catholique de Paris/Le Centre d'Études du Saulchoir, 1995), 11–23.

'Une confidence du Père Chenu', in *La vie spirituelle,* 147, novembre-décembre (1993), 757.

Epp, René, 'A propos de la «Doctrine Sociale» de l'Église comme idéologie, de M.-D. Chenu', in *Revue des Sciences Religieuses,* 54/1 (1980), 79–88.

Fouilloux, Étienne, 'The Antepreparatory Phase: The Slow Emergence from Inertia (January 1959—October 1962)', in *History of Vatican II.* volume I, edited by Giuseppe Alberigo and Joseph A Komonchak (Maryknoll/Leuven: Orbis/Peeters, 1995), 55–166.

'Autour d'une mise à l'index', in *Marie-Dominique Chenu: Moyen-Âge et Modernité,* edited by Guy Bedouelle OP (Paris: L'Institut Catholique de Paris/Le Centre d'Études du Saulchoir, 1995), 25–56.

La Collection «Sources Chrétiennes». Éditer les Pères de l'Église au XXe siècle (Paris: Cerf, 1995).

'Le Saulchoir en procès (1937–42)', in M.-D. Chenu OP, *Une École de théologie: Le Saulchoir* (Paris: Cerf, 1985), 39–59.

Franco, Antonio, 'La teología de M.-D. Chenu: itinerario histórico-culturel', in *Ciencia Tomisto,* 112/2 (1985), 231–65.

Froidure, M, 'L'essence de la manifestation', in *Revue des sciences philosophiques et theologiques,* 51 (1967), 39–52.

Gallo, Luis-Antonio, *La concepción de la salvacion y sus presupuestos en M.-D. Chenu* (Rome: LAS, 1977).

Geffré OP, Claude, editor, *L'hommage différé au Père Chenu* (Paris: Éditions du Cerf, 1990).

'Le Réalisme de l'incarnation dans la théologie du Père M-D Chenu', in *Revue des sciences philosophiques et théologiques,* 69 (1985), 389–99.

'Révélation et expérience historique des hommes', in *Laval Théologique et Philosophique,* 46/1 (1990), 3–16.

'Théologie de l'incarnation et théologie des signes des temps chez le Père Chenu', in *Marie-Dominique Chenu: Moyen-Âge et Modernité* edited by Guy Bedouelle OP (Paris: L'Institut Catholique de Paris/Le Centre d'Études du Saulchoir, 1995), 131–53.

Giorgis, Ettore de, 'Padre Chenu: una teologia incarnata nella storia', in *Vita Sociale*, XLVII.240/2 (1990), 109–19.

'Rigore teologico e presenza al mondo', in *Vita Sociale*, XLII.217/4–5 (1985), 303–08.

Greenstock TOP, David L, 'Thomism and the New Theology', in *The Thomist*, 13 (1950), 567–96.

Gucht, Robert van der, and Herbert Vorgrimler, editors, in *Bilan de la théologie du XXe siècle*, 2 volumes (Paris: Casterman, 1970).

Guelluy, Robert, 'Les Antécédents de l'Encyclique «Humani Generis» dans les sanctions romaines de 1942: Chenu, Charlier, Draguet', in *Revue d'Histoire Ecclésiastique*, LXXXI (1986), 421–97.

Haight SJ, Roger, *Dynamics of Theology* (New York: Paulist Press, 1990).

Hauerwas, Stanley, 'Work as Co-Creation: A Critique of a Remarkably Bad Idea' in J John W Houck and Oliver F Williams (editors) *Co-Creation and Capitalism: John Paul II's Laborem Exercens* (Lanham: University Press of America, 1983), 42–58.

Hayen SJ, André, 'La théologie comme science aux XIIe, XIIIe et XXe Siècles', in *Nouvelle Revue Théologique,* 79 (1957), 1009–28.

Hebblethwaite, Peter, 'Maverick Theologian Chenu "Emerges" into Dim Light', in *National Catholic Reporter,* 21/4 (February 8, 1985), 4–5.

Hoogen, Toine [Antonius Josephus Maria] van den, *Pastorale Teologie: Ontwikkeling en Struktuur in de Teologie van M-D Chenu* (Alblasserdam: Offsetdrukkerij Kanters BV, 1983).

Hughes, John, *The End of Work* (Oxford: Blackwell, 2007).

Imbach, Ruedi, 'L'étude historique de Saint Thomas et les Thomismes', in *Marie-Dominique Chenu: Moyen-Âge et Modernité*, edited by Guy Bedouelle OP (Paris: L'Institut Catholique de Paris/Le Centre d'Études du Saulchoir, 1995), 121–30.

G Jacquemet, 'Chenu', in *Catholicisme: hier, aujourd'hui, demain* (Paris: Letouzey et Ané, 1949).

Jenkins CSC, John I, *Knowledge and Faith in Thomas Aquinas* (Cambridge: Cambridge University Press, 1997).

Jolivet, Jean 'Les Études consacrée par le Père Chenu au Moyen Age', in *Marie-Dominique Chenu: Moyen-Âge et Modernité*, editor by Guy Bedouelle OP (Paris: L'Institut Catholique de Paris/Le Centre d'Études du Saulchoir, 1995), 67–83.

'M.-D. Chenu médiéviste et théologien', in *Revue des sciences philosophiques et theologiques*, 81 (1997), 381–94.

Jossua OP, Jean-Pierre, 'Fin de la Chrétienté ou nouvelle Chrétienté, selon M-D Chenu', in *Cristianesimo nella storia*, 26/3 (2005), 769–80.

Le Père Congar. La théologie au service de peuple de Dieu (Paris: Cerf, 1967).

'Le Saulchoir revisité: 1937–1983', in M-D Chenu OP, *Une école de théologie: Le Saulchoir* (Paris: Cerf, 1985), 81–90.

'Le Saulchoir: une formation théologique replacée dans son histoire', in *Cristianesimo nella storia*, 14 (1993), 99–124.

The Condition of the Witness, translated by John Bowden (London: SCM, 1985).

Kerr OP, Fergus, 'Chenu's Little Book', in *New Blackfriars*, 66 March (1985), 108–12.

Twentieth Century Catholic Theologians (Oxford: Blackwell, 2007), chapter 2.

'Yves Congar and Thomism', in Gabriel Flynn (editor), *Yves Congar Theologian of the Church* (Louvain: Peeters, 2005), 67–97.

Komonchak, Joseph A, 'Marie-Dominique Chenu', in *Commonweal*, 117/8 (1990), 252–3.

Küng, Hans, *Christianity: Its Essence and History*, translated by John Bowden (London: SCM Press, 1995).

Lacoste, Jean-Yves, 'De la technique à la liturgie: un pas ou deux hors de la mÿodernité', in *Communio*, IX/2 (1984), 26–37.

Ladrière, Jean, 'Théologie et historicité', in M-D Chenu OP, *Une école de théologie: le Saulchoir* (Paris: Cerf, 1985), 63–79.

Laudouze OP, André, *Dominicains français et Action Française: 1899–1940. Maurras au couvent* (Paris: Les Éditions Ouvrières, 1989).

Le Goff, Jacques, 'Au Moyen Age: temps d'église et temps du marchand', in *Pour une autre Moyen Age: Temps, travail et culture en Occident* (Paris: Gallimard, 1977). Section I, Chapter 2.

'Au Père Chenu', in *Lumière et Vie*, 39/196 (1990), 138–39.

La civilisation de l'occident médiéval (Paris: B Arthaud, 1964).

'L'intellectualité dominicaine au Moyen-Age et sa relation au monde de la ville et de l'université', in *Marie-Dominique Chenu: Moyen-Âge et Modernité*, edited by Guy Bedouelle OP (Paris: L'Institut Catholique de Paris/Le Centre d'Études du Saulchoir, 1995), 57–65.

'Le Père Chenu et la société médiévale', in *Revue des sciences philosophiques et theologiques,* 81 (1997), 371–80.

Leprieur, François, *Quand Rome condamne: Dominicains et prêtres-ouvriers* (Paris: Plon et Cerf, 1989).

Little, Lester K, *Religious Poverty and the Profit Economy in Medieval Europe* (London: Paul Elek, 1978).

Lécrivain SJ, Philippe, 'Les semaines sociales de France', in *Le Mouvement social catholique en France au XXe siècle*, edited by Denis Maugenest SJ (Paris: Cerf, 1990), 151–65.

Lubac SJ, Henri de, *Mémoire sur l'occasion de mes écrits* (Namur: Culture et Vérité, 1989).

Maugenest SJ, Denis, editor, *Le Mouvement social catholique en France au XXe siècle* (Paris: Éditions du Cerf, 1990).

Mazzarello, Maria Luisa, 'Gli scritti del P Marie-Dominique Chenu 1963–1979', in *Salesianum,* 42 (1980), 855–66.

Il Rapporto Chiesa-mondo nel pensiero del P. Marie-Dominique Chenu (Città del Vaticano: Tipografia Poliglotta Vaticana, 1979).

Melloni, Alberto, 'Les Journaux privés dans l'histoire de Vatican II: Introduction', in M.-D. Chenu OP, *Notes Quotidiennes Au Concile: Journal De Vatican II 1962-1963* (Paris: Cerf, 1995), 7–54.

Miller OSF, Paula Jean, 'Technology and the Theology of Earthly Realities in M.D. Chenu', in *Chicago Studies,* 40/3 (2001), 299–312.

Mills OP, John O, 'Chenu: 90, Vatican II: 20', in *New Blackfriars,* 66 February (1985), 54–55.

Moeller, Charles, 'Pastoral Constitution on the Church in the Modern World. History of the Constitution', in *Commentary on the Documents of Vatican II*, edited by H Vorgrimler, volume V (New York: Herder, 1969), 1–76.

Montages, Bernard, 'L'ultime chagrin du Père M.-J. Lagrange', in *Revue des sciences philosophiques et theologiques,* 78 (1994), 3–29.

Murphy, Francesa A, 'Gilson and Chenu: The Structure of the Summa and the Shape of Dominican Life', in *New Blackfriars,* 85 (May 2004), 290–303.

Nédoncelle, Maurice, R Aubert, P Evdokimov and Y Congar *et al,* editors, in *L'ecclésiologie au XIXe siècle* (*Unam Sanctam* 34) (Paris: Cerf, 1960).

Nichols OP, Aidan, *From Newman to Congar: The Idea of Doctrinal Development from the Victorians to the Second Vatican Council* (Edinburgh: T&T Clark, 1990).

Yves Congar (London: Geoffrey Chapman, 1989).

Petit, Jean-Claude, 'La Compréhension de la théologie française au XXe siècle. Vers une nouvelle conscience historique: G Rabeau, M-D Chenu, L Charlier', in *Laval théologique et philosophique*, 47/2 (1991), 215–29.

Potworowski, Christophe F, *Contemplation and Incarnation: The Theology of Marie-Dominique Chenu* (Montreal: McGill-Queens University Press, 2001).

'History and Incarnation in the Theology of M-D Chenu', *Sciences et Esprit*, 42 (1990), 237–65.

Poulat, Émile, *Église contre bourgeoisie. Introduction au devenir du Catholicisme actuel* (Paris: Casterman, 1977).

Naissance des prêtres ouvriers (Tournai/Paris: Casterman, 1965).

Refoulé, François. 'Les Éditions du Cerf, cinquante ans de débats et des combats (Des hommes de presse editeurs et journalistes)', in *Mémoire Dominicaine*, 5 automne (1994), foreword and 151.

Salamito, J-M, 'La Croix du Travail, le travail de la croix', in *Communio*, IX/2 (1984), 4–15.

Schmitt, Jean-Claude, 'L'oeuvre médiéviste du Père Chenu', in *Revue des sciences philosophiques et theologiques*, 81 (1997), 395–406.

Schoof OP, Mark (Ted), *Breakthrough: Beginnings of the New Theology* (Dublin: Gill and MacMillan, 1970).

Schüssler-Fiorenza, Francis 'Religious Beliefs and Praxis: Reflections on Catholic Theological Views of Work', *Concilium*, 131 (1980), 92–102 (97–8).

Sommet SJ, J, 'Catholicisme et Résistance', in *Revue des Sciences Religieuses*, 80/3 (1992), 327–44.

Synan, Edward A, 'Aquinas and His Age', in *Calgary Aquinas Studies*, edited by Anthony Parel (Toronto: Pontifical Institute of Medieval Studies, 1978), 1–11.

Teichweier, Georg, 'Versuch einer Theologie der Arbeit', in *Theologische Quartalschrift*, 138 (1958), 307–29.

Te Velde, Rudi, *Aquinas on God: The 'Divine Science' of the Summa Theologiae* (Farnham: Ashgate, 2006).

Thornhill SM, John, 'Is Religion the Enemy of Faith?', in *Theological Studies*, 45 (1984), 254–74.

Tijero OP, Alberto Escallada, 'La pasión por la verdad. Tríptico con Chenu al fondo', in *Ciencia Tomista*, 112/2 (1985), 267–76.

Tracy, David, 'The Uneasy Alliance Reconceived: Catholic Theological Method, Modernity, and Postmodernity', in *Theological Studies*, 50 (1989), 548–70.

Tranvouez, Yvon, *Catholiques d'abord. Approches du mouvement catholique en France (XIXe-XXe Siècle)* (Paris: Les Éditions Ouvrières, 1988).

Tucci SJ, Roberto, 'Introduction historique et doctrinale: Ferments rénovateurs durant la Troisième Session Conciliaire (14 Septembre—21 Novembre 1964)', in *L'église dans le monde de ce temps—Réflexions et perspectives*, volume II (*Unam Sanctam* 65 B), edited by Yves M-J Congar OP and M Peuchmard OP (Paris: Cerf, 1967), 73–127.

Vilanova, Evangelista, 'Réception de la théologie du Père Chenu en Espagne', in *Revue des sciences philosophiques et theologiques*, 75 (1991), 457–68.

Vorgrimler, Herbert (editor), *Commentary on the Documents of Vatican II*. 5 volumes (New York: Herder, 1969).

Wattebled, Robert, *Stratégies Catholiques en monde ouvrier dans la France d'après-guerre* (Paris: Éditions Ouvrières, 1990).

Weisheipl OP, James A, 'Review: *Is Theology a Science?*', in *New Scholasticism*, XXXV (1961), 241–43.

Wittstadt, Klaus, 'On the Eve of the Second Vatican Council (July 1—October 10, 1962)', in *History of Vatican II*, volume I, edited by Giuseppe Alberigo and Joseph A Komonchak (Maryknoll/Leuven: Orbis/Peeters, 1995), 405–500.

Other Sources

Adam, Karl, *The Christ of Faith: The Christology of the Church*, translated by Joyce Crick (New York: Mentor-Omega, 1962).

The Spirit of Catholicism translated by Dom Justin McCann (London: Sheed and Ward, 1938).

Alberigo, Giuseppe, 'The Announcement of the Council: From the Security of the Fortress to the Lure of the Quest', in *History of Vatican II*. Volume I, edited by Giuseppe Alberigo and Joseph A Komonchak (Maryknoll/Leuven: Orbis/Peeters, 1995), 1–54.

'The Christian Situation after Vatican II', in *The Reception of Vatican II*, edited by Jean-Pierre Jossua, Giuseppe Alberigo, Joseph A Komonchak, translated by Matthew J O'Connell (Washington: Catholic University Press of America, 1987), 325–48.

Alberigo, Giuseppe, and Joseph A Komonchak, editors, *History of Vatican II. Announcing and Preparing Vatican Council II: Toward a New Era in Catholicism*, volume I (Maryknoll/Leuven: Orbis/Peeters, 1995).

History of Vatican II. The Formation of the Council's Identity: First Period and Intersession October 1962—September 1963, volume II (Maryknoll/Leuven: Orbis/Peeters, 1997).

Ambrosiano, Marcellino d', '*Ressourcement* Theology, *Aggiornamento*, and the Hermeneutics of Tradition', in *Communio*, 18 Winter (1991), 530–55.

Anderson, Benedict, *Imagined Communities: Reflections on the Origin and Spread of Nationalism* (London: Verso, 1983).

Ashley, James Matthew, *Interruptions: Mysticism, Politics, and Theology in the Work of Johann Baptist Metz* (Notre Dame: University of Notre Dame Press, 1998).

Barnes, Michel René, 'Augustine in Contemporary Trinitarian Theology', in *Theological Studies*, 56 (1995), 237–50.

Baum, Gregory, *The Priority of Labor: A Commentary on Laborem Exercens* (New York: Paulist, 1982).

Bell, Richard H, 'Simone Weil and the civilisation of work', in *Simone Weil's Philosophy of Culture: readings toward a divine humanity* (Cambridge: Cambridge University Press, 1993), 189–213.

Berdyaev, Nicholas, *The Fate of Man in the Modern World*, translated by Donald A Lowrie (London: SCM Press, 1935). *Une nouveau Moyen Age* (Paris: Plon, 1927).

Bigo, Pierre, *La 'doctrine sociale' de l'Église* (Paris: Presses Universitaires de France, 1966).

Blanchette, Oliva *The Perfection of the Universe according to Aquinas: A Teleological Cosmology* (University Park: Pennsylvania State University, 1992).

Blondel, Maurice, *Letter on Apologetics and History and Dogma*, translated by Alexander Dru and Illtyd Trethowan (London: Harvill Press, 1964).

Bonsor, Jack, 'History, Dogma, and Nature: Further Reflections on Postmodernism and Theology', in *Theological Studies*, 55 (1994), 295–313.

Boyle, Nicholas *Who are we Now? Christian Humanism and the Global Market from Hegel to Heaney* (Notre Dame: University of Notre Dame Press, 1998).

Breclaw, Keith A, '*Homo Faber* Reconsidered: Two Thomistic Reflections on Work', in *The Thomist*, 57/4 (1993), 579–607.

Brito SJ, Emilio, 'Deux modèles du Dieu unique: Thomas d'Aquin et Hegel', in *Église et Théologie*, 21 (1990), 33–64.

Buckley SJ, Michael J, *At the Origins of Modern Atheism* (New Haven: Yale University Press, 1987).

Burrell CSC, David B, 'Incarnation and Creation: The Hidden Dimension', in *Modern Theology*, 12/2 (1996), 211-20.

Camus, Albert, 'L'Incroyant et les chrétiens (1948)', in *Essais* (Paris: Gallimard, 1950, 1967)), 371-75.

Cavanaugh, William T, '"A Fire Strong Enough to Consume the House" The Wars of Religion and the Rise of the State', in *Modern Theology*, 11/4 (1995), 397-420.

Certeau, Michel de, *La Fable mystique: XVIe-XVIIe siècle* (Paris: Gallimard, 1987).

L'écriture de l'histoire (Paris: Éditions Gallimard, 1975).

'La faiblesse de croire', *Esprit*, 4-5 (nouvelle série) (1977), 231-345.

Charlier OP, L, *Essai sur le problème théologique* (Paris: Maison Casterman, 1938).

Congar OP, Y. M. J., *La Foi et la théologie* (Paris: Desclée, 1962).

Jalons pour une théologie du laïcat (*Unam Sanctam* 23) (Paris: Cerf, 1953).

Esquisses du mystère de l'Église (*Unam Sanctam* 8) (Paris: Cerf, 1953).

'Preface', *Church and World in the Plan of God: Aspects of History and Eschatology in the Thought of Père Yves Congar OP*, edited by Charles MacDonald (Frankfurt: Verlag Peter Lang, 1982), vii-viii.

'Comptes Rendus [on *Sacra Doctrina*]', in *Bulletin thomiste*, 5/8 (1938), 490-505.

Curran, Charles E, *Catholic Social Teaching, 1891-Present: A Historical, Theological and Ethical Analysis* (Washington, Georgetown University Press, 2002).

Daly OSA, Gabriel, *Transcendence and Immanence: A Study in Catholic Modernism and Integralism* (Oxford: Clarendon, 1980).

Dansette, Adrien, *Religious History of Modern France*, volume II, translated by John Dingle (London: 1950).

DiNoia OP, Joseph A, 'American Catholic Theology at Century's End: Postconciliar, Postmodern, Post-Thomistic', *The Thomist*, 54 (1990), 499-518.

Doyle, Dennis M, 'Journet, Congar, and the Roots of Communion Ecclesiology', *Theological Studies*, 58 (1997), 461-79.

Dubarle OP, Dominique, *Dieu avec l'être* (Paris: Beauchesne, 1986).

Humanisme scientifique et raison chrétien (Paris: Desclée de Brouwer, 1953).

Pour un dialogue avec Marxisme (Paris: Cerf, 1964).

Duffy, Stephen J, *The Graced Horizon: Nature and Grace in Modern Catholic Thought* (Collegeville: Michael Glazier/The Liturgical Press, 1992).

Dupré, Louis, 'Experience and Interpretation: A Philosophical Reflection on Schillebeeckx', in *Theological Studies*, 43 (1982), 30–51.

Passage to Modernity (New Haven: Yale University Press, 1993).

Dupuy, Bernard. D, 'Schisme et primauté chez J. A. Möhler', in *L'ecclésiologie au XIXe siècle* edited by Maurice Néondecelles, *et al* (*Unam Sanctam* 34) (Paris: Cerf, 1960), 197–231.

Duval OP, André, 'Aux Origines de l'Institut historiques d'études thomistes du Saulchoir (1920 et *ss*). Notes et documents', in *Revue des sciences philosophiques et théologiques*, 75/3 (1991), 423–48.

Erlander, Lillemor, *Faith in the World of Work: On the Theology of Work as Lived by the French Worker-Priests and British Industrial Mission* (Stockholm: Almquist and Wicksell, 1991).

Fessard SJ, *La Main Tendue? Le Dialogue Catholique-Communiste Est-Il Possible?* (Paris: Éditions Bernard Grasset, 1937).

Flynn, Gabriel, *Yves Congar's Vision of the Church in an Age of Disbelief* (Aldershot: Ashgate, 2004).

Fouilloux, Étienne, 'Jalons pour une histoire de dix ans [1968–78]', in *Esprit*, 4–5 (nouvelle série) (1977), 40–57.

Fransen SJ, Piet, 'Criticism of Some Basic Theological Notions', in *Authority in the Church*, edited by Piet Fransen SJ (Leuyen: KU Leuven Press, 1983), 48–74.

The New Life of Grace, translated by Georges Dupont SJ (London: Geoffrey Chapman, 1971).

Gardeil OP, Ambroise, *Le Donné révélé et la théologie*, second edition (Juvisny: Les Éditions du Cerf, 1932).

Garrigou-Lagrange OP, Reginald, 'La nouvelle théologie où va-t-elle?', in *Angelicum* 23 (1946), 126–45.

Gauchet, M, *Le Désenchantement du monde. Une histoire politique de la religion* (Paris: Gallimard, 1985).

Geffré OP, Claude, 'La théologie au sortir de la modernité', in *Christianisme et modernité*, edited by Danièle Hervieu-Léger, Roland Ducret, Paul Ladrière (Paris: Cerf/Centre Thomas More, 1990), 189–209.

Gilson, Etienne, *L'Esprit de la philosophie médiévale* (Paris: Vrin, 1932).

Le Thomisme: Introduction à la philosophie de Saint Thomas d'Aquin (Paris: Vrin, 1947).

Goldie, Rosemary, 'Personal Correspondence' (6 January 1997).

Greenstock TOP, David C, 'Thomism and the New Theology', *The Thomist,* 13 (1950), 567-96.

Guarino, Thomas, 'Between Foundation and Nihilism: Is *Phronesis* the *Via Media* for Theology?', in *Theological Studies,* 54 (1993), 37-54.

'Postmodernity and Five Fundamental Theological Issues', in *Theological Studies,* 57 (1996), 654-89.

Gutiérrez, Gustavo, *A Theology of Liberation,* translated by Sr Caridad Inda and John Eagleson (Maryknoll, New York: Orbis, 1973).

We Drink from our own Wells (Maryknoll, New York: Orbis, 1988).

Haight SJ, Roger, *Dynamics of Theology* (New York: Paulist Press, 1990).

Halls, WD, *Politics, Society and Christianity in Vichy France* (Oxford: Berg, 1995).

Healy, Nicholas, 'Indirect Methods in Theology: Karl Rahner as an Ad Hoc Apologist', in *The Thomist,* 56 (1992), 613-34.

Hebblethwaite, Peter, *Paul VI: The First Modern Pope* (London: Harper Collins, 1993).

'The Popes and Politics: Shifting Patterns in "Catholic Social Doctrine"', in *Daedalus,* III Winter (1982), 85-99.

Heidegger, Martin, 'The Question concerning Technology', in *Basic Writings,* translated by David Farrell Krell (San Francisco: Harper, 1977), 287-317.

Hennessy, J, 'Leo XIII's Thomistic Revival. A Political and Philosophical Event', in *The Journal of Religion,* 58 supplement (1978), S185–S97.

Himes, Michael J, *Ongoing Incarnation: Johann Adam Möhler and the Beginnings of Modern Ecclesiology* (New York: Crossroad Herder, 1997).

Jacquemet, Gabriel editor, *Catholicisme: hier, aujourd'hui, demain,* volume 2 (Paris: Letouzey et Ané, 1949).

Jossua OP, Jean-Pierre, *La Père Congar: La Théologie au service du peuple de Dieu* (Paris: Éditions du Cerf, 1967).

Jáki OSB, Stanislas, *Les Tendances nouvelles de l'ecclésiologie* (Rome: Herder, 1957).

Kasper, Walter, *The Methods of Dogmatic Theology,* translated by John Drury (Shannon: Ecclesia, 1969).

Theology and Church, translated by Margaret Kohl (London: SCM Press, 1989).

Kennedy OP, Philip, *Deus Humanissimus: The Knowability of God in the Theology of Edward Schillebeeckx* (Ökumenische Beihefte 22) (Fribourg: University Press Fribourg, 1993).

Kerr OP, Fergus, 'French Theology: Yves Congar and Henri de Lubac', *The Modern Theologians* edited by David Ford, second edition (Oxford: Blackwell, 1997), 105-17.

Kilby, Karen Elizabeth, 'The *Vorgriff Auf Esse*: A Study in the Relation of Philosophy to Theology in the Thought of Karl Rahner' (unpublished PhD thesis Yale University, 1994).

Komonchak, Joseph A, 'Ecclesiology and Social Theory. A methodological Essay', in *The Thomist*, 45 (1981), 262-83.

'Modernity and the Construction of Roman Catholicism', in *Cristianesimo nella storia*, 18 (1997), 353-85.

'Theology and Culture at Mid-Century: The Example of Henri de Lubac', in *Theological Studies*, 51 (1990), 579-602.

'Vatican II and the Encounter between Catholicism and Liberalism', in *Catholicism and Liberalism* edited by RB Douglas and D Hollenbach (Cambridge: Cambridge University Press, 1994), 76-99.

Krieg CSC, Robert A, *Karl Adam: Catholicism in German Culture* (Notre Dame: University of Notre Dame Press, 1992).

Lacroix, Jean, *Maurice Blondel: An Introduction to the Man and his Philosophy* (New York: Sheed and Ward, 1968).

Larkin, Maurice, *Religion, Politics and Preferment in France since 1890: La Belle Epoque and its Legacy* (Cambridge: Cambridge University Press, 1995).

Lash, Nicholas, *A Matter of Hope: A Theologian's Reflections on the Thought of Marx* (London: Darton, Longman and Todd, 1981).

Latourelle, René, and and Gerald O'Collins, editors, *Problems and Perspectives of Fundamental Theology* (New York: Paulist Press, 1982).

Latreille, A, 'La pensée catholique sur l'état depuis les dernières années du XIXe siècle', in *L'ecclésiologie au XIXe siècle,* edited by M Nédoncelle *et al* (Paris: Éditions du Cerf, 1960), 281-95.

Laudoze OP, André, 'Un Théologien d'action française, le Père Janvier', in *Revue d'histoire l'Église de France*, LXXV 195 (1989), 343-57.

Le Bras, Gabriel, *Etudes de sociologie religieuse*, 2 volsumes (Paris: Presses Universitaires de France, 1955/56).

Lebret OP, L-J, *Montée Humaine* (Paris: Les Éditions Ouvrières, 1951).

Lebrun, François, *et al*, *Histoire des Catholiques en France: du XVe siècle à nos jours* (Toulouse: Privat, 1980).

Les Prêtres Ouvriers, *The Worker-Priests: A Collective Documentation*, translated by John Petrie (London: Routledge & Kegan Paul, 1956).

Loew OP, Jacques, *En mission prolétarienne: étapes vers un apostolat intégral* (Paris: Économie et Humanisme, 1946).

Lubac SJ, Henri de, *Catholicisme. Les aspects sociaux du dogme* (*Unam Sanctam* 2) (Paris: Les Éditions du Cerf, 1938).

Corpus Mysticum: L'eucharistie et l'Église au Moyen Age: étude historique (Paris: Aubier, 1948).

Mémoire sur l'occasion de mes écrits (Namur: Culture et Vérité, 1989).

Résistance Chrétienne à l'antisémitisme. Souvenirs 1940–1944 (Paris: Fayard, 1988).

MacDonald, Charles, *Church and World in the Plan of God: Aspects of History and Eschatology in the Thought of Père Yves Congar OP* (Frankfurt: Verlag Peter Lang, 1982).

MacKinnon, Donald, *Borderlands of Theology and Other Essays* (London: Lutterworth, 1968).

'The Future of Man', in *Explorations in Theology 5* (London: SCM Press, 1967), 1–10.

The Problem of Metaphysics (Cambridge: Cambridge University Press, 1974).

Marin-Sola OP, Francisco, *L'évolution homogène du dogme catholique* (Fribourg: Imprimerie et Librairie de l'Oeuvre de Saint-Paul, 1924).

Matheson, Peter, 'The Inductive Methodology of "Gaudium Et Spes"', in *Australasian Catholic Record*, LXIII/3 (1986), 280–93.

McCool SJ, Gerald A, *Catholic Theology in the Nineteenth Century: The Quest for a Unitary Method* (New York: Seabury Press, 1977).

McInerney, Ralph, *Aquinas on Human Action* (Washington: Catholic University of America, 1992).

McMullin, Ernan, editor, *The Concept of Matter in Greek and Medieval Philosophy.* (Notre Dame: University of Notre Dame Press, 1965).

The Concept of Matter in Modern Philosophy (Notre Dame: University of Notre Dame Press, 1978).

Menozzi, Daniele, 'Opposition to the Council (1966–84)', *The Reception of Vatican II*, edited by Jean-Pierre Jossua, GuiseppeAlberigo, Joseph A Komonchak (Washington: Catholic University Press of America, 1987), 325–48.

Merleau-Ponty, M, *Phenomenology of Perception*, translated by Colin Smith (London: Routledge & Kegan Paul, 1962).

Messina, Jean-Paul, 'L'Église d'Afrique au Concile Vatican II: Origines de l'assemblée speciale du Synode des Évêques pour L'Afrique', in*Mélanges de sciences religieuse*, 51/3 (1994), 279–95.

Metz, Johannes B., *Theology of the World* translated by William Glen-Doepel editor (London: Burns & Oates/Herder and Herder, 1969).

Milbank, John, '"Between Purgation and Illumination": A Critique of the Theology of Right', *Christ, Ethics and Tragedy: Essays in Honour of Donald Mckinnon* edited by Kenneth Surin (Cambridge: Cambridge University Press, 1989), 161–96.

Theology and Social Theory: Beyond Secular Reason (Oxford: Blackwell, 1990).

The Word Made Strange: Theology, Language, Culture (Oxford: Blackwell, 1997).

Neusch, Marcel, and Bruno Chenu OFM, *Au Pays de la théologie* (Paris: Centurion, 1994).

O'Connell, James, 'Is There a Catholic Social Doctrine? The Problem of Content and the Ambivalence of History, Analysis and Authority', in *Heythrop Journal*, XXXII (1991), 511–38.

O'Meara OP, Thomas F, 'Thomas Aquinas and Today's Theology', in *Theology Today*, 55/1 (1998), 46–58.

'Toward a Subjectve Theology of Revelation', in *Theological Studies*, 36/3 (1975), 401–27.

Ormerod, Neil, 'Quarrels with the Method of Correlation', in *Theological Studies*, 57/4 (1996), 707–19.

Pasture, Patrick, 'Diverging Paths: The Development of Catholic Labour Organisations in France, the Netherlands and Belgium since 1944', in *Revue d'histoire ecclésiastique*, LXXXIX/1 (1994), 54–90.

Pelletier, Denis, *Economie et humanisme: de l'utopie communitaire au combat pour les tiers-monde 1941–1966* (Paris: Éditions du Cerf, 1996).

Pope John XXIII, *Humanae salutis* (1961), *Pacem in Terris* (1963).

Pope John Paul II, *Sollicitudo Rei Socialis* (1988).

Laborem Exercens (1982).

Letter of His Holiness to Artists (Easter Sunday 1999).

Pope Paul VI, *Populorum Progressio* (1967).

Les théologiens et le Collège Episcopal: autonomie et service. [Istituto Paolo VI, Brescia, *Insegnamenti di Paolo VI*, volume VII] (Vatican: Libreria editrice Vaticana, 1977).

Popper, Karl, *The Poverty of Historicism* (London: Routledge, 1957).

Potterie SJ, Ignace de la, 'History and Truth', in *Problems and Perspectives of Fundamental Theology*, edited by René Latourelle and Gerald O'Collins (New York: Paulist, 1982).

Poulat, Émile, *Histoire, dogme et critique dans la crise moderniste* (Paris: Casterman, 1962, revised edition 1979).

Intégrisme et catholicisme intégral: un réseau secret international anti-moderniste: la 'Sapinière' (1909-1920) (Tournai: Casterman, 1961).

Une Église ébranlée. Changement, conflit et continuité de Pius XII à Jean-Paul II (Paris: Casterman, 1980).

'Critique historique et théologique dans la crise moderniste', in *Recherches des sciences religieuses*, 58 (1970), 535-50.

Rahner SJ, Karl, 'A Scheme for a Treatise of Dogmatic Theology', in *Theological Investigations* Volume 1 (London: Darton, Longman and Todd, 1961), 24-29.

'The Unity of Matter and Spirit in the Christian Understanding of Faith', translated by Karl-H and Boniface Kruger, in *Theological Investigations*, Volume VI (London: Darton, Longman & Todd, 1969), 153-77.

'Theology and Anthropology', in *Theological Investigations*, Volume IX, translated by Graham Harrison (London: Darton, Longman and Todd, 1972), 28-45.

'Theological reflections on the problem of secularisation', in *Theological Investigations*, Volume X, translated by David Bourke (London: Darton, Longman & Todd, 1973), 318-48.

'Theological considerations of secularization and atheism', in *Theological Investigations*, Volume XI, translated by David Bourke (London: Darton, Longman & Todd, 1974), 166-84.

Ratzinger, Joseph, 'The Dignity of the Human Person', *Commentary on the Documents of Vatican II*, volume V, edited by H Vorgrimler, translated by WJ O'Hara (New York: Herder, 1969), 115-63.

Theological Highlights of Vatican II translated by H Traub, GC Thormann and W Barzel (New York: Paulist, 1966).

Reit, Georges van, *Thomistic Epistemology: Studies Concerning the Problem of Cognition*, volume 1, translated by Gabriel Franks OSB (St Louis/London: B Herder, 1963).

Reno, Russell R, *The Ordinary Transformed: Karl Rahner and the Christian Vision of Transcendence* (Grand Rapids: Eerdmans, 1995).

Roncalli, Angelo Giuseppe (Pope John XXIII), *Mission to France 1944-1953*, translated by Dorothy White (London: Geoffrey Chapman, 1966). (orig: *Souvenirs d'un Nonce Cahiers de France* (Rome: Edizioni di Storia e Letteratura, 1963).

Schillebeeckx OP, Edward, *Church: The Human Story of God*, translated by John Bowden (London: SCM Press, 1990).

'The Crisis in the Language of Faith as Hermeneutical Problem', in *Concilium*, 5 9 (1973), 34.

Schoonenberg SJ, Piet, 'The Theologian's Calling, Freedom, and Constraint', in *Authority in the Church*, edited by Piet Fransen SJ (Leuven: KU Leuven Press, 1983), 92–118.

Simonin OP, H-D, 'La Théologie thomiste de la foi et le développement du dogme', in *Revue Thomiste*, XVIII (1935), 537–56.

Solages, Bruno de, 'Pour L'honneur De La Théologie: Les Contresens Du RP Garrigou-Lagrange', in *Bulletin de littérature ecclésistiques* (1947).

Spiazzi OP, R, *P Mariano Cordovani dei Frati Predicatori* (Rome, 1954).

Surin, Kenneth, 'Some Aspects of the "Grammar" of "Incarnation" and "Kenosis": Reflections Prompted by the Writings of Donald Mckinnon', in *Christ, Ethics and Tragedy: Essays in Honour of Donald Mckinnon*, edited by Kenneth Surin (Cambridge: Cambridge University Press, 1989), 93–116.

Sutton, Michael *Nationalism, Positivism and Catholicism: The Politics of Charles Maurras and French Catholics 1890–1914* (Cambridge: Cambridge University Press, 1982).

Torrell OP, Jean-Pierre, 'New Trends in Fundamental Theology in the Postconciliar Period', *Problems and Perspectives of Fundamental Theology*, edited by René Latourelle and and Gerald O'Collins, translated by Matthew J O'Connell (New York: Paulist, 1982), 11–22.

Saint Thomas Aquinas. The Person and His Work, volume 1, translated by Robert Royal (Washington: Catholic University of America Press, 1996).

Tracy, David, 'The Uneasy Alliance Reconceived: Catholic Theological Method, Modernity, and Postmodernity', in *Theological Studies*, 50 (1989), 548–70.

Turner, Denys, *Marxism and Christianity* (Oxford: Basil Blackwell, 1983).

Valadier SJ, Paul, 'Signes des temps, signes de Dieu?', in *Études*, 335 (1971), 261–79.

Wannenwetsch, Bernd, 'The Political Worship of the Church: A Critical and Empowering Practice', in *Modern Theology*, 12/3 (1996), 269–99.

Weigel SJ, Gustav, 'The Historical Background of the Encyclical *Humani Generis*', in *Theological Studies*, 12 (1951), 208–30.

Weisheipl OP, James A, 'The Meaning of *Sacra Doctrina* in *Summa Theologiae* I, Q.1', in *The Thomist*, 38 (1974).

White OP, Allan, 'Father Bede Jarrett OP and the Renewal of the English Dominican Province', *Opening the Scrolls: Essays in Catholic History in Honour of Godfrey Anstruther OP*, edited by Dominic Aidan Bellenger OSB (Bath: Downside Abbey, 1987), 216–34.

White OP, Victor, *Holy Teaching: The Idea of Theology According to St Thomas Aquinas* (London: Blackfriars Publications, 1958).

Williams, AN, 'Deification in the *Summa Theologiae*: A Structural Interpretation of the *Prima Pars*', in *The Thomist,* 61/2 (1997), 219–54.

'The Logic of Genre: Theological Method in East and West', in *Theological Studies,* 60/4 (1999), 679–707.

'Mystical Theology Redux: The Pattern of Aquinas' *Summa Theologiae*', in *Modern Theology,* 13/1 (1997), 53–4.

www.ingramcontent.com/pod-product-compliance
Ingram Content Group UK Ltd.
Pitfield, Milton Keynes, MK11 3LW, UK
UKHW042005230426
12048UKWH00009B/555